PILLS, POWDER, AND SMOKE

Antony Loewenstein is a Jerusalem-based Australian journalist who has written for *The New York Times*, *The Guardian*, the BBC, *The Washington Post*, *The Nation*, the *Huffington Post*, *Haaretz*, and many others. He is the author of *Disaster Capitalism: making a killing out of catastrophe*, writer/co-producer of the documentary *Disaster Capitalism*, and co-director of an Al Jazeera English film on the opioid drug tramadol. His other books include *My Israel Question*, *The Blogging Revolution*, and *Profits of Doom*, and he is also the co-editor of the books *Left Turn* and *After Zionism*, and a contributor to *For God's Sake*.

antonyloewenstein.com @antloewenstein

ANTONY
LOEWENSTEIN

PILLS,
POWDER,
AND
SMOKE

INSIDE THE BLOODY
WAR ON DRUGS

SCRIBE
Melbourne • London

Scribe Publications
18–20 Edward St, Brunswick, Victoria 3056, Australia
3754 Pleasant Ave, Suite 100, Minneapolis, Minnesota 55409, USA
2 John St, Clerkenwell, London, WC1N 2ES, United Kingdom

First published by Scribe in Australia, New Zealand and North America 2019
Published by Scribe in the United Kingdom 2020

Typeset in Minion Pro by the publishers

Printed and bound in the UK by CPI Group (UK) Ltd, Croydon CR0 4YY

Scribe Publications is committed to the sustainable use of natural resources
and the use of paper products made responsibly from those resources.

9781947534940 (US edition)
9781925713367 (Australian edition)
9781912854240 (UK edition)
9781925693768 (e-book)

Catalogue records for this book are available from the National Library
of Australia and the British Library.

scribepublications.com
scribepublications.com.au
scribepublications.co.uk

*To the millions of drug-war victims around
the world who deserve a life of peace.*

Contents

Introduction

'Every one of the bastards that are out for legalizing
marijuana is Jewish. What the Christ is the matter with the
Jews? I suppose it is because most of them are psychiatrists.'
US PRESIDENT RICHARD NIXON

Washington has never fought a war on drugs, but it has fought multiple wars fuelled by drugs. Controlling drug supply was rarely if ever a priority. Understand this, and you get how powerful the drug war has been in the public imagination for over one hundred years. Trillions of dollars spent, millions of lives lost, surging drug use and abuse around the world, and apocalyptic violence caused by illicit substances all look like failures. But don't be fooled; this was always the inevitable by-product of trying to control an industry that's led by the insatiable appetite for drugs in every corner of the globe.

From US president Richard Nixon, who unleashed the war on drugs in 1971 and called drug abuse 'public enemy number one', to President Donald Trump, who called in 2018 for drug dealers to be given the death penalty, this war has been fought across multiple administrations, nations, continents, communities, and generations. It has killed, maimed, enslaved, and imprisoned millions, with the annual global value of drug-trafficking worth hundreds of billions of dollars, second only to the illicit industries of pirated goods and counterfeiting.

These facts are central to understanding what the drug war has always meant to its architects in Washington, London, Canberra, and beyond. Despite these astronomical figures and lives lost and jailed, there's no sign that drug use has declined. If anything, it's become more ubiquitous and devastating due to the unregulated potency of illicit substances, organised criminal networks that profit from the misery, and huge state resources dedicated to chasing and targeting all levels of the drug-trade. It's been a colossal waste of resources and money, with more than US$50 billion spent annually in the US alone towards fighting a war that will never eradicate drugs from our societies. And yet on and on it goes, year after year.

Victory in the traditional sense was never really the point. One of Nixon's key advisors admitted years after he left power that the drug war was designed to neuter domestic opponents of the president. 'The Nixon campaign in 1968, and the Nixon White House after that, had two enemies: the anti-war left and black people,' Nixon's domestic policy head, John Ehrlichman, said:

> You understand what I'm saying? We knew we couldn't make it illegal to be either against the war or black, but by getting the public to associate the hippies with marijuana and blacks with heroin, and then criminalizing both heavily, we could disrupt those communities. We could arrest their leaders, raid their homes, break up their meetings, and vilify them night after night on the evening news. Did we know we were lying about the drugs? Of course we did.[1]

It's easy to be cynical about this comment, dismissing the entire drug war as nothing more than government control of minorities through the strong arm of the state. As this book will show, from the US to Honduras to Australia, every country dresses up its rhetoric against drugs in different ways, but the overarching aim is the same, publicly stated with such regularity that it's arguably become the most propagandised message of the modern age: *Drugs are bad. Drug takers must be punished. Imprison the weak souls who sell hard drugs. A military-style response is the only answer to crush and control the trade.*

The war on drugs is both an overt and covert conflict with visible and largely ignored victims. There are few winners, except drug cartels that make billions of dollars in profits, and law-enforcement bodies in multiple jurisdictions that enjoy a steady flow of state funds to pursue their goals. Mass incarceration in the US, with 2.3 million adults held in penitentiaries on a daily basis, is one of the inevitable outcomes of Nixon's policies and ideological obsessions. US president Ronald Reagan deepened it, as did every subsequent US president, with the notable exception of Barack Obama, who was the first US leader to take a more critical view.

In this war, Latinos, African-Americans, and the poor are principally targeted for exclusion, and drugs are the convenient excuse. Not all inmates are locked up because of the drug war; close to half of all people in US federal institutions are there for drug charges (though it's less in state and local jails). Whites and African-Americans use drugs at a roughly similar rate, but blacks are nearly six times more likely to be charged with a drug offence and far more likely to be incarcerated for it.

The US-led drug war operates on multiple levels. On the one hand, it's a real war with deadly consequences, reckless in its aims and dismissive of civilians. Although officials know that drug-trafficking and use won't end by militarising the conflict, Washington hopes to at least partially control the trade and infiltrate its key players. On the other hand, though, it's also a phoney war pushed by the US to control segments of its own population, manage client states near and far, enrich the US defence industry, and benefit close allies. Think of it as a form of neo-imperialism. No war can last this long without utilising all the rhetorical devices in the playbook.

The explosion of privatised prisons and entire industries that have profited from the prison boom since the 1980s proves that this isn't an accident of the war on drugs but a deliberate part of it. On any moral reading, this has been a catastrophic failure that has destroyed communities and families; but in another interpretation, mass incarceration has served its purpose. As writer Michelle Alexander, author of *The New Jim Crow*, explains, 'Like Jim Crow (and slavery), mass incarceration operates as a tightly networked system of laws, policies, customs, and institutions that operate collectively to ensure the subordinate status of a group defined largely by race.'[2]

Washington didn't invent the rhetoric. During the Nazi era in Germany, illicit drug use was framed as menacing, with anti-Semitic overtones. In his ground-breaking book *Blitzed*, about the Nazis' use of drugs, including by Adolf Hitler, author Norman Ohler explains that the National Socialists 'combined their twin bogeymen, Jews and drugs, into racial-hygiene propaganda that was used in schools and nurseries … Anyone who consumed drugs suffered from a "foreign plague". Drug dealers were presented as unscrupulous, greedy, or alien, drug use was "racially inferior", and so-called drugs crime as one of the greatest threats to society.'[3]

Jews are no longer labelled as the cause of drug dealing, but instead different racial groups are targeted. Less has changed in our discussion about drugs than we may like to believe. Western media reports still routinely blame the designated enemies of the day: the black drug dealer, the Latino cartel boss, and the poor white or black heroin user.

Public opinion in the US has evolved since the height of the drug war in the 1980s. A 1988 CBS News/*New York Times* poll found that 48 per cent of people surveyed thought that drug-trafficking was the top foreign-policy issue. Stopping communism was only of main concern to 21 per cent.[4] By 2018, according to Gallup polling, immigration was the biggest concern of voters. Drugs were way down the list, lower than the environment, poverty, and education, but higher than school shootings and terrorism.

What's changed is that for the vast bulk of people, drug taking is a normal part of life with no negative consequences. In this book, I examine how this profound societal shift has occurred in virtually every Western country in the last 30 years. Drugs are no longer the bogeyman that threatens lives; they're taken for fun on weekends, with friends, and in homes, clubs, and bars. But, too often, how drugs reach people, and those who have suffered in their production, isn't considered by those who take them. How about a movement that pushes for fair-trade cocaine, heroin, and cannabis?

The infrastructure of the war on drugs would collapse tomorrow if demand for cocaine, cannabis, ecstasy, methamphetamine, heroin, synthetic cannabinoids, opioids, or fentanyl suddenly stopped. But so long as humans have lived on planet earth, drugs have been used and abused. Humans have been getting high on alcohol, opium, and magic mushrooms since prehistoric times.

Many countries have been consumed by drug policies designed in Washington. Just think of Honduras, Mexico, and Colombia alone. These states aren't consumed by drug violence because locals are inherently criminal. Washington claims it's about stopping drug networks, but this book questions those claims. In fact, the aim is not to stop drug-trafficking or drug use, an impossible task when demand for drugs in the West continues to surge, but to ensure that Washington and its allies work with drug producers and cartels from whom they can glean intelligence. This book investigates largely untold examples in Honduras and West Africa where the pursuit of traffickers is less about stopping smuggling and more to do with pursuing US foreign-policy goals.

There's copious evidence that shows how broken the US DEA [Drug Enforcement Administration]-led war has become, from DEA agents attending cartel-funded sex parties in Colombia between

2009 and 2012 to the DEA leaking sensitive information about cartel activity in Mexico to corrupt Mexican officials in 2011.[5] This led to the vicious Zetas organisation murdering hundreds of people that it considered snitches.[6]

In Mexico alone, according to its corruption-tainted government (which means the figure was likely much higher), there were a record 33,341 homicides in 2018, the highest number recorded since authorities started releasing figures in 1997. The drug war was a leading cause of the carnage. In such circumstances, it's unsurprising that so many Mexicans want to flee to safer territory in the US. Mexico's top human-rights official announced in 2019 that the government aimed to search for and find the estimated 40,000 individuals missing due to the drug war.

In the city of Tijuana, methamphetamine, or *cristal* in Spanish, is a cheap drug that's causing civil war–level violence. There were 2,518 people killed in 2018, close to seven times higher than in 2012. With 140 murders per 100,000 people, Tijuana has become one of the most dangerous cities on the planet.[7]

Mexico is a grim reminder that the drug war is designed as a violent, cynical game. When infamous cartel leader Joaquin 'El Chapo' Guzman escaped from a supposedly high-security Mexican prison in 2015 — he was eventually recaptured and faced extensive charges in a US court trial, though his Sinaloa cartel boomed despite his incarceration — it was suggested that the Mexican government had wanted him to escape, and had even helped.

During the trial of El Chapo in 2018 and 2019 in a New York courtroom, there were explosive allegations about the drug war that revealed its real agenda (and lack of accountability). Colombian drug lord Alex Cifuentes Villa, who worked with El Chapo between 2007 and 2013, alleged that a former president of Mexico, Enrique Pena Nieto, had taken a US$100 million bribe from El Chapo. Pena Nieto has always denied taking any money from drug-traffickers.

Other equally damning details during the trial included testimony from cartel witnesses that El Chapo's Sinaloa cartel was in regular contact with the DEA and had given the US government information about rival drug groups for over a decade, and that in doing so these individuals received immunity (or reduced sentences) from US prosecution. The DEA denied that any deals were ever made.[8] Nonetheless, El Chapo was replaced by his sons and former colleague so that the Sinaloa cartel is still alive and well today, and it has 'the most expansive footprint in the United States', according to the DEA's 2018 assessment of the drug-trade.

El Chapo was found guilty of all ten charges laid against him, and will likely spend the rest of his life in a US prison. After the verdict was announced in 2019, Richard P. Donoghue, the United States attorney for the Eastern District of New York, claimed that the decision was a victory for the 100,000 dead in Mexico and the drug war itself. 'There are those who say the war on drugs is not worth fighting,' he argued. 'Those people are wrong.'

The trial encapsulated so much that was futile about the drug war. While El Chapo was undeniably a brutal drug boss who caused misery for many, his trial and imprisonment will neither reduce violence in Mexico nor address the industrial-scale amount of drug taking in the US. Believing that law enforcement can solve the issues of drug use, abuse, and trafficking fundamentally ignores the last 50 years of history. The Sinaloa cartel, and other major Mexican drug groups, are increasingly producing fentanyl for the US market as demand for heroin decreases.[9] El Chapo's incarceration will do nothing to stop this.

To truly understand the drug war in Mexico is to appreciate how few facts appear in the mainstream media about it. Former Mexican journalist turned academic Oswaldo Zavala wrote a controversial book in 2018 that detailed the reality of cartels in his home country. He argues that the cartels have never overwhelmed the nation, despite successive governments claiming that they have, but instead work for the state to bolster both their powers. The logic of the violent drug war gives Mexican administrations the ability to grant multinational corporations access to natural resources. Violent militias or drug gangs do the dirty work for companies by forcibly cleansing people from their areas. Zavala argues that this is the unspoken reason behind the Mexican war on drugs, the alliances between authorities, multinationals, and cartels.[10]

On 31 January 2018, the last day of the El Chapo trial, authorities in Arizona announced that they had seized the largest amount of fentanyl ever found in the US — enough for 100 million lethal doses — in trucks at a legal entry point into the US. The Nogales port of entry, connecting Arizona and Mexico, was a regularly used transit point by the Sinaloa cartel.[11] El Chapo had left the scene, but the drug-trade that he had undeniably worsened was still operating with ruthless efficiency. Removing El Chapo from the scene gave a warning to other potential drug kingpins, but the sheer amount of money that could be earned in the industry rendered his verdict almost irrelevant. The future of cartels may lie with IT experts who code, encrypt, and lead global networks of untraceable drug distribution.

In reality, El Chapo's incarceration had never done anything to stem the bloodshed. Violence had soared during his time in jail, and a senior cartel operative explained that officials hoped El Chapo would 'restore peace' by cracking down hard on his rivals, whom authorities found difficult to control. Whoever was left standing would be weakened but victorious, at least momentarily until another cartel rose to challenge its power. 'There's no real fight against drugs,' a Mexican intelligence official admitted. 'It's all a perverse game of interests.'[12]

Mexican President Andrés Manuel López Obrador offered a sensible response to this situation by announcing in May 2019 that his country should decriminalise all illicit drugs, shift funding to treatment programs, and negotiate with the US to follow suit. This is the drug war in a nutshell: futile, powerful, and self-sustaining.

Perhaps Mexico should follow the lead of Bolivia, which took the important step of kicking out the DEA in 2009, legalised coca, and regulated production. Cocaine production has dropped ever since.

Consider Colombia, the world's biggest supplier of cocaine. (Peru is second.) According to the United Nations Office on Drugs and Crime, there had been a 31 per cent increase in cocaine production in Colombia in 2018 from the year before. Despite a 2016 peace deal between warring sides of the country's long-standing civil war, cracks had appeared due to a lack of support for demobilised Farc rebels, some of whom produced cocaine, and other groups that remained committed to trafficking.

Washington's relationship with Colombia is a salient warning in how not to approach drugs. In 2000, the Clinton administration and Colombia initiated Plan Colombia to tackle drug cartels and Farc militants. More than US$10 billion was sent from Washington with bipartisan backing.[13] Both governments claimed victory 15 years later, but the price had been steep. Over 220,000 people had died since 1958, a toll which accelerated during Plan Colombia. Foreign investors were pleased with the results, however — a key, often unstated, aim of the policy. There was an increase in the amount of cocaine being produced on the ground (output fell for a time, but it didn't last), and gross human-rights abuses by a militarised approach included collusion between security forces and right-wing death squads.[14]

~

I began working on this book before Donald Trump had the faintest chance of becoming US president. It was conceived during the Obama years when there were some positive, albeit small, changes to the drug war in the US and globally. The rate of incarceration in US prisons declined, a handful of US states legalised cannabis without federal government censure, and, on the international stage, Washington was less belligerent about enforcing a zero-tolerance prohibitionist agenda.

These were significant departures from previous US administrations, and sent a signal globally that nations could explore alternatives to policies that had killed millions while enriching drug cartels and organised-crime gangs. Legalisation and decriminalisation were finally on the agenda. Uruguay was the first nation on earth to legalise marijuana in 2013. Canada was the first Western country to do so in 2018.

In this book, I report from Honduras and Guinea-Bissau in West Africa, two nations that are at the centre of the US-led drug war, though they receive little media coverage. Honduras experiences some of the worst violence in the world outside a traditional war zone. The bulk of cocaine arriving in America and Europe transits through both these countries. As the white powder grows in popularity in Western capitals, it's the people of Honduras and Guinea-Bissau that feel it most acutely. I speak to the farmers, authorities, peasants, and victims of a war that they didn't start and have no idea how to stop.

The Philippines is also a focus, and has recently suffered a brutal war on drugs launched by its president, Rodrigo Duterte. More than 30,000 people have been killed since he took office in 2016, and the bloody streets of Manila are a salutary tale of what happens when state-sanctioned murder becomes official policy. How and why so many Filipinos back Duterte in his drug war is perhaps the most disturbing part of the story.

As the intellectual heart of the drug war, the US is a key battleground. I investigate how marijuana has gone mainstream, a reality that seemed impossible just ten years ago, while the state still implements a drug war that it knows will disproportionately affect people of colour and poor whites. The darkest policies of the Nixon and Reagan eras are rearing their heads again in the Trump age with demonised drug users back at the rhetorical heart of law enforcement, the Justice Department, and the DEA. I uncover some of the secrets behind the DEA and how it entraps vulnerable people in West Africa and Honduras.

In the UK and Australia, two US client states, there's a growing awareness that prohibition has failed to impede drug use or criminality, but political cowardice means that little is done about it. In Australia, I find some reasons for optimism — for example, safe injecting rooms are increasingly accepted by the community as a necessary tool in tackling addiction — but the authorities remain fearful of moving too fast on drug-policy reform in case they incur a tabloid media backlash. In Britain, with extreme austerity, soaring poverty, and hopelessness evident from the heart of London to Newcastle, it feels like generations of young people are being left to suffer amidst an influx of deadly drugs.

I detail the ways in which drug users increasingly access the dark net to shop for drugs as a safer way to source illicit substances. Alongside this positive development is growing research into and adoption of psychedelic substances such as LSD, ecstasy, and magic mushrooms to treat depression and other mental-health problems. Finally, the debate that's long overdue is slowly entering the mainstream: tangible plans to regulate and legalise all drugs. What was once considered radical and unrealistic has never been more important to discuss and implement.

I've picked these countries and themes because they reveal a cross-section of the drug war. I wanted to examine places that receive little mainstream media attention but play a huge role behind the drugs that are consumed nightly in such major cities as London, Sydney, New York, and Paris.

~

The Donald Trump era has brought the drug war back with a vengeance, though it's arguably far less effective in convincing people than in the past. President Trump claimed that his proposed border wall with Mexico was the answer to ending drug importation. 'The drugs are pouring in at levels like nobody has ever seen,' he said. 'We'll be able to stop them once the wall is up.' But a DEA intelligence report found the complete opposite, explaining that the vast bulk of illicit substances entered the country by air and sea. 'The majority of the heroin available in New Jersey originates in Colombia and is primarily smuggled into the United States by Colombian and Dominican groups via human couriers on commercial flights to the Newark International Airport,' the document said.[15]

During the El Chapo trial, witness after witness testified that his network imported drugs largely at legal US border crossings in cars, tanker trains, and trucks. A Trump-style wall would do virtually nothing to change this.

Trump was using rhetoric that Nixon, Reagan, and Bill Clinton had used in the past, whipping up fear against black and Latino drug dealers and users. The DEA still operates with almost complete impunity, and Trump has boosted its budget by US$400 million. But with a majority of Americans now supporting cannabis legalisation, and increasingly high support for this policy in Britain, Australia, and many other Western states, what kind of drug war is it fighting and with what public mandate?

Nonetheless, the drug war has served the political class well for decades, providing an ideological framework and language while talking 'tough' on drugs. On the DEA's 45th birthday in 2018, two leading US senators, Republican Chuck Grassley and Democrat Dianne Feinstein, issued a congratulatory resolution in Congress to thank the department for its work. The DEA had served the US 'with courage', and had 'helped protect the people of the United States from drug-trafficking, drug abuse, and related violence'.

The drug war has developed its own momentum that is incredibly hard to stop. It's not dissimilar to the war on terror, declared after the terrorist attacks on 11 September 2001, that unleashed a multibillion-dollar industry to thwart and deter terrorism, if not stop it entirely. It has not achieved any of its stated goals — terror threats and actions from both Islamists and far-right extremists have worsened in the years since 2001 — but the justification for its continuation has not diminished. The DEA routinely links drug-trafficking to terrorist group financing, so the wars on drugs and terror are both sold as vital to protecting the homeland.

There are always new ways to create threats and then provide solutions to them. The US Coast Guard now locks up low-level drug-smugglers in international waters, in floating Guantanamo Bays of dubious legality, and keeps them there for weeks or months before bringing them to US courts.[16] This didn't cause a scandal when it was revealed in 2017.

We've seen this narrative before when the US government's drug policies knowingly worsened the drug-trade. Soon after the Soviet Union invaded Afghanistan in 1979, US president Jimmy Carter reacted by sending armaments to the mujahideen rebels. Dr David Musto, a White House advisor on drugs who had been appointed by Carter to the White House Strategy Council on Drug Abuse, expressed concern. 'We were going into Afghanistan to support the opium growers in their rebellion against the Soviets', he told Alfred McCoy, professor of South-East Asian History at the University of Wisconsin-Madison, and author of one of the finest books on the drug war, *The Politics of Heroin: CIA complicity in the global drug-trade*.[17] After Washington backed Islamist rebels in Afghanistan and Pakistan, heroin poured into the US, and drug-related deaths soared.

McCoy had uncovered a vast, largely hidden, history of CIA and US government complicity in the production of heroin in Laos, Thailand, and Burma from the late 1940s until the 1980s, sustained by the murderous Vietnam War and its brutal legacy. The CIA contracted airlines to transport opium, and turned a blind eye to its distribution. Global supply skyrocketed, the drug caused a huge increase in overdoses around the world, and it was all done in the name of fighting the Cold War.

'Since ruthless drug lords made effective anti-Communist allies and opium amplified their power, CIA agents, operating half a world away from home, tolerated the illicit trade', McCoy wrote:

The CIA's role in the heroin traffic was an inadvertent consequence of its Cold War tactics … Once a CIA secret war ended, its legacy persisted in rising narcotics production. American agents may have departed, but the covert war zone's market linkages and warlord power remained to make these regions major drug suppliers for decades to come.[18]

These were the early days of the global war on drugs. I show how Britain, Australia, Honduras, and a range of other nations signed up to Washington's militarised drug war, usually through coercion as well as a desire to stay in the US's good books, and are still playing the game today.

I'm not shy about my own views after four years of research around the world for this book; the drug war must end, but the question is how. I view ending the war on drugs as akin to killing a zombie. It's not impossible, if you know how to destroy the brain with a stake through its centre, but it's like playing whack-a-mole because there are too many institutions with a vested interest in its continuation. Nonetheless, voices of sanity, calls for legalisation and regulation, and politicians who reject the drug-war rhetoric are becoming less of a whisper and more like a scream, from the halls of Washington to the bloodied capitals of Latin America that have suffered the most.[19]

Although I began this book with strong views against the drug war, writing it took me in directions that I didn't necessarily expect. I've spent my career investigating the abuse of corporate and state power — from occupations in Palestine and Afghanistan to private prisons and internet censorship — but the drug war was inarguably bigger than them all. It's a conflict that's never-ending and completely global, so I aim to reveal what this means for the millions of civilians caught in the middle of it. Capturing the scale of the war — its rhetorical justifications, militarisation, faux arguments, and yet brutal outcomes — is what this book hopes to achieve.

I view this book as a work of journalistic investigation infused with a curious mind. It's true that, before I embarked upon it, I wasn't open to supporting the prohibition of drugs — I've never believed such a policy works effectively to improve human rights — but in the course of my research I certainly listened to individuals who worried about the societal effects of full legalisation and regulation. And although my work over the years has often been accompanied by activism on particular issues, from Palestine to privatised wars, the journalism has been a priority because I believe that fine reporting is often connected to opposing injustice. Speaking out against the drug war inevitably makes me an advocate in the broadest sense of the word, but it's nothing compared to the bravery of countless men and women on the frontlines whom you'll meet in these pages.

Before I began researching the war on drugs, I would casually and unthinkingly use the word 'addict' to describe a person who used drugs excessively. But current thinking about drugs has forced me to challenge my thinking and biases. The Associated Press updated its widely used *AP Stylebook* in 2017 to accommodate the new ideas. 'Addict' would no longer be used as a noun. 'Instead', it said, 'choose phrasing like *"he was addicted"*, *"people with heroin addiction"* or *"he used drugs"*'.

John Kelly, an associate professor of psychiatry at Harvard University, and founder and director of the Recovery Research Institute at the Massachusetts General Hospital, welcomed the move, because he had found in a 2010 study that doctors took a more punitive stand against patients who were described as 'substance abusers' as opposed to 'people with substance use disorder.'[20]

This equally applied to the general public when reading stories in the media. Addiction researchers at the University of Pennsylvania found in a 2018 study that people responded negatively when a person was described as an 'addict', 'alcoholic', or 'substance abuser.' 'Terms that seem to label the person — and invoke the negative attitudes toward the person rather than the disease — those are the ones that have the higher levels of bias,' said lead study author Robert D. Ashford.[21]

For all these reasons, I've tried to modify my language throughout the book to reflect the most appropriate way to discuss drugs and the people who use them.

Aside from checking my language, this book challenges the vast bulk of what passes for reporting on the drug war. Too often, government spin is what journalists publish. I've highlighted many examples throughout the text when embedded reporters visit a dangerous country, barely meet anyone not taken to them by a government minder, and end up endorsing US foreign-policy goals. The fact that Washington and the West are often behind a nation's descent into violence, drug use, or gang warfare is ignored or softened.

This isn't to downplay the hideous brutality unleashed by cartels — they were committing the kinds of abuses that ISIS shocked the world with, years before the Islamist terror group emerged — but it's too easy to just cast them as the bad guys.

The drug war is exactly that — a war — and yet it's too frequently viewed through the prism of a public-health emergency or national panic. Neither is entirely untrue, but journalism requires more than simply repeating grim statistics and speaking to experts who talk about the crisis. I spent time in the middle of the war so I could explain what it looks and smells like from the streets of Sydney to the killing fields of Honduras. Nothing can replicate being on the frontline of a war that's a conflict against both a domestic population and vast swathes of the global population.

Unpacking the ways in which the war has survived and thrived for decades is a trickier proposal, but no less important. How can a war be both created in the minds of its advocates and practitioners, with slogans and weapons at the ready, while also designed as an effective tool of control over what are viewed as unruly populations?

The answer is partly that this is how empires operate. Washington is the latest iteration of an age-old tradition, but I think it goes deeper than this to the very heart of modern capitalist societies and those who aim to protect their wealth at any cost.

~

Popular culture has a lot to answer for when it comes to romanticising the drug war and deliberately ignoring its ugly realities. Take the Netflix series *Narcos*, on the rise of cocaine in Colombia from the 1980s. Framed as a noble DEA effort to curtail the growing cartel business, the program portrays Colombia as a backwards country that needs some good, old-fashioned American help in the form of imposing violence and making immoral choices working with the 'good' traffickers. This battle in Colombia was never about a war on drugs, but was a war fought over drugs. *Narcos* dishonestly claims otherwise.[22]

It's impossible to count the number of drug-war books that glorify the industry. Drug-war tourism is thriving, too. In Medellin, Columbia, the city that experienced the notoriety of narco-trafficker Pablo Escobar, visitors can go on tours to some of Escobar's famous sites. Escobar's accountant and brother, Roberto Escobar, who served 14 years in prison, now takes tourists to the family's former safe houses.[23]

There's no evidence that prohibition has curtailed drug use. I've often wondered during the writing of this book what our world would have looked like if the prohibitionists hadn't gained control of the levers of power in the 20th century. In Portugal, a nation that decriminalised all drugs in 2001, drug use has declined amongst the most at-risk group, 15–24-year-olds. The sexiness or allure of illegal drugs was removed; they're now just a normal part of life, ignored or mostly consumed safely. This is a sensible approach that I examine in a number of countries. Could it work elsewhere around the world?

This book is a local and global investigation to determine a better way to manage drugs, and a challenge to end the most destructive war of the last half century.

CHAPTER ONE
Honduras

'They are afraid of us because we are not afraid of them.'

BERTA CACERES, HUMAN-RIGHTS ACTIVIST

Indigenous leader Berta Caceres was murdered in a house on the out-skirts of La Esperanza, her birthplace. The property was painted in green and white, and its red metal roof glistened in the sun on the day I visited. The grass was overgrown and already creeping up the outside walls. It was an active crime scene, with police tape around its entire perimeter. Killed by armed men on 2 March 2016, Caceres had been a marked woman, an enemy of a state that targeted environ-mental campaigners and opponents of its rule.

Her house was situated amidst a beautiful valley of trees and low hills. A solitary police car sat outside, and one policeman and soldier walked up to me, asking what I was doing there. It was eerily quiet, and not difficult to imagine Caceres' murder on an evening in 2016.[1] Her possessions from inside the house had been removed, and the policeman told my fixer, Raul, that the property was still 'contami-nated', months after the murder.

Caceres was 44 years old and the winner of the Goldman Environmental Prize in 2015 for 'a grassroots campaign that success-fully pressured the world's largest dam builder to pull out of the Agua Zarca Dam' on the Gualcarque River in western Honduras. That high-profile work, along with co-founding the Council on Popular and Indigenous Organisations of Honduras (Copinh), a group dedicated to protecting the environment and defending the indigenous Lenca people, brought her global admiration and local dangers.[2]

She knew the risks, as she told Al Jazeera English in 2013: 'I want to live. There are many things I still want to do in this world, but I have never once considered giving up fighting for our territory, for a life with dignity, because our fight is legitimate. I take lots of care, but in the end, in this country, where there is total impunity, I am vulnerable. When they want to kill me, they will do it.'

Her simple grave sat in a local cemetery. Her burial place featured an image of her made in ceramic. Flowers and plants were scattered across the concrete gravestone.

Honduran authorities arrested a former intelligence officer in March 2018 for allegedly masterminding Caceres' murder and giving logistical support to one of the hitmen. David Castillo Mejia was the executive president of the company Desa, which was building the Agua Zarca dam. Caceres had expressed fear of Mejia, accusing him of hounding her with threats and intimidation. He was the ninth person arrested for the murder — Honduran prosecutors only brought formal charges against him in 2019 — and the fourth with ties to the Washington-backed and -funded Honduran military. A former soldier said that Caceres had been placed on a hit list just before she was killed.[3]

A trial for some of the accused concluded in Honduras in late 2018: seven men were found guilty, but it was beset by irregularities after the victim's lawyers were thrown out of court. It remains unclear who within the Honduran establishment was complicit in her death.

Honduras remains one of the most violent nations in the world outside a designated war zone. I've never felt more unsafe reporting in a country, apart from Afghanistan, and locals routinely told me not to walk the streets alone. Many of the cities were charming with old, decaying architecture, but the threat of violence was ubiquitous.[4] NGO Global Witness reported in 2017 that Honduras was the deadliest country on earth for environmental activism; at the time, more than 120 people had been killed since 2010 for opposing land grabs and environmental destruction.

Since the turn of the century, the death toll throughout Latin America and the Caribbean has been horrific. More than 2.5 million people have been murdered in this period, according to research group Igarapé Institute. With just 8 per cent of the world's total population, this region accounts for 38 per cent of the planet's murders.

The Caceres family home was near the centre of La Esperanza, four hours' drive from the violent capital, Tegucigalpa. I was welcomed in by Berta's mother, Austra Bertha Flores Lopez, a sprightly 84-year-old wearing a wooden cross around her neck and long, grey hair in a ponytail. 'The first day after the murder was devastating', she said. 'I thought I would die. Solidarity has been amazing from family and around the world.'

Like her daughter, Austra Flores was a strong opponent of capitalism — 'it's the destruction of all countries' — and her Catholic faith sustained her after Berta's death. 'Berta wasn't religious, and she hated some priests who sided with the US empire', she told me. A former midwife who delivered 5,000 babies over a 52-year career, often in remote areas populated by indigenous Lenca women, she had also been a Congresswoman and mayor of La Esperanza two times. 'I was the first woman then, and still now to hold the position', she said.

Austra Flores showed me around the house, built in 1977. It was a sprawling but modest property where members of the family still lived. One room had been transformed into a memorial to Berta, and featured many photos of her, the famed Goldman Environmental Prize, and the last image taken of her in a corn field. Austra Flores was proud of the room, though visibly saddened by its necessity.

Berta's daughter Laura was also staying at the family home. She told me that police were now stationed outside the entrance since her mother's death, but that this didn't make her feel any safer. Nobody trusted the police. Born in 1992 and having studied obstetrics in Buenos Aires, Laura was one of Berta's four children. Many of them lived outside the country for their own security; one daughter, Bertha Isabel Zuniga Caceres, survived an assassination attempt in central Honduras in 2017.

Laura had seen drastic changes in her nation after the 2009 coup against the democratically elected president, Manuel Zelaya. She told me that threats against Berta increased after this event. Laura blamed the US for worsening violence and repression in her country by its funding of the government's military.

In the months before her mother's killing, she wasn't allowed to stay overnight in the house where Berta was murdered. It was deemed too unsafe after Berta had received at least 33 text-message threats from the Desa company since 2013. Desa's key backers were supporters of the 2009 coup, and the company was given the dam contract as a reward.

Desa had received huge financial support for its plans. Initial funding came from the World Bank and Sinohydro of China, and then the Central American Bank for Economic Integration (CABEI), the Dutch development bank FMO, and the Finnish Fund for Industrial Cooperation, Finnfund. They all backed the project, although these organisations withdrew after Honduran prosecutors filed murder charges against a former employee of Desa in 2016. They had long supported the development despite credible allegations of corruption, money laundering, and suspect government concessions surrounding the project for years.[5]

'In order for this company [Desa] to function in Honduras it needs military and police, some of them trained and financed by the US', Laura said. 'They operate by hiring hit men to create fear in the population. This form of project implementation is normal in Honduras.'

Despite the devastating loss of her mother, Laura vowed to continue her struggle. The government constantly tried to buy her family's support, coming to their home offering small bags of groceries, rice, sugar, and beans, but the family refused to take them. 'I grew up with a mother as a mother but also comrade and role model', Laura told me. 'I believed all of her arguments and struggles that she fought for.'

The Caceres murder had no direct link with the drug war, and yet it was intimately connected to it. The surge in violence and instability across Honduras is caused by an authoritarian government led by President Juan Orlando Hernandez, unaccountable police and military, and rampant gang activity. Fuelling the killings is huge US funding for corrupt state institutions[6] and the complicity of Honduran authorities; they've turned the country into a major Central American transit route for cocaine, although there are increasing signs of traffickers growing coca plantations in Honduras. This explains why so many Hondurans continue fleeing to the US for a safer life despite the Trump administration aiming to stop them at the border.[7] Climate change is also causing increasing chaos in the country's agricultural cycles, forcing many to flee.

The US money destined to fight its drug war in Honduras has led to apocalyptic violence against civilians. It fits a global pattern: the more money flows from Washington to tackle traffickers, the more attacks on the population increase. After being colonised by the Spanish in the 16th century and declaring independence in 1821, Honduras has become embroiled in Washington's dirty wars for more than 50 years.

~

The modern history of Honduras is strewn with blood and tyranny. A tiny, engorged elite maintains control over vast resources, land, and access to business opportunities. Those opposing this arrangement are targeted. The bulk of people living in major cities such as San Pedro Sula and Tegucigalpa don't walk the same streets as the wealthy and connected. They toil in poverty, forced to pay a regular 'war tax' by vicious gangs to operate even the smallest of enterprises.[8] There are at least 36,000 gang members in the country.[9] I met taxi drivers who paid hundreds of US dollars per month to simply stay alive; they feared death if they didn't make a payment. At night, most of the cities become ghost towns; locals don't dare emerge from the shadows while gangs and police fight for control of the streets, often working together to extort money from anybody unfortunate enough to cross their paths.[10]

Corruption is endemic. When Jose David Aguilar Moran was appointed national police chief in January 2018, he was credibly accused of helping a cartel leader in 2013 to secure a delivery of nearly one ton of cocaine worth US$20 million. He didn't lose his job.

I flew into San Pedro Sula, in 2013 rated as the most violent city in the world outside a war zone due to its extraordinarily high murder rate,[11] and was told by my driver that the area near the airport was too dangerous to visit. He said that I'd lose my life and possessions, so he drove fast and barely stopped at red lights. American fast-food chains such as McDonald's, Burger King, Pizza Hut, Denny's, and Wendy's littered the landscape near the centre of town. It felt like an American enclave, and reminded me of poor neighbourhoods I'd visited in Atlanta, Georgia. My driver said that most locals couldn't afford even the cheapest food on offer at these restaurants because salaries were low and unemployment high.[12] The population of the country was barely over nine million.

Washington's tentacles enveloped Honduras from the early 20th century, and it revolved around bananas. The United Fruit Company, one of the most successful and brutal multinationals of the last 100 years, was integral to the term 'banana republic' being coined, and Honduras was the first nation to fall victim. By the end of the 19th century, Americans didn't want to grow fruit in their own country and much preferred to import it from the warmer environs of Central America.[13]

But this industry came at a steep price for the Honduran people. The United Fruit Company dominated vast sections of nearly 12 nations in the Western hemisphere for much of the 20th century. John Ewing, a US minister in Tegucigalpa, sent a letter in 1914 to the US state department and explained the power of the United Fruit Company to 'enter actively into the internal policies' of many nations.[14]

Dictatorships scarred the Honduran landscape for decades. From the 1930s and 1940s there were countless regimes that were decided by the US embassy and the United Fruit Company. It was a cosy arrangement that continually excluded the Honduran population. The US trained thousands of Honduran soldiers, and these men ran the country for years. US financial assistance to the Honduran military — totalling hundreds of millions of dollars over decades from the 1950s onwards — made it the most developed political institution in the country. The Honduran army, today one of the more brutal and lawless arms of the state, developed a culture of unaccountability during these years.

The country did not see the violence experienced by its neighbours, El Salvador, Nicaragua, and Guatemala, during much of the 20th century, but everything changed from the early 1980s. Washington used Honduras as a staging post for its war against Latin American communism. When the communist Sandinista government emerged in Nicaragua from the late 1970s, the US under President Ronald Reagan initiated a plan to overthrow it by backing, funding, and arming the right-wing parliamentary Contras.[15] Honduras was at the centre of this ugly fight, positioned as an active front in the war against the Sandinistas.

The most notorious feature of this period was the establishment of a US-backed military-intelligence unit, Battalion 316, which unleashed a campaign of terror and murder against Honduran civilians. It began in August 1980 when 25 Honduran military officials arrived in the US to receive CIA training in interrogation techniques.

Battalion 316 was also instructed by Pinochet's Chile and Argentina's junta.[16]

US ambassador John Negroponte, who served in Honduras between 1981 and 1985, turned a blind eye to the most egregious abuses committed by his Honduran hosts. He ensured a huge increase in US military aid from US$4 million to US$77.4 million per year, and enthusiastically promoted Reagan's militarised anti-communist agenda.[17] During the administration of George W. Bush, Negroponte was US ambassador to Iraq in 2004 and 2005 when Washington backed Shiite and Kurdish death squads. He endorsed Hillary Clinton during the 2016 presidential campaign.

It was during the 1980s that the seeds of today's drug war in Honduras were planted.[18] The CIA released a report in 1988 which acknowledged for the first time that it had purposely ignored drug-smuggling by its Contra allies in the 1980s. With the Reagan administration zealously working to overthrow communism in the US sphere of influence, colluding with CIA director William Casey and National Security Council Lieutenant Colonel Oliver North, former CIA inspector general Frederick Hitz detailed countless examples of its mission being corrupted from the start. The CIA worked with a Honduran businessman, Alan Hyde, a notorious cocaine trafficker, for logistical support. The pilots that flew military supplies to the Contras were known by the CIA to take 'guns down, drugs up'; cocaine filled the cargo holds of the planes returning to the US.[19]

Even after the Iran–Contra scandal broke in the mid-1980s — when the Reagan administration sold weapons to Iran to free US hostages held by Tehran and fund the Contras — the CIA continued colluding with drug-traffickers. The Hitz report proved that the second-in-command of Contra forces in Honduras had admitted to being a fugitive from a Colombian drug conviction, and the CIA knew it. The CIA worked with major drug-traffickers across the region, including individuals who were behind the so-called Cocaine

Coup in Bolivia in 1980, turning that country into the region's first narco-state.[20]

A secret 1981 CIA cable which was made public in the 1990s revealed that the CIA had been told by 'an asset' that the Contras were going to sell drugs in the US to support their work.[21] American investigative journalist Gary Webb published an explosive exposé in the 1990s that showed how the CIA was implicated in bringing crack cocaine to the US in the 1980s.[22]

At the beginning of the 1990s, the DEA (Drug Enforcement Administration) was paying Honduran military officers for every kilogram of cocaine they'd present; the process was only abandoned when it was impossible to ignore the fact that these men were involved in drug-trafficking. The presidency of Manuel Zelaya, from 2006 until he was deposed in a 2009 coup, was the first administration that began to seriously examine both the legacy of US involvement in the Honduran drug-trade and to challenge the Washington consensus on drug prohibition.[23]

After the coup, Zelaya was smeared by a vicious PR campaign as a friend of drug-traffickers. US cables, leaked by Wikileaks and written by former US ambassador Charles A. Ford, accused the ex-president of colluding with narco-traffickers and organised crime. (Though he provided no evidence of either, I also heard credible allegations against Zelaya.) Despite this, Wikileaks cables confirmed that the US embassy in Tegucigalpa had accepted it was a coup. The cable was titled, 'Open and Shut'.[24]

Zelaya was deposed after his opponents falsely claimed he had made attempts to stay in power indefinitely through changes to the constitution. He was kidnapped by the military and flown out of the country in his pyjamas on 28 June 2009. The coup leader, Honduran General Romeo Vasquez Velasquez, was a graduate of the notorious School of the Americas in the US, where at least 11 Latin American dictators were trained after it opened in 1948.[25] Honduras dispatched senior colonels to Washington to lobby for the coup's legitimacy. They accused Zelaya of being a communist, a message warmly received by Republicans.[26]

Leaders across Latin America protested the coup, but then US secretary of state Hillary Clinton later admitted that the Obama administration had supported Zelaya's removal. A senior US military official met the coup plotters in Honduras the night before the coup, indicating knowledge and support for the impending event.[27] In the hardback edition of her memoir *Hard Choices*, in sections curiously omitted from the paperback version, Clinton wrote that, 'In the subsequent days [after the coup] I spoke with my counterparts around the hemisphere, including Secretary [Patricia] Espinosa in Mexico. We strategized on a plan to restore order in Honduras and ensure that free and fair elections could be held quickly and legitimately, which would render the question of Zelaya moot.'[28]

The coup triggered an avalanche of murders, rising 50 per cent between 2008 and 2011, along with killings of opposition leaders and peasant organisers. Gangs and unaccountable Honduran security forces had complete impunity, exploiting already weak state institutions.

Zelaya had made some powerful enemies in the US and Latin America for daring to question Washington's militarised drug war. In November 2008, he pushed for the decriminalisation of drug consumption, and urged policy to shift from interdiction to prevention. 'Instead of pursuing drug-traffickers', Zelaya said, 'societies should invest resources in educating drug addicts and curbing their demands.' Soon after, he wrote to then president-elect Obama and stated his opposition to US 'interventionism' under the guise of a drug war.[29] Zelaya's scepticism about the drug war was echoed across Latin America, with many ex-leaders acknowledging the failures of Washington's violent approach.[30] Nonetheless, Brazil's far-right president, Jair Bolsonaro, and Colombia's president, Ivan Duque Marquez, favour a more aggressive drug war, both finding favour with the Trump administration.

Zelaya allied himself with more independent regional nations such as Bolivia and Venezuela, states that increasingly refused to accommodate DEA activities on their soil, and he wanted to convert the US airbase at Soto Cano into a civilian airport. Today it remains the largest US military installation on foreign soil in the hemisphere, with hundreds of US military personnel. The base was used for Pentagon drug-surveillance flights, and thousands of US troops were housed there in the 1980s.

Zelaya had taken US military aid and signed up to the so-called Merida Initiative, a multi-billion-dollar drug war aid package for Mexico and Central America. But his sin was to accuse the US of being the 'chief cause' of drug-trafficking in the region because of the ever-growing appetite for illegal drugs within the US.

The 2009 coup was a pivotal event in modern Honduran history, revealing the extent to which Washington wanted to keep the country fully engaged in its drug war, whatever the civilian cost.[31] Since 2009, the US has given hundreds of millions of dollars in aid and security assistance to Honduras, but in 2019 President Trump pledged to cut all aid to Honduras, El Salvador, and Guatemala in retaliation for what he viewed as the three countries failing to stop their citizens fleeing to the US. The facilitation of human rights, transparency, and good governance had received only 15 per cent of funds before Trump's cuts. Washington first designated Honduras as a major drug-transit country in 2010, and had pumped in funds ever since to allegedly combat it.[32] The facts on the ground suggested otherwise.

The US response to this reality was explained in *The New York Times* in a 2012 story headlined, 'Lessons of Iraq Help US Fight a Drug War in Honduras'.[33] Acknowledging a 'messy' US history in the country, embedded journalist Thom Shanker explained how America's 'small-footprint missions' would give local police and military the lead in fighting cartels. There was no mention of the 2009 coup, government complicity in the drug-trade, or mass violence caused by Honduran security forces. It was akin to a press release written by the Pentagon. Too often, the US media ignored the coup and Washington's complicity in its violent aftermath.[34]

The DEA's collaboration with Honduras was always murky. After the Honduran air force used American intelligence and shot down two planes in 2012, claiming that they were full of drugs, only for no illicit substances to be found, Washington rethought its strategy. It initiated Operation Anvil, a plan without clear lines of authority or accountability.[35] The DEA deployed commandoes known as FAST (the Foreign-deployed Advisory and Support Team), which had operated in Afghanistan and failed to dent that country's explosion in opium production. Fanning across Latin America since 2008, they were often a law unto themselves, working with local law enforcement in notoriously corrupt states such as Haiti and Guatemala. FAST was shut down in 2017 after a bungled 2012 mission in Ahuas, Honduras, that killed four civilians.

The 2009 coup was a godsend to Colombian traffickers, who changed their route days later and began ferrying cocaine through Honduras; Mexican cartels were the main recipients, and facilitated the transit of between 140 and 300 tons of cocaine annually. (The exact amount was impossible to know.)[36]

Vast parts of the country were under narco control, and at least 50 per cent of Honduran police were estimated to be corrupted by the drug-trade.[37] From 2007 onwards, when the US succeeded in shutting down a drug route from South America through Mexico and the Caribbean, Honduras was targeted by cartels.[38] In 2012, the US state department estimated that 79 per cent of all cocaine-trafficking flights leaving South America for the US first landed in Honduras (with 90 per cent of cocaine passing through Central America and Mexico).[39]

President Juan Orlando Hernandez has led Honduras since

January 2014 (although he was already a Congressman during the 2009 coup and began amassing power after then).[40] He was embraced by Washington and lavished with funds.[41] The country also signed a military deal with Israel.[42] The Obama administration pushed through Congress a US$750 million package to Guatemala, El Salvador, and Honduras in late 2015, with US$98 million slated for Honduras. It was a stated attempt to boost stability in the three nations, but it was equally about strengthening local security services to stop potential migrants travelling to the US. Obama bribed Mexico to detain and deport desperate people fleeing gang-infested suburbs in Guatemala, El Salvador, and Honduras.[43]

But rumblings of dissent were stirring in the US Congress. Democratic representative Hank Johnson co-introduced a bill in 2016 called the Berta Caceres Human Rights in Honduras Act that aimed to cease all US military support to the Honduran regime.[44] It was supported by the Caceres family. One of the most outspoken congressmen was Democrat Patrick Leahy. 'Over the past 25 years, the United States has provided hundreds of millions of dollars in aid to Honduras, with little to show for it', he told the *Los Angeles Times* in 2016.[45]

Hernandez was re-elected in 2017 despite widespread allegations of fraud, with the Trump administration viewing the regime as supportive of its war against immigration.[46] Honduras was a compliant ally in its drug war, so Washington confirmed the Hernandez election victory despite opposition from some Democratic representatives. The US embassy in Tegucigalpa under chargé d'affaires Heide B. Fulton worked behind the scenes to solidify the Hernandez win.[47] Trump's then-ambassador to the United Nations, Nikki Haley, visited Honduras in February 2018, praised the regime, and thanked the president for his country being one of the very few nations in the world to support the US decision to move its embassy to Jerusalem.[48]

Trump's White House chief of staff John Kelly referred to Hernandez in early 2017 as a 'great guy' and 'good friend'. When Kelly was head of the US military's Southern Command from 2012 to 2016, before being briefly appointed by Trump to lead the Department of Homeland Security, he formed a bond with Hernandez. Kelly told the US Congress in 2015 that, 'human-rights groups have acknowledged to me that Honduras is making real progress', against drug-trafficking and criminality.[49] In fact, human-rights groups were saying the complete opposite.

Dozens of protestors were murdered by security forces in post-election violence in 2017 and 2018 while Hernandez cracked down even harder on the population. At least 1,500 people were imprisoned on false charges — I knew one political activist who remained behind bars despite having committed no crime — and my friends in Honduras feared a return to the darkest days of the 1980s. The huge numbers of Hondurans fleeing today in large migrant caravans towards the US are the direct result of drug cartels forcing people to choose between leaving or dying. On the tenth anniversary of the 2009 coup, Hondurans protested the repressive government despite police violence against them.

~

Travelling through the Honduran interior revealed the extent of the country's descent into chaos. It wasn't a war zone in the traditional sense — insurgents weren't targeting foreigners or engaging in attacks that killed indiscriminately — but the countryside was home to rampaging soldiers and gangs, along with police who routinely harassed locals. Virtually everybody I met was scared or cautious when talking about the government and security forces.

Relative calm was deceptive even in a pretty city such as La Esperanza. At its centre were bustling fruit and vegetable markets, and children played football on a green pitch. The name 'Berta' (Caceres) was everywhere, spray-painted on various surfaces. Even on the outside walls of the prison were two massive colour murals of her face. Next to one was a message about police death squads that read, 'Police dickface'. Elsewhere it read, 'Police hit man'. I was astounded that the authorities hadn't removed them.

Copinh operated a network of community services in the area, including the House of Healing for domestic-violence victims. Its manager, Lilian Esperanza Lopez, told me that its purpose was to 'fight machismo', support assaulted women in a society that rarely did so, and back families who had been displaced by deforestation. 'Berta taught us to resist', she said. After the 2009 coup, emergency contraception for women was outlawed, and abortion is now banned in all circumstances, despite the country having one of the highest rates of sexual violence in the world outside an official war zone.

The Copinh headquarters, which was called 'Utopia', was in a luscious green field. It had the feel of a community centre with training facilities, dorm rooms, and large meeting spaces. Leader Jose Asuncion Martinez was a kind-looking man wearing a cap, colourful scarf, denim jacket, and jeans. He lived in Santa Elena, a community near the border with El Salvador. We sat around an undercover wooden table as the rain began to pour. A dog started chasing a nearby bull, causing the chickens to revolt and squawk. Like so many Copinh members, the political analysis offered by Martinez wasn't theoretical but gained from living with the daily threat of state assassination.

'The role of Washington is to work with the Honduran government to repress indigenous communities in the country', he said. 'Thirty-five per cent of Honduras has concessions for oil, gas, and hydro-electric projects on indigenous lands. Concession means the national government hands out resources and lands without consultation. It's illegal. The concessions are mostly given out to transnational companies, "projects of death", for mining and hydro-electric projects.'

Martínez opposed the presence of the US and the European Union in his country, because their agenda was never publicly admitted. 'They say they're here to back the Honduran government and strengthen the military, but it's really just a way to grow US bases. The Honduran government allows more US bases even though it claims it's fighting the war on drugs. It's militarising indigenous land. It's a throw-back to the 1980s, but resistance is more criminalised now than then.'

Although Martinez believed that the murder of Caceres had strengthened the Copinh struggle, he recognised that Honduras was infected with drug money, akin to Mexico. 'Our country is a narco-state with narco-mayors and narco-MPs', he said. 'They get funded by drug-traffickers, and when they get into power they have to pay traffickers back.'

In the north of the country, citizens faced similar threats. In the city of La Ceiba, gangs increasingly controlled the streets. Public buses were attacked, with drivers threatened and killed. I was shown a shocking video on a mobile phone, in black and white with no audio, of a female gang member pulling a gun on a bus driver while he was driving. She shot him dead. The passengers were terrified, and the bus crashed. The woman was eventually caught after being identified on Facebook.

In nearby Tocoa, a poor town with low-rise buildings, it was indigenous leaders and peasants who felt the wrath of the state. Vitalino Alvarez, 53 years old with seven children, was a high-profile member of the United Peasant Movement (Muca) and a campesino (peasant farmer) leader. His name appeared on a military hit list, alongside Berta Caceres and dozens of other environmental and social activists, used by US-trained special forces to eliminate enemies.[50] Having survived at least four assassination attempts since 2010, Alvarez was named by the Inter-American Commission on Human Rights (IACHR) in 2014 as needing urgent protection. He never received it.

'When Berta was killed, I became top of the [hit] list', he told me. 'I think they'll have to get rid of us all. I saw the hit list on social media months ago.' I was also shown the hit list by activists, with many names on it, but it was impossible to verify its accuracy.[51]

'Seventeen days after Berta's murder, they tried to kill me,' Alvarez said. 'I had participated in protests and supported her. Men on motorcycles came to my landlord and wanted to know where I was, but I wasn't home. They were angry. I left the area with my two kids immediately by taxi. I gave them money in case I was killed or injured.'[52]

As we spoke, a poll appeared on Honduran state TV: 'How believable for you is the fact that the Virgin Mary is seen crying today?' Seventy-seven per cent said it was very believable.

Another campesino leader was Johnny Rivas, a member of the United Peasant Movement in the Bajo Aguan region. He was also placed on the military hit list. During a meeting of agrarian farmers in Tocoa, he told me that much of his people's farmland in this agricultural heartland had been turned into palm oil plantations owned by multi-millionaire Miguel Facusse Barjum's company, Dinant. The West's obsession with reducing its carbon footprint was directly connected to this dirty war in Honduras and the mass expansion of palm oil production. Ten oligarch families dominated the industry.[53]

'Drug-traffickers buy land and have cattle here, but this is cover for building landing strips [to deliver drugs]', Rivas said. 'Drugs are not produced here, just delivered. Drug-trafficking affects the Aguan. It's reduced the campesinos' area of land. We have no friction with drug-traffickers, but private security companies, protecting the landowners, work with police, military, and traffickers. The traffickers keep to themselves and don't bother us. The aim of the US drug war isn't to win it but control it.'

Wikileaks' state department cables released in 2011 confirmed what I had heard in the Aguan. Since the 2009 coup, the government had worked with landowners in the area to secure territory for biofuel production through intimidation, coercion, and bribery. One of the leading businessmen was coup backer Miguel Facusse, and his private security guards stood accused of killing dozens of peasant activists who resisted these moves. His guards worked with the Honduran police and military, both of whom received huge amounts of funding from the US to fight its drug war.

The cables confirmed that the US government had been aware of Facusse's role as a cocaine importer since 2004, but had done nothing to stop its money going to fund, train, and maintain Honduran forces working alongside his men.[54] Facusse controlled at least one-fifth of the land in the Aguan — 22,000 acres — with African palms covering the territory for his burgeoning biofuel business.[55]

Facusse was accused of being behind the killing of human-rights lawyer Antonio Trejo. Facusse told the *Los Angeles Times* in a rare interview in 2012 that, 'I probably had reasons to kill him but I'm not a killer.'[56] When confronted by the newspaper about his alleged complicity in the drug-trade, Facusse claimed that he had tried to stop small planes loaded with cocaine for Mexican and Colombian traffickers landing on his property by putting chains on the runways. 'I'm controlling it', he said. 'The narcos are building airports all over the place. It's a perfect place to land. Nobody is around.'

Wikileaks cables offered detailed evidence of Facusse's involvement in the drug-trade. On 19 March 2004, US ambassador Larry Palmer wrote a cable that read in part: 'A known drug-trafficking flight with a 1,000-kilo cocaine shipment from Colombia, which resulted in a fruitless air interdiction attempt ... successfully landed March 14 on the private property of Miguel Facusse.' The cable explained how sources had told police that 'its cargo was off-loaded onto a convoy of vehicles that was guarded by about 30 heavily armed men'. The plane was burned and its wreckage buried by a 'bulldozer/front-end loader'. According to the cable, 'Facusse's property is heavily guarded and the prospect that individuals were able to access the property and without authorization use the airstrip is questionable.' Facusse was allegedly on the property at the time.[57]

Ambassador Palmer had no doubt who was at fault, writing

that 'this incident marks the third time in the last fifteen months that drug-traffickers have been linked to this property owned by Mr. Facusse'. In a follow-up cable in late March, Palmer detailed the capture by Honduran officials of around 700 kilograms of cocaine, and stated that the drugs likely came from the destroyed plane seen on Facusse's land. None of these details had any impact on US officials meeting with Facusse both before and after the 2009 coup.[58] Facusse died in 2015 at the age of 90, but nothing has since changed positively for the affected communities.

We drove for 45 minutes from Tocoa along a rocky road that led to vast African palm plantations, on land owned by the Facusse family. Armed guards patrolled the fields; it was kilometre after kilometre of tall African palm trees, though some sections had died, leaving smaller palms to grow around them. Speckled sun burst through the branches. It was an eerie sight of death and destruction as well as new, greener life. My fixer, Raul, said that the road was inaccessible at night because drug-traffickers controlled the area. They would kill us.

Heading further into drug territory revealed even greater desperation amongst civilians. The drive from Tocoa to Vallecito (meaning 'little valley') village was mostly on dirt tracks. There were 30 families in brick and concrete homes, with many new structures being built in tin and wood. On arrival, we were given a basic meal of freshly caught fish, rice, and beans. White-painted pole fences stretching for kilometres signified that, years ago, the property behind the fence had belonged to the Los Cachiros drug-cartel family. They used to control the land, but heads of the family were extradited to the US on drug charges, and their property was transferred to the Honduran state.

What happened to the two brothers behind the Los Cachiros gang revealed a familiar tactic employed by the DEA in Honduras and globally: offer leniency in exchange for evidence of collaboration between traffickers and the elites. What the victims' families in Honduras thought of the arrangement was impossible to know, as they were never asked. Devis Leonel Rivera Maradiaga and Javier Eriberto Rivera Maradiaga ran a brutal enterprise while living lavishly, killing at least 78 people since 2003 and building an empire as middlemen by moving huge amounts of drugs from hidden airstrips in Honduras to Mexican cartels (who then sent it onto the US). They bought off politicians, including former president Porfirio Lobo, his son Fabio, and allegedly president Juan Orlando Hernandez.[59]

The Rivera brothers approached the DEA and made it an offer as early as 2013; they knew that the agency was investigating them, so this gave the DEA a unique opportunity to catch some senior figures in the drug-trade. Although both men had to admit guilt for the crimes that they had committed, they escaped long jail terms, and some of their family members were granted permission to move to the US. Witness protection was an option for the brothers. The DEA accepted the deal and claimed it would decrease the use of Honduras as a drug-transit country. There was no evidence to support this claim.

As we continued to drive, we were constantly stopped by military checkpoints along the track. Well-armed men and police asked for our IDs and wanted to know where we were headed. Bribes were never demanded. Some of the roads had once been used by drug-traffickers as landing strips. Our driver, Ruben, said that years before he'd seen planes landing here at night, and roadblocks established to stop all traffic and allow the cartel time to unload the drugs. I saw alternative paths off the main road where landing strips existed today. I was told that during President Zelaya's government before the 2009 coup, there was a 'happy hour' in the area when radar was switched off by officials for an hour a day to allow drug-traffickers to fly in and deliver drugs.

The landscape during this journey was luscious, often on tracks adjacent to the Atlantic Ocean. There were green, rolling hills with cows and sheep grazing the fields. This was the home of the indigenous Garifuna people, numbering in the tens of thousands, who lived in many communities along the Caribbean coast. Vallecito was the only town not so close to the water, around one kilometre away, and our Garifuna guide, Guillermo, explained that nearly all of the neighbouring areas faced rising sea levels due to climate change. Guillermo was a tall, large black man with dreadlocks, a tight-fitting white T-shirt, and a brown Kangol cap.[60]

The Garifuna people had one of the country's most eloquent spokespeople. Miriam Miranda was head of Ofraneh, the Black Fraternal Organisation of Honduras, and she told me in Tegucigalpa that the drug war directly impacted her people. She faced constant threats to her life. 'The Garifuna people have had to organise not only because their land is where the drugs are being transported from and to, but also because authorities are involved in drug-trafficking', she said. She condemned the US presence, and had told them to leave.

This was the heart of drug-trafficking territory in Honduras. It didn't feel particularly unsafe or violent, but we were passing through during the day, and didn't stop and loiter.

At a point along the red dirt road from Cusuna to Ciriboya, Guillermo said that the long, relatively straight path was used by drug-traffickers as a landing strip. It had been used as recently as five months ago, he believed. The Garifuna people used to protest, but the traffickers were too powerful to be stopped. They had to accept that their lands were now prime targets for a lucrative trade over which they had no say.

This was how it worked: a small plane landed after 6.00pm when it was getting dark. Traffickers used a generator to power lights along the landing strip. The drugs were removed — they usually came from Colombia — and then the plane was burned and ditched in the Atlantic. Heavy moving equipment was brought in for the job. The municipal government regularly smoothened the road, which, Guillermo said, was just one way that the state supported the cartel trade. He knew of three pilots who had died because they had crashed on approach to the landing strip.

'The Garifuna fights against traffickers', Guillermo told me, 'but it's hard when you're fighting a state that colludes with the traffickers.'

A little down the road, we spotted another checkpoint, but this was no ordinary roadblock. We'd accidently hit a major anti-drug operation in the town of San Jose De La Punta by the Honduran military, police and its investigations unit, the US-trained Honduran Tigres force and the elite Cobra team. Dozens of heavily armed men, some with black ski masks, prowled the area. They were looking for Eliel Sierra, a key trafficker in the area, and they took into custody the manager and employees of his business. Guillermo said that they would interrogate them for information about the whereabouts of Sierra, possibly torture them to get information, and then release them. Authorities were also seizing assets in his business.

Local officials played a double game, sometimes trying to stop drug-smuggling through aggressive means — at times to impress Washington and ensure continuing funds — but they largely allowed the most egregious examples of trafficking to continue under their very noses, due to bribery and corruption. The US knows this, but doesn't care. After decades of this unhealthy relationship, the US under successive administrations is content to partner with a client state that's willing to fight Washington's war on its own territory. Innocent civilians die in the crossfire.

Civilians were staring on the side of the road while others just walked past as if they saw such sights every day. Authorities had brought eight to ten open-top trucks and 45 men in bullet-proof vests, some carrying grenades, and they ran around with high-calibre weapons. I was unable to see their faces, a tactic to protect themselves from identification by traffickers.

One of the operation heads ordered us out of the car. Police searched it thoroughly, and told us to speak to an officer whose face was covered. He wanted to know why we were there, and asked to see my ID and international journalist card. While we were conversing, and my fixer, Raul, translated, I kept my eye on the dozens of men to make sure I didn't miss any outbreak of gunfire. 'What's happening?' Raul asked. 'Too many traffickers, even during the day', the officer replied.

After 15 minutes of being questioned, we were allowed to drive away. Within seconds, open-backed trucks sped past us — we counted seven cars — and raced ahead. Our vehicle was enveloped in dust. We soon arrived at the next town, Iriona Puerto, and saw the seven trucks stopped with masked men surrounding a house. A few had drawn their weapons. It was the house of trafficker Eliel Sierra's business manager. We hung back for a while, not wanting to be in the middle of anything violent if the situation exploded, but there were no gunshots.

I asked Guillermo if he saw such operations regularly. He said no, but explained why there was scepticism about these missions. The mayor of Iriona Puerto was involved in drug-trafficking and murdered in 2014, so the absurdity of the day's operation was soon apparent. The house of drug-trafficker Eliel Sierra was a large wooden structure overlooking the river in Iriona Puerto, adjacent to the municipal building and across the road from the main police station. It was still standing, he hadn't been arrested, and it was obvious that he was protected by those in government. The Honduran government was infected with drug-traffickers and their supporters, so they couldn't be expected to adequately fight the trade.

Before the end of a long day, we took a small boat to a poor village on the Atlantic coast, Sangrelaya, one of the many tiny and largely ignored places affected by the drug war. It was the magic hour, and the trees, branches, birds, and Zika-infested mosquitoes all glistened in the fading sun. There was no electricity there, but generators and solar power provided a few lights when darkness fell. It was a hot and sweaty night in a hotel room more like a concrete box, barely bigger than an average prison cell.

Despite the apparent peace of the village on a hot day, the drug war and its victims were never far away from daily life. Marian Colon was 28 years old with two children and long black dreadlocks. She was the sister of Elvis Armando Garcia Martinez, a 19-year-old man who was murdered by the Honduran military on 27 December 2015. I met her on the tiled porch at her family home. Elvis and his friend were killed near Iriona Puerto while crossing a nearby river around five in the morning. He was murdered on the way to his transportation job in Tocoa.

Marian said that Elvis was a 'relaxed student' who never took drugs or drank alcohol. The government alleged that Elvis and others had shot at the military during an early-morning confrontation when they were in the middle of an operation against drug-trafficking. There was no evidence to support this claim, a common accusation after civilians were shot dead, and Marian had been told nothing by officials after his death. 'Elvis always showed respect to everybody', she said. 'Life cannot be given back, but we want government support.' During my conversation with Marian, her grandmother held the framed photo of Elvis and stared into the distance. Marian said that she'd never recovered from her grandson's death.

A few hours later, I met a survivor of the incident that killed Elvis. The organiser of the transportation trips from Sangrelaya to Tocoa where Elvis worked was Maynor Mejia, a 29-year-old with two children. He lived in Cocalito, but I met him in Iriona Puerto while he was fixing his vehicle, which had been attacked by the military on that fateful December day in 2015. It still had many visible bullet holes in the exterior; some bullets had even gone through the seatbelt. Maynor was shirtless, with greasy hands and red shorts.

'I saw the military take position in the weeds, and they shot us from there', Maynor began. 'There was no communication between us. The two boys were killed outside the car pushing it [the vehicle had engine trouble that day], so they were vulnerable. I survived by luck. Bullets hit the car and flew past me when I was in the front passenger seat. I yelled to the seven other passengers to lie down. Windows shattered. The military approached us while still firing at us and to check if we were drug-traffickers. I saw one man, my work partner, die instantly. The military made us lie face down on the ground and looked for guns and drugs, but found nothing.'

Straight after the incident, Maynor and his passengers were smeared in the media as violent drug-traffickers. 'When I saw the government claim in the press that we had weapons, I was outraged', he said. 'I want compensation for my car, psychological care, and the soldiers charged with attempted murder.' Maynor's understanding was that 'the soldiers [on the day of the incident] were high [on drugs], and the military confused us with drug-traffickers. They were shooting to kill, aiming for our body and head.'

~

The most notorious example of Washington's botched efforts to control the drug-trade in Honduras occurred on 11 May 2012. In the eastern Mosquitia region near the isolated community of Ahuas, the DEA and Honduran military were working on Operation Anvil to stop drugs moving north. On that evening, the authorities intercepted traffickers who were attempting to transport more than 400 kilograms of cocaine, so they quickly moved the illicit substance to a motorised canoe.

Four government helicopters appeared, and in the ensuing confusion the traffickers fled into the jungle. Honduran police and the DEA were pursuing the canoe when another canoe suddenly appeared — a civilian water taxi carrying a dozen passengers. It steered towards the drugs-laden boat and collided with it. The anti-drug officials opened fire on the passengers as they jumped into the water for protection. Four civilians, including two pregnant women, were killed, and three were injured.

To this day, the DEA claims that there was an 'exchange of gunfire' and that they were responding to an attack from the water taxi. There was no evidence to back this allegation, and surveillance footage shot by the DEA on the night, eventually available in 2017 after a long freedom-of-information battle, confirmed that the DEA had been lying.[61] A devastating 424-page joint report from the inspectors general of the justice and state departments released in 2017 detailed how the DEA lied for years to the US Congress, the public, and the justice department about the nature of the raid and its deadly aftermath. Despite claiming otherwise, the DEA led the mission, and Honduran forces were at best joint partners.

The DEA is a notoriously secretive organisation, and despite multiple requests I've lodged over the last years for information on this incident and others, it has rarely given me more than a sentence in response. I asked to embed with DEA forces while in Honduras, but this request was denied.

However, since 2016 I've spoken by phone to the former US embassy's DEA attaché in Honduras, Jim Kenney, from his home in Florida. He arrived in Honduras just before the 2012 coup and supported the overthrow of president Zelaya because of the 'corruption' (though he said that Washington officially opposed the change of government). Then US ambassador Hugo Llorens told Kenney to stop co-operating with the new regime for a 'short time' on narcotics investigations, but one month later authorised its continuation. 'No one else really had that authority', Kenney told me. 'I was the only one.' He believed that the DEA assisted the Honduran authorities to successfully fight drug cartels, and said that the country was in better shape today because of this collaboration.

In multiple conversations with me over many years, Kenney

continually denied that his DEA team had screwed up on the 2012 mission, and took no responsibility for the deaths of the four Hondurans. He said that at least two people on the water taxi had fired gunshots at his anti-drug team (though he said it was 'crazy' to think the boat was a water taxi; he said a confidential informant had claimed it was protecting the cocaine). Kenney expressed regret that they had died, but argued that the Honduran government, not US authorities, should be the one maybe giving compensation.

Throughout the entire 2012 mission, Kenney was in Tegucigalpa and in constant contact by satellite phone with his men in the helicopters. He praised their professionalism, and was proud of the Honduran officers being 'vetted' by him.[62]

'The bottom line is, we were there to stop an interdiction of a major load of cocaine coming into the country', Kenney told me. 'We were doing our job. When we started becoming very successful over the two to three years beforehand, they [the drug cartels] started beefing up their response to us. They had SWAT teams, very tactically trained, and their mission was to take down one of our helicopters and kill us to protect their load.'

Years after the incident, the survivors remained penniless and forgotten. They were unworthy victims in the eyes of the US government, the DEA, and much of the media that covered the drug war. I tracked down two of the survivors who had rarely spoken to the media about that fateful evening in May 2012.

On the Caribbean island of Roatan in northern Honduras, I met Clara Woods.[63] Her son, Hasked Brooks Woods, was killed. She wore a black top, white shorts, and pink thongs. We sat and ate at a Bojangles fast-food restaurant, where the food options were fried chicken, fried nuggets, French fries, and sugary drinks. Clara's mother-in-law, Julia Simmons, joined us. She spoke English in a Creole style, partly understandable, but often incomprehensible. She shook while sitting, and occasionally mumbled a few words about Clara and her murdered grandson. She constantly raised her head in anger and despair, and said that there was no justice.

Clara lived in Roatan before the 2012 incident, and had travelled to Ahuas to visit her mother. She recalled, in the past, hearing drug-trafficker's planes landing when she went to the area, but this time everything was quiet. Soon after seeing Black Hawk helicopters hovering above the water taxi, she realised something was wrong.

'I was looking through the fog on the river', she said. 'It was 2.00am, and I couldn't see very well. I saw a boat approaching us, but nobody was driving it; it was just floating in the current. When I looked closely, I saw two American military men come down from the helicopter with ropes onto the other boat. I heard four gunshots. I was screaming, crying, and praying to God. I called for my son, but he did not respond.' She was quietly sobbing while recounting the story.

Clara called out for her son, but she couldn't find him for two days. When she eventually discovered his body, 'he was unrecognisable'. By then his body was terribly swollen, and she had no choice but to bury him in a bag still wearing the clothes he had worn on his last night. Clara buried him on Mother's Day.

What happened after Hasked's murder was unlike any other drug-war death that I'd investigated, though it fitted into a long history of DEA attempts to tamper with the truth. Starting in mid-2013, Clara said that a Honduran man called Eddie began contacting both her and a family member of one of the female victims of the incident. Eddie urged them to drop their legal representation and to find other support through him. Twice in February 2014, Eddie accompanied Clara to Tegucigalpa for questioning by American officials (it was never clear if they were from the DEA or the US embassy). The Americans — one identified as Mr Andres — urged her to change her testimony and to allege that people in the water taxi had opened fire on the DEA, therefore justifying their deadly response.[64] Eddie said that Clara would receive US$5,000 if she altered her testimony, but she refused.

On her second visit to the nation's capital, Clara said that she was taken to the US embassy for a polygraph test. The man administering it said he was from the DEA, but the test didn't proceed because she had recently taken pills to calm her nerves given to her by Eddie, and the DEA representative claimed that this meant Clara didn't want to tell the truth.

I asked Clara what she thought had happened on that awful 2012 evening. 'I think the US and Honduran forces were confused', she said. 'It may have been an accident, but there still needs to be justice.' She told me that some of the victims had received financial assistance from the US government, but she'd seen nothing. 'I feel forgotten. I want the grave of my son to be rebuilt with a little shack and a garden where I can feel it's nice. They want to wash their hands of all this. That's why they wanted to polygraph me. Why would they take me in such a sneaky way to test me if they didn't have anything to hide?'

Speaking to her was one of the most difficult interviews I've ever done. At various times during our conversation, she wept, with tears streaming down her face. She was never likely to receive compensation from the US for her devastating loss. She lived with her husband in Roatan without a job, and looked after two children — one given to her by a poor female friend who couldn't afford to look after her four-year-old daughter, and an 11-year-old boy given to her by another close friend. I sensed she wanted to be around children after her own son had been murdered. I feared that she was being re-victimised by me interviewing her, and I didn't feel entirely comfortable doing it.[65]

Spending time with Clara challenged my ability to be a neutral journalist simply reporting what she said. Objectivity felt inappropriate in the face of such suffering. Her story was horrific, and she deserved justice. I didn't believe that featuring her testimony would radically change her situation, but I'd long believed that a journalist should advocate for the most marginalised members of society. It's the least we could do when using our powerful platform.

Woods' story was confirmed by one of the country's leading human-rights bodies. Bertha Oliva runs Cofadeh, the Committee of Relatives of the Disappeared in Honduras, based in Tegucigalpa, and she told me that her group had legally represented the victims of the massacre (though the Honduran state had kept vital legal documents secret). The dead were buried by locals after the event, but were exhumed soon after by Americans and Hondurans to determine which bullets were used and how the victims were shot.

Oliva visited Washington to meet the then head of the DEA. She left disappointed. 'The meeting was tense', she said. 'We went with evidence about the case and with what the families gave us. We went with the demand that the US needed to repair the damage for the victims and survivors. It wasn't an easy meeting, but at least there was tolerance of being heard. We wanted action.'

Oliva dismissed the DEA's claim that it had sent US$200,000 to the La Mosquitia group Ingwaia, because she had seen no evidence that funds had reached the affected families, rather than just this minor group. 'The DEA said what they always do: it was not their intention, and they didn't aim to violate human rights.'

Another massacre survivor was Lucio Adan Nelson Queen, a 25-year-old agricultural worker who hadn't been able to work since the 2012 incident. I met him and his girlfriend, Glancy, in Tocoa. They were quiet and shy, and had recently had a baby. His right arm had never functioned properly since he'd been shot on the boat, and its bending flexibility was limited. He suffered constant cramps when he walked in the sun, and the arm swelled. He couldn't walk much, since he had a limp, and he had to take constant pain medication. He'd recently had surgery to partially fix his arm, backed by the Honduras Solidarity Network, but he didn't have the money to fund the entire treatment. He couldn't do any activities that required strength.

Lucio Adan ran errands between Ahuas and Patuca in 2012, which explained his presence on the boat that May night. He had been hit by four bullets during the event, and they had all been removed. When, years later, he pulled up his T-shirt and pointed to two bullet holes on his back, they still looked unhealed.

He described the chaos of the moment in Ahuas; he jumped into the water soon after the firing began. 'I felt the bullets go through me as I was in the water', he told me. 'I was bleeding from three different places. I was bleeding too much.'

Lucio Adan had received no financial assistance since the massacre. 'When I start talking about this issue, I feel bad, nervous and traumatised', he said. 'I go into shock again. I forget about things since the incident. I have bad memories. Sometimes I run errands and then forget what I'm doing. I want to get psychological treatment to see what issues I have.'

~

It was hard to find many Hondurans who viewed Washington's role in their country with anything other than suspicion. I wanted to challenge my own negative perceptions, so I initiated contact with the US state department in Washington to determine how much access I could get while in Honduras. After months of negotiation, with Washington and the US embassy in Tegucigalpa, I was eventually granted a two-day embed with the head of public affairs, Eric Turner, to be shown US-funded programs in two major cities.

I met Turner in San Pedro Sula soon after I arrived. He was a friendly man in his fifties, a former journalist who was now a state department Foreign Service careerist, and had worked in Costa Rica, Iraq, Ireland, and Guinea before his posting to Honduras. I was driven to one of the poorest and more violent areas in the city, Chamelecon.

At a police-training facility, 46-year-old district commander Lorenzo Adilio Pineda Reyes explained how he oversaw 135 police, eight of whom were women, and around 150,000 civilians living in the area. He praised the US support he received, and told me that he was 'seeing results'. His team worked with the US-based Bureau of International Narcotics and Law Enforcement Affairs, an agency with an annual budget of more than $1 billion, to target traffickers.

Reyes cited figures that sounded impressive. 'There's been a 60 per cent drop in homicides in the last two years', he said. 'Less than 100 murders in this area. Deaths are over fights for territory and drugs. The big gangs are 18th Street and MS-13.'[66]

The US embassy wanted me to meet what it viewed as the elite local forces tackling the drug war. The Tigres were the jewel in the crown, established in 2014 under president Juan Orlando Hernandez as an acknowledgment that the police were too corrupt to reform. In late 2014, 21 Tigres members were suspended (with dozens more under investigation) over the theft of US$1.3 million during a mission against traffickers. These police had been assigned to the US embassy, and despite the US claiming that they'd been heavily vetted and trained by them, it was clear that this process had failed.[67] Tigres forces were used to suppress public protests after the stolen 2017 presidential election.[68] Before I arrived in Honduras I requested an embed with the Tigres to see how they operated, but it was refused.[69]

Police inspector Julio Sierra was a 30-year-old member of the Tigres force. Dressed in full uniform with a gun attached to his right leg, he praised US backing. Washington gave 'specialised training to minimise risk to us, reduce human-rights violations and supply equipment. Before this, the Tigres didn't have education and breached human rights. With US support, the Tigres has reduced organised crime.'

The rest of the first day was spent visiting USAID-funded outreach centres in Chamelecon (Washington sponsored 46 of them in the country). Some of these facilities tried to steer a small number of citizens away from gang life.[70] I met Agar Gaverrate, the 25-year-old co-ordinator of the outreach centre, and she told me that her main goal was keeping young people on the right path.

'We try to teach values, like good behaviour, waiting your turn if you're playing a game, and finding creative use of time for the youth', she said. 'It's to help youth get a job and reduce violence, because we keep the kids busy and off the streets. Over the last three years, violence has reduced here. I don't see any drugs. Some youth are attracted to gangs due to lack of family communication. Gang leaders become parental figures.'

The centre had a gym — young kids played on the treadmill — and popular video games. A beauty salon taught skills for men and women, and helped them get jobs in hairdressing and make-up. There were breakdancing classes because the local kids loved local and American hip-hop.

Violent gangs were a daily reminder of the country's dysfunction. Gaverrate told me that she was often scared. 'This year I had to go to a gang leader to rescue a kidnapped man. I had to tell the gang that you were coming today, because otherwise I would have questions afterwards. They know you're here.' I was later told that gang members were watching us during the visit.

In the evening, I flew to the capital, Tegucigalpa, for a final day of US embassy touring. I had spent months arranging the visit, and was granted authority to interview the then US ambassador, James D. Nealon, the following morning at the US embassy. He insisted on speaking off the record, but US representative Eric Turner told me that officials in Washington would ensure that some of his quotes could be used for publication. However, after submitting some of his statements, I was informed they were all forbidden. Nealon had uttered little more than platitudes about the US role in Honduras, and had defended his government's record.[71] Turner blamed his superiors in Washington for my inability to use Nealon's direct quotes, but I told

him that 'the US in Honduras claims to be open and transparent …
but the reality is secrecy and refusing to provide answers to my many
questions'. Communication between us ceased after this exchange.

After the completion of his term (2014–17) as ambassador in
Honduras, Nealon was appointed assistant secretary of international
engagement within the Department of Homeland Security's Office of
Strategy, Policy, and Plans.

The strangest and most disturbing part of my tour occurred when
I arrived at a mobile checkpoint in the Durazno area around 30 minutes from the centre of Tegucigalpa. It was on the major highway
between San Pedro Sula and Tegucigalpa. US spokesman Eric Turner
said that it had been mostly set up for my benefit to see how it worked,
though such checkpoints were common on this route. I was uncomfortable seeing dozens of Honduran police stopping and pulling over
buses, asking civilians to get out and show their IDs. Sniffer dogs
roamed the area looking for drugs, people-smuggling, or large sums
of US dollars.

I spoke mostly to Carlos (not his real name, because I was told
I couldn't quote him directly), an American Homeland Security
representative, on the side of the noisy highway. He wore a black
bullet-proof vest, and packed a handgun. He was proud of what his
Honduran colleagues were doing.

While I was speaking to Carlos, a Honduran police officer
approached us and showed him a small wrapped-up piece of paper. It
contained marijuana, picked up by the sniffer dog, and it was in the
pocket of a 70-year-old man. They confiscated it, checked if he had
any outstanding warrants against him, and let him go, saying that
they were sure it was just for his personal use, perhaps for medical
reasons. The idea that somebody could be arrested to show me how
effective they were in fighting drugs made me sick. I was inadvertently placed in a position where I might have felt complicit in the
misfortune of a person being arrested for drug possession.

Most of my two days with the US embassy were highly cho-reographed, with little left to chance. Eric Turner said it was like 'a dog and pony show'. It was smooth media management, but more spontaneity would have made me feel less like they were trying to hide something, or were at least more open to accepting American blemishes.

Accessing the Honduran regime was close to impossible without connections on the inside. After days of pressure, I was granted an interview with the country's security minister, General Julian Pacheco Tinoco. I never found out exactly how the US embassy had helped me secure the meeting, but they had clearly encouraged or even pres-sured him to see me.

The minister's office was barely furnished, with a large meeting table and light-blue painted walls. He stayed mostly on message, except when I asked him directly if the 2009 coup was a coup, which he categorically denied. The minister had written a book about it, and supported the forced change of government. His record was colourful, at best, with serious allegations of complicity in drug-trafficking. He had received training in the US from the late 1970s in counter-insurgency tactics.[72]

During the interview, a young Honduran man sat beside me. He'd studied abroad, as an employee of the US embassy implementing the Alliance for Prosperity Plan, in one of many Washington-pushed ini-tiatives to reduce migrants' incentives to leave their countries.

I asked Pacheco if he could call his country independent, con-sidering the amount of US interference. 'Despite many weaknesses, we consider ourselves sovereign with dignity', he said. He praised his government's investigation into the killing of Berta Caceres, claiming that the defence ministry had negotiated with her on what kind of security she wanted due to the threats, and helped her stay safe. He said that the state prosecutor had 'solved' Berta's murder case — a blatant untruth.

Pacheco was keen to praise Washington's help in fighting drug cartels. He said that Honduras had been involved in 20 extraditions of drug-traffickers to the US, but the US embassy had told me the number was 13 (with 30 unofficially in process).[73] When I challenged him on his figure, he remained resolute. 'There are many efforts to stop the flow of drugs into the US', he told me. 'We don't aspire to end the war on drugs because it's a monumental task, but we're trying not to corrupt the police, army, Supreme Court, and the prosecutor's office, which are the pillars that keep order in the country.'

The 2012 DEA-massacre in Ahuas was a 'regrettable incident', Pacheco said. He alleged that the Honduran government was 'still working to provide reparations to the victims, and this issue hasn't been closed'. This was news to the victims I spoke to, who had never received any money or even communications from the government.

~

Resistance to the Honduran regime could take your life. For this reason, it was rare to meet outspoken leaders who were willing to challenge the government's brutality, so I cherished the moments when I did.

Opposition politician Maria Luisa Borjas sat on the Regidora (City Council representative) and was a member of the Libre party. She was also the former head of internal affairs of the Honduran national police, who was kicked out because she'd dared to investigate senior officers and found them guilty of corruption and murder. She was found guilty of defamation by a Honduran court in 2019 for accusing the president of a local bank of being one of the masterminds behind the 2016 killing of activist Berta Caceres.

We met in her small office, which had a large Honduran flag in the corner. Borjas was blunt. 'Because of the level of impunity in the country, we have narco-mayors, narco-judges, narco-police,

narco-magistrates of the Supreme Court, and a narco-president ...
I, along with my husband and kids, have had attempts on our lives.
They're all alive. My two oldest kids were arrested without reason and
put in jail. They were released after 24 hours. It was intimidation.'

She was unafraid to name President Hernandez of complicity in
the drug-trade. The president's brother, Tony, was also allegedly connected to trafficking drugs, and was arrested by the DEA in Miami
in late 2018 for cocaine trafficking, weapons offences, and false statements.[74] 'The president must know what his brother is doing', she said.

The arrest of Tony Hernandez proved that the DEA was still committed to fighting the drug war, despite knowing that victory in any
reasonable sense was impossible. The DEA was playing a complex
game in Honduras, both working with officials who were complicit in
the drug-trade, but also going after big figures who could be held up
as examples of the organisation's toughness against the trade.

The dark echoes of history reverberated during my visit. Honduras
was a country that seemed unable to escape its violent past. Bertha
Oliva, head of the NGO Cofadeh (the Committee of Relatives of
the Disappeared in Honduras), understood this better than most.
We spoke in her office in Tegucigalpa, a venue that was attacked by
security forces after the 2009 coup, now adorned with awards from
around the world both for herself and the organisation. The group
was founded in 1982 by 12 families whose family members had been
disappeared by the US-backed dictatorship. This included Oliva,
because her husband, professor Tomas Nativi, vanished in 1981 four
months after they were married. They had one son together, and his
remains had never been found.

She had suffered unimaginably during the last decades, but
warned me that the current situation was deteriorating. 'I can sadly
report that submission and dependency of Honduras to the US after
30 years is worse than before, with some great differences', she said.
Oliva said that in the 1980s, citizens weren't speaking about human

rights, but today they knew they had international conventions to protect them. 'Back then, death squads were in hiding and being advised by the US; now, the army is bloodier and in the open', she told me. 'The orders are planned in the Pentagon and sent here. We're like the arse of the US.'

Oliva condemned President Hernandez for opposing human-rights groups because they dared to challenge his dictatorial rule. 'He just came back from a trip to the US saying that human-rights organisations are doing damage to his government by requesting a cut in US military aid. He considers human-rights groups to be treacherous and against the interests of the country.'

In 2014, Oliva told *The Guardian* that, 'The police and military are using the cover of the US-led war on drugs in Honduras to eliminate many people, maybe including me: I am on the death list again.'[75] When I met her, her pessimism had deepened. 'Many enemies have tried to kill me', she said. 'I'm afraid of dying by gunfire. I want changes that aren't just cosmetic but structural.'

In a country wracked by civil strife and massive state repression, this was a noble but faint hope. Honduras has never been truly free, able to chart its own independent path, because it's too valuable as an obedient client state of Washington. After so many decades of corrupt institutions and drug-war violence, Honduras seems destined to remain a dysfunctional state — unless demand for illicit drugs disappears in the US, or drugs are legalised and regulated to remove the black market.

CHAPTER TWO

Guinea-Bissau

'In the nineteenth century, Europe's hunger for slaves
devastated West Africa. Today, its appetite for cocaine could
do the same. The former Gold Coast is turning into the
Coke Coast.'

THE UNITED NATIONS OFFICE ON DRUGS AND CRIME (UNODC), 2008

Kassumba was a tiny speck on the map in the far south-east of the country. A poor village near the Atlantic Ocean that lacked electricity, it was like so many other idyllic locations along the coast, but this place was special. Kassumba had become a vital transit point for huge shipments of cocaine coming from South America. Europe was the final destination.

Little of this was apparent when I visited. When we rode by motorcycle from the nearest town, Cacine, the dirt path was filled with potholes and rain-water. We raced past countless villages in which women in colourful dresses walked by, and carried food and clothes on their heads. There were growing signs of Islam, with mosques funded by Saudi Arabia.[1] These were remote places with no electricity and only the occasional solar panel. They were reliant on the seasons for sustainable agriculture. There was no easily accessible fresh water, so pumps had to be built to access the underground water.

As we headed towards the coast, the palm trees, water lilies, and rice fields formed a beautiful scene. It felt like modern technology had barely changed the landscape (with the exception of mobile-phone towers every few kilometres). Pure white sand was soon underfoot, a vast expanse with the tide far out to sea. Fishermen were fixing an old boat on the shore, listening to reggae music and drinking strong tea. One man wore a Bob Marley beanie. Cows lay and slept on the sand. Large trees were sitting on their sides, the victims of strong tides. On the horizon was the neighbouring country of Guinea-Conakry.

This entire space was a no man's land, not policed by any authorities, and therefore a perfect place on which to deposit large amounts of cocaine. On the journey to get there, we had crossed at least 100 kilometres and seen no officials or police. Because it is logistically impossible to smuggle drugs directly from South America to Europe, traffickers have been forced to find a way via Africa. The US government had choked old cocaine routes through the Caribbean — an example of Washington simply pushing the drug war from one territory to another — and cartels saw Africa as the new, often lawless frontier.

The Caribbean was a key smuggling route into the US in the 1970s — cocaine was mostly produced in Colombia — but more assertive US interdiction efforts massively slowed down the trade in the 1980s. By the mid-1990s, however, the Caribbean had again become a key transit zone for heroin and cocaine. The Obama administration warned that the region was being used by traffickers, alongside Central America, and the DEA's 2015 National Drug Threat Assessment claimed that 90 tons of cocaine passed through the Caribbean in 2014.

The message was clear: the DEA was never going to stop the drug-trade, traffickers would always adapt to changing circumstances, and demand for drugs in the US was sky-high. Africa offered a relatively untouched continent for smugglers to transport their goods through.

Nowadays, smugglers arrive in Guinea-Bissau by flying a plane from Colombia and refuelling in Brazil, or by chartering a boat from Venezuela or Brazil. It is nearly 2,600 kilometres across the Atlantic Ocean. The boats only travel at night, taking four to five days. They use blue tarpaulins to cover up during the day and avoid air detection.[2] Traffickers choose unstable nations such as Guinea-Bissau, Sierra Leone, and Liberia through which to ply their wares.

Most people around Kassumba were farmers and fishermen who were just trying to survive. Given their rampant poverty and limited education, they were wide open to exploitation if somebody came along with a bag of cash and asked them to recover, store, hide, or transfer drugs; even if they didn't know what the goods were, many would accept such a deal to have a better life. I was told this by both UN drug experts in the capital, Bissau, and by locals in the area. I had complete sympathy with their predicament, and in their situation I was sure I would act similarly.

It was difficult to find hard evidence of drug-smuggling in the area. Asking people directly about drugs was ill-advised, so I had to pose questions in code. My veteran local fixer, Allen, said that the circumstantial details were strong. He told me that I was the first foreign journalist he knew of who had visited the area.

While standing on the beach near Kassumba village, I saw Guinea-Conakry beyond the palm trees. This was a buffer zone under no official control. To the people in both countries, there was no border; they crossed back and forth, as they spoke the same language. Drug-traffickers loved this area. They knew that if they landed there, nobody would see them. Forests on the shore provided protection, and they could hide packets of cocaine until there was safe passage to Bissau, up through Africa and on to Europe.

This was the process: at various times of the year, though usually during the dry season when accessibility was easier, drug-smugglers dropped off drugs in the water by plane or by boat just off the coast near Kassumba in water-proof sealed packages. Often weighing between 600 and 1,200 kilograms, the packages were then picked up by locals, who were paid to do so. Military and political figures from Guinea-Bissau regularly visited the area to oversee the safe transport of drugs from the beach to Bissau, and often used depots in military zones for storage.[3]

Kassumba village was basic. Sea-shells were pushed into the dirt paths around people's mud homes. Baby goats slept and leapt. A man from Senegal, who had troubles with his construction business back home, had just arrived because he'd heard the area had healing and spiritual powers.

Aly Bangura was a fisherman fixing a net on the beach. Born in Sierra Leone, but living in Kassumba with his brother, he told me that officials from Guinea-Bissau came to the area regularly for 'business trading'. I sensed, even in his very broken English, that he knew more than he was saying. These poor fishermen knew to keep their assistance in the drug-trade quiet. Some had become rich, bought expensive cars, and built houses, but others simply had no idea what they had been asked to do. There were documented cases of fishermen seeing bricks of cocaine bobbing in the sea and using them for fertiliser on their crops (which soon died), putting it on their bodies during traditional ceremonies, and using them as condiments in their food.

Back from the shore, while a few boys played on a home-made draughts board, I spoke to Djibril Keita, Lassana Keita, and Ampa Keita, three brothers who lived in Kassumba. They all wore shorts and T-shirts. Djibril was the most talkative, telling me that, 'The Guinea-Bissau military last visited a few days ago. They come and offer nothing to us, and don't help the poor. They just come and watch the beach. We would like the government to build a hotel for tourism, but these officials don't listen. They say they want to control the border zone with Guinea-Conakry, to monitor and patrol goods such as clothing.'

Djibril continued, 'In the dry season, white people come from Portugal, Spain, Brazil, and Holland, and stay for a few days in the area. They offer to repair roads and water pumps, give medicine for hospitals, and build schools. They sometimes deliver these goods, but the smugglers want to be left alone on the beach.' These 'white people' were undoubtedly drug-traffickers monitoring their business.

Ansumana Keita was 87 years old and the father of the three brothers. A Muslim, he wore an orange, green, and white prayer cap, a white singlet, and loose blue pants. He was uncharacteristically old for Guinea-Bissau — most people died younger — and he remained articulate and active.

He was scathing about the drug-trade and how little of its profits went to the local people. 'We don't get benefits from the beach, but we need fresh water and better schools', he said. 'Many people come here and want land, but don't ask what we want. When white people and Guinea-Bissau officials come, nobody tells us why. Some are fishermen, and others are involved in something else [which was the closest he came to acknowledging that the drug-trade had a presence there]. In 1998, a Portuguese man was the first white man who came with bags of cocaine. After that period, we thought guns and ammunition were being smuggled, but we later realised it was drugs.'

~

The United Nations Office on Drugs and Crime (UNODC) issued a stark warning in 2008: 'In the nineteenth century, Europe's hunger for slaves devastated West Africa. Today, its appetite for cocaine could do the same. The former Gold Coast is turning into the Coke Coast.'[4] The UNODC gave figures to back up its claims, while acknowledging that it was impossible to know the exact amounts of drugs flowing through Guinea-Bissau, and they were stark: at least 33 tons of cocaine were seized on the way to Europe between 2005 and 2007.

In the decades before this, it was rare to seize even one ton across the whole African continent. Between 1998 and 2003, around 600 kilograms of cocaine was seized. The UNODC worried that most of the 33 tons was captured in only 23 large seizures, 'many of which were accidental and partial. This indicates the existence of a much larger underlying flow.'[5] The UNODC admitted that they were only able to seize 46 per cent of the total global traffic in drugs, with the majority of illicit substances reaching their final destinations.

The UNODC estimated in 2008 that around 27 per cent (or 40 tons) of the cocaine taken annually across Europe transited through West Africa, with a wholesale value of US$1.8 billion. By 2012, the UNODC believed that nearly 60 per cent of cocaine taken in western Europe transited through the region. The UN report found that nearly 1,000 kilograms of cocaine was being flown into Guinea-Bissau every night, co-ordinated by 50 Colombian drug lords based in the country.[6]

The street value of these drugs in London or Rome was at least US$18 billion. In 2007, the UN Security Council said that 'drug-trafficking threatens to subvert the nascent democratization process of Guinea-Bissau, entrench organized crime, and undermine respect for the rule of law'.

The reasons for the country falling victim to South American drug cartels were familiar: a corrupt political and judicial class with few resources, a police department with no petrol to drive their few patrol cars, the lack of a functioning prison, and wealthy drug-traffickers who could afford sophisticated equipment to avoid detection.

The modern history of Guinea-Bissau proves that transitioning from a colonised nation to a democratic and independent state, when beset by transnational organised-crime groups, is close to impossible — especially when demand for drugs in the West is so high. Colonised by the Portuguese in the 16th century and achieving liberation in 1974 after an 11-year armed struggle, Guinea-Bissau has been ruled by a succession of autocrats ever since. The country ranks 178 out of 188 countries on the United Nations Human Development Index.

The first multi-party elections were held in 1994, but stability was elusive. The army routinely overthrew the civilian government; there have been nine coups or attempted coups since 1980, including a so-called cocaine coup in 2012 whereby the military facilitated a massive increase in trafficking.[7] A civil war between 1988 and 1999 saw the death of thousands and the displacement of hundreds of thousands of people.

One of the most consistent political leaders was Joao Bernardo 'Nino' Vieira, who was president three times from 1980 until his murder by the country's military in 2009.[8] He once described himself as 'God's gift' to Guinea-Bissau, but it wasn't a view shared by many of his people. A political rival, Kumba Yala, accused Vieira in 2008 of being the country's 'biggest drug-trafficker'.[9] There was already evidence in the early 2000s that drugs were moving through West Africa from Latin America with the assistance of officials in Guinea-Bissau and Guinea-Conakry.[10]

A senior, unnamed official with the DEA told *The Observer* in 2008 that it made sense for Guinea-Bissau to be chosen by cartels as their transit country of choice. 'You walk in, buy the services you need from the government, army and people, and take over', he said. 'The cocaine can then be stored safely and shipped to Europe, either by ship to Spain or Portugal, across land via Morocco on the old cannabis trail, or directly by air using "mules".'[11]

Constant rivalries between the military and government have bedevilled the country for decades. Many of the fights within the Guinea-Bissau elites have been over power and control, with little care for the citizenry. Generals often paid their soldiers from sacks of cash, heightening corruption. Many local journalists told me that self-censorship was rampant — the government also routinely censored material in state-run media it didn't like — because nobody wanted to directly accuse politicians or the military of complicity in the drug-trade. They risked assault or worse if they dared.

Workers from the state-run radio station told me that citizens reported problems to them instead of to the police or courts, because they didn't trust these institutions. The president of the Guinean Human Rights League, Augusto da Silva, labelled Guinea-Bissau a police state in 2018, and said that police officers acted 'without a warrant'.

Former finance minister Jose Mario Vaz became president in 2014, but was unable to bring stability; in-fighting caused four prime ministers to be turned over in one year. Very few elected leaders have served a full-term since independence. Out of frustration, the West African regional bloc ECOWAS slapped sanctions on Guinea-Bissau officials in 2018.

With a country population of 1.9 million people and vast, largely uninhabited coastlines, the remote Bijagos archipelago comprised 88 mostly inhabited islands. The country's natural beauty had rarely been seen by international tourists, due to its remoteness and lack of infrastructure. Poverty was rampant — affecting 69 per cent of the population in 2010, according to the World Bank — and foreign investment had been limited due to continuing political troubles. In 2015, international donors pledged more than one billion euros to help the nation get back on its feet, but the UN Security Council warned that the funds would only be delivered if there was stability.

Today, Guinea-Bissau is one of the poorest countries in the world, with cashew nuts, timber, and fish being major sources of income for many citizens and the main source of foreign exchange. Nearly 70 per cent of the population lives on less than US$2 a day. Exports only total roughly US$250 million annually.

~

The head UNODC official in Guinea-Bissau, Mario Jose Maia Moreira, was clear about why cartels targeted the country. 'If you were a drug-smuggler from South America, wouldn't you chose Guinea-Bissau, considering the system and the fragility of the country itself?', he asked.

At his office in central Bissau, the Portuguese-born official told me that he had worked in Guinea-Bissau as a police advisor for the UN mission between 2012 and 2014. The UN peacebuilding initiative started in 2009 to promote stability in the country, and could end in 2020.

Moreira said that he was trying to expand the abilities of the police and legal system to tackle the crisis in drug-trafficking. He hoped to achieve this by being a co-ordinator of the UN's West African Coast Initiative (WACI), launched in 2009 to fight transnational crime; it now operates in Sierra Leone, Liberia, Guinea-Bissau, and the Ivory Coast, alongside Interpol and other international bodies to track, arrest, and prosecute drug cartels. In 2013, the UNODC claimed that WACI had reduced the infiltration of South American traffickers in the region.

Yet, according to the 2017 UN World Drug Report, two-thirds of the cocaine smuggled between South America and Europe still went through West Africa, especially Benin, Cape Verde, Ghana, Guinea-Bissau, Mali, Nigeria, and Togo. Some routes were controlled by Islamist militants. Officials in Guinea-Bissau said that they were worried that Islamists were funding their activities from drug-smuggling in the region. In February 2019, police in Cape Verde seized close to ten tons of cocaine on a Russian vessel, the country's biggest haul in its history. In Guinea-Bissau, one of the largest drug busts in more than a decade took place in 2019 when nearly 800 kilograms of cocaine was found near the capital, Bissau, in a truck filled with fish. Authorities claimed that the truck was owned by an associate of the militant group Al-Qaeda.

African demand for drugs also grew, especially methamphet-amines, and countries such as Senegal and Nigeria were hardest hit.[12] East Africa experienced an explosion of heroin trafficking.[13]

The appetite for cocaine across Europe remained high. In 2017, the UNODC found that the countries with the highest percentage of users included England, Scotland, Spain, Wales, and Albania (along-side the US, Australia, and Uruguay).

Moreira proudly told me how, the week before we met, the judi-cial police and transnational crime unit had seized around three kilograms of cocaine at the Bissau international airport.[14] The culprits had Guinean citizenships, and had swallowed the drugs. Some would do jail time in horribly cramped conditions. He said that only 11 kilo-grams of cocaine had been seized so far that year — a paltry amount — but Moreira blamed this on 'operational capacity'. He knew that at least 20 tons of cocaine passed through Guinea-Bissau annually. 'For every kilogram of drugs that we seize, five or six kilograms probably go through', he said.

The scale of the problem was well articulated by Moreira, but there was little consideration for the source of the problem: Western demand for drugs. Law enforcement would always be a drop in the ocean against this ever-growing appetite. 'In Bissau, since the transnational crime unit was established in 2011', he explained, 'we've only had 41 cases of drug-trafficking investigated, 54 people prosecuted, and seized 31.13 kilograms of cocaine and 216.96 kilograms of marijuana.'

I asked Moreira if he believed that the legalisation of drugs, or at least marijuana, would alleviate some of his headaches. He wasn't entirely opposed to the idea, but wondered how it would operate practically. 'Will all the world decriminalise drugs at the same time?' he asked. 'If so, things would change, it would become a business, and Guinea-Bissau could be rich because they would get their share of the business. You could have an option where personal use of drugs wouldn't be a crime but a misdemeanour.'[15]

Moreira didn't see this option as viable in Guinea-Bissau — 'People here aren't even ready to address drug-trafficking' — so he advocated for more stringent legal frameworks to catch traffickers.

But much of the world remained unconvinced of this plan of action. When the UNODC attempted to raise from donors several hundred million dollars for a program in 2006 to reform the security forces in Guinea-Bissau, it was unable to do so. After scaling down its ambitions, the UNODC asked for $19 million, but only received pledges for $6.5 million in late 2007.[16]

This trend has continued in the decade since. The UN Security Council noted in 2018 that donors 'seemed reluctant to provide contributions in light of the current [political] situation'. When I contacted the UNODC regional representative for West and Central Africa, Pierre Lapaque, in 2018 for an update on Guinea-Bissau, he would only say that the situation was 'difficult' due to political instability.

When I interviewed the head of the mission in Bissau, Miguel Trovoada, the 78-year-old former prime minister and president of Sao Tome and Principe, he challenged the international community to do more than just 'put out fires during a crisis without having a long-term strategy'.

UNODC continued to work across West Africa, acknowledging the growing threat of transnational drug-smuggling in increasing numbers of states. But it, too often, followed the US lead in supporting a militarised response to the threat. According to a 2014 report by the Global Drug Policy Observatory at Swansea University, the UN was repeating the same mistakes made in Latin America:

> It is legitimate to question whether the hyped-up narrative that has been constructed of a lethal problem is meant to justify placement of military, surveillance and anti-terrorism hardware and software in the region at a time when the US-led 'war on drugs' is losing support within many Latin American countries.[17]

The former Guinea-Bissau justice minister, Dr Carmelita Pires, acknowledged some of the country's problems, and blamed corruption as public enemy number one. I met Pires at her palatial home on the outskirts of Bissau, in an area where former and current politicians lived alongside drug dealers and traffickers. Subtle design wasn't the style. Dr Pires's house was large and yellow. Dressed in a floral skirt, she was friendly and approachable, claiming that she was too principled for politics in a tough country such as Guinea-Bissau. She had been justice minister three times, having trained as a lawyer in Portugal. During one of her terms in office in 2008, she received death threats for daring to arrest suspected drug-traffickers.

'We are still a new country, 40 years old and 20 years a democracy', she said. Her experience had taught her that women were far less corruptible than men, and yet too few women were in positions of power. She told me that South American drug cartels had overwhelmed the poor capabilities of Guinea-Bissau, and there were never enough funds allocated to tip the balance in the government's favour.

Pires said that in 2007 there were only 60 judicial police agents. By 2008, she had raised this number to 260 by working with parties in Brazil, Portugal, and Russia to help with recruitment and training. But when she assumed the role of justice minister again in 2015, there were only 150 judicial police. Constant coups and political instability had destroyed any chance of continuity. The UN and economy ministry in Guinea-Bissau reported in 2018 that the country's total security and justice budget for the year was less than half of the average street value of one ton of cocaine in Europe.[18]

'We are not a narco-state', she insisted. 'We don't produce drugs, and people here don't have enough money to consume drugs.' However, according to Abilio Aleluia Co Junior, who ran the country's research body Observatory for Drugs and Drug Addiction, around one-quarter of the drugs transiting through Guinea-Bissau were increasingly being consumed locally, with crack cocaine and marijuana leading the list.[19]

Very few officials in Bissau wanted to talk about the role of Washington fighting its drug war in West Africa. Pires was a notable exception. She said that when she was in office in 2008, she had received a fax from the US embassy in neighbouring Dakar, Senegal, informing her that US ships were soon to arrive off Guinea-Bissau to fight drugs. The document was dated 18 September 2008, and read in part: 'Together the US and Guinea-Bissau governments can send a strong message to the traffickers that their destructive activities will not be tolerated.' Pires welcomed the assistance, though the US gave her government no choice; it was a friendly letter that masked a diktat.

~

The country's sole drug-control laboratory was situated at the back of police headquarters on a quiet and dusty street in Bissau. Funded by the European Union, the room had bars on the windows but no visible security. I met the facility's co-ordinator, Sargento Natcha, a large, softly spoken man who talked passionately about his work. He opened all the cupboards in the room displaying drug-testing units, while new deliveries still in boxes, including scales and a fridge, sat in the corner. Six people worked at the lab and had trained in Portugal, Senegal, Ghana, and Guinea-Bissau.

UNODC first delivered the drug-testing kits in 2015. Natcha explained that if a drug suspect arrived at the Bissau airport, officials first checked if that person had swallowed cocaine capsules — a common method of smuggling drugs into (and out of) the country. A doctor had to be present to test the suspect. Before the opening of the laboratory, Natcha said that it had been nearly impossible to get accurate test results.

'Our law is against all substances except alcohol and tobacco', he said. He stressed that he had 'never smoked or snorted anything. I like my job. We want to diminish 80 to 90 per cent of the drug-trade flowing into Guinea-Bissau.'

Natcha performed a test on a small sample of cocaine he kept in the lab, stored in a small jar. He also showed me a bag of dried marijuana. It was an effective chemistry experiment, but would have no impact against sophisticated South American cartels.

I asked Natcha if he had details of people recently found with drugs at Bissau airport. He happily passed me a sheet of paper with the names, country of origin, and other personal details of the seven people who had been stopped at Bissau's airport and found with coke capsules. If they faced jail time at all, they'd likely get around four years behind bars. Most drug-smugglers escaped prison due to court corruption.

'Guinea-Bissau is still a country of cocaine', said Fernando Jorge Barreto Costa, the deputy director of the judicial police, in his air-conditioned Bissau office around the corner from the drug-testing lab. 'I cannot deny the reality. This is a poor country.' He opposed drug legalisation because he worried his nation would transition from a transit to consumption country.

The lack of money to investigate and pursue drug-traffickers was commonplace. 'Drugs are arriving more by sea than by plane', he told me, 'and we don't have the capability to intercept boats. If we get news about drugs at sea, it takes two to three days to get an answer from authorities for action. This is too slow, and by then the drugs and people may have moved on. When we pursue drugs, we only tell a few officers in the team about it to avoid information leaking.' The judicial police sporadically burned kilograms of cocaine in attempts to show that they were serious about the problem. In January 2019, 28 kilograms of cocaine and 500,000 units of counterfeit medicine were burned in Bissau.

Many authorities gave me similar arguments: don't blame us for the flow of drugs when we don't have the means to stop them. Corruption was rampant, and Costa was frustrated that 'the government has the power to withhold resources— it's economic corruption — for us to fight drugs. In the government corruption unit, there are no means to fight corruption.'

Poverty and economic insecurity were directly linked to many officials either turning a blind eye to the problem or taking money from cartels to fuel it. Costa said that his government regularly didn't give him and his colleagues enough money for them to work effectively. 'You will not be able to buy fuel for our cars to find drug-smugglers. Sometimes public servants aren't paid. In 2014, I wasn't paid for six months. It was very difficult. In my case, my wife is a judge and we had saved some money.'

~

The creation of a 'narco-state' was deceptively simple. Although Guinea-Bissau has never seen the levels of extreme violence unleashed in Honduras, Mexico, or the Philippines around the drug war, this tiny West African state was vulnerable because of its weak political structures and the scant foreign attention it was subject to. 'While the narco-traffickers did not seize power, they were indeed extremely close to the centre of power', writes the Gambian historian Hassoum Ceesay. 'And while drugs did not run the country, traffickers took advantage of the state's inherent weakness and exacerbated it by their presence.'[20]

Media reports from 2008 provided anecdotal evidence of South American traffickers driving expensive cars through the streets of Bissau, purchasing lavish, hacienda-style estates, and drinking in ways that the vast bulk of the population couldn't afford. During my visit, I never saw any signs of such wealth, but I was told that cartels had become less ostentatious in flaunting their money.

There is some resistance from Guinea-Bissau watchers to the country being labelled a 'narco-state'. It's a rejection, writes British academic Toby Green and editor of a rare book on Guinea-Bissau in 2016, of 'Western-imposed narratives that create stories of "success" and "failure" in Africa in order to shore up a hubristic self-image and entrench the status quo; such narratives support the idea that successful change can only come from outside the country.'[21]

Whether Guinea-Bissau qualifies as a narco-state is more than an academic question for a desperate population.[22] A clear definition is whether a country's institutions are infiltrated at every level by the drug-trade.[23] Many other nations around the world could have qualified over the last decades, from Afghanistan to Myanmar, and Mexico to Colombia, but Guinea-Bissau operates at a much quieter and less violent pace.[24] This is a blessing for its citizens, but does nothing to alleviate the grinding poverty I witnessed in every town and village.

There were few public signs that drugs had consumed the country — namely violence or gang activity that was rife across Latin and South America — but crumbling infrastructure and buildings were visible indicators of misplaced priorities by those in power. The constant soaring humidity had cracked many painted surfaces, and spirits were languid. Many people sold apples, bananas, and nuts on the side of the dusty, often fraying roads. With only 500 tourists arriving annually, outside visitors were rare. Most signs were in Portuguese or French. The parliament building was decaying, with mould crawling up the walls. Bissau was filled with Portuguese-era colonial-style architecture.

In Honduras, humour about the country's dire predicament was uncommon, but when I visited the health ministry in Bissau, the chief of staff to the health minister joked with me and asked whether I'd like to buy Guinea-Bissau. 'It's very cheap', he said.

Outside of Bissau, much of the country felt distant from the influence of law enforcement, but it wasn't dangerous. Instead,

Guinea-Bissau had settled into a seemingly relaxed aura of detach-ment. Most citizens just wanted to survive, and had no connection to the drug-trade.

In village after village, there were colourful clothes being dried on the ground, motorbike-repair shops, countless spare tyres littering the dirt, small markets selling food and cleaning products, cooked and slightly burned corn on the cob for sale, and worn-out buildings.

As a journalist, I was acutely aware of how little the world knew about Guinea-Bissau, and therefore the framing of the country in this book forced me to reflect on my own reporting. It was too simple to dismiss the nation as a narco-state with few redeeming fea-tures. It was also untrue, and yet countless reporters after my visit contacted me to ask why and how Guinea-Bissau was a narco-state. There was little interest in nuance. It felt like a catch-22 situation, because the country was largely ignored by the global media and only received attention because it had been colonised by South American drug cartels. I wanted my reporting to inject subtlety and colour to Guinea-Bissau, and give its people a voice beyond unwilling or com-plicit drug-traffickers.

'Narco-states' are built with surprisingly few participants. When a state is unwilling or unable to provide services for its people, the vacuum is filled by opportunists, and citizens are forced to rely on their own ingenuity to survive. International drug-traffickers are some of the cleverest business people on the planet, exploiting a never-ending demand. Making billions of dollars every year takes effort, brains, and violence.

After travelling for around three hours from Bissau, I arrived in the Saltinho area at the Hotel Pousada Do Saltinho, close to the vil-lage of Sintcha Sambel. It was advertised, including on its colourful outside wall, as a tourist hotel, but I soon learned that it never received tourists. It was a regular base for South American drug-smugglers. Mostly from Venezuela, Brazil, and Colombia, they stayed anywhere between one and three months, and waited for safe passage for drugs to Bissau, up through Africa and on to Europe. One route out of Guinea-Bissau involved Venezuelans using speedboats to take the drugs to Cape Verde and then on to the Canary Islands before moving the product to the West.[25]

The hotel was a peaceful place, with the sound of a river in the near distance and chickens wandering around the garden. Two were killed by the hotel's staff and prepared in front of us for lunch. The birds were so tough as to be almost inedible. Only the hotel's boss knew when the smugglers arrived, but the busiest time of year was in December and January, the dry season.

Traffickers arrived by small plane, road, or high-speed boat on the nearby river, the Rio Corobal. Local Guinea-Bissau messengers would arrive and tell the smugglers their next stop along the long path towards the drug's final destination. There were no smugglers when I came, but the place had the feeling of a relaxing rest-stop. Many small rooms were equipped with Ikea-branded queen-sized beds, and each room had a different name, such as 'Banana'. A small bar for whisky, gin, and Cinzano was empty, but I was told that, during their long stints, smugglers would arrange prostitutes and enjoy copious amounts of alcohol. There were three similar hotels on the Guinea-Bissau mainland, and more on the Bijagos Islands, whose sole purpose was drug-trafficking.

Cartels had refined the delivery process. Drugs were dropped off by plane on the Rio Corobal. They came from Guinea-Conakry; often, the Bissau port was heavily policed, though I heard that the port was increasingly used for smuggling, so it was easier to deliver the drugs near the hotel. A lieutenant-colonel from the Guinea-Bissau military often came from Bissau to oversee the smooth transfer of cocaine. He provided protection for the goods — sometimes up to 500 kilograms of cocaine — and ensured they were stored in safe houses in Bissau before leaving for other African countries.

Guinea-Bissau had perfected the trafficking of cocaine, but other drugs were also smuggled: morphine pills and tramadol, an opioid pain medication. Islamist fighters in Africa and the Middle East, including the Islamic State, loved this drug because it reduced pain in the case of injury — pills of abuse-grade strength, along with the amphetamine-type stimulant Captagon, gave militants an inflated sense of strength and bravery, with no need to sleep for days. Legitimate medical patients in Guinea-Bissau couldn't get this drug, even though it was pouring into the country (around 4,000 tramadol pills entered monthly). Smugglers take the drugs from Bissau to Mauritania, and sell them to Ansar Dine, an Al-Qaeda–aligned group in Mali, Mauritania, and Senegal, and to Boko Haram in Nigeria.

A key aspect of a 'narco-state' is the ability of outsiders to regularly infiltrate it and to leave undetected. This was the case with Guinea-Bissau.[26] So-called humanitarian caravans have arrived from Eastern Europe in the last decade. People from Poland, Hungary, and Romania fill a convoy with clothes, medicines, and second- and third-hand ambulances to mask their activities, and they hand out these goods along the route from Europe to Africa.

They arrive in Guinea-Bissau to pick up drugs, and receive around 10,000 euros for the work. They then take the cocaine through Mali and to the Toubou people living in Chad, Sudan, Niger, and Libya. This group completes the mission towards northern Libya, and then trusted smugglers take it on to Europe. Such a 'humanitarian caravan' may seem like an arduous and dangerous path to ensure the safe passage of drugs, but the economics work out for the traffickers and the drug mules.

Guinea-Bissau has never suffered a debilitating civil war as devastating as neighbouring states such as Liberia or Sierra Leone have experienced, but the elites made a clear choice in the late 1990s and early 2000s that the drug-trade was the best and often only option for income, aside from war profiteering, when investment, foreign

NGOs, and natural resources were scant. In my view, it was a fateful and inexcusable decision, and many locals damned officialdom for its failings. However, what also couldn't be ignored were the ways in which the West had long viewed West Africa: a dysfunctional region beset by war and conflict, with the legacy of slavery, resource exploitation, and colonialism conveniently ignored.

This paternalistic thinking held that while West Africa hadn't negatively affected 'us' in the West, a country like Guinea-Bissau was forgettable. It was only when huge amounts of cocaine began arriving in Europe that had come through West Africa that some Western states took notice and demanded action against the drug-trade. In the process, they did little to assist state-building in Guinea-Bissau.

~

On 5 April 2013, the Manhattan US attorney's office announced that it had made major arrests. 'Drug kingpin' Jose Americo Bubo Na Tchuto, the former head of the Guinea-Bissau navy and a fighter in the country's independence war, had been captured in West Africa. After an intricate undercover operation, the DEA claimed it had interdicted Na Tchuto and six others who were attempting to receive cocaine off the coast of Guinea-Bissau that was to be sent to them by Farc rebels in Colombia. They had agreed to store it securely on the mainland before it was to be transported to Europe and the US. The money made from the sale of the drugs would have benefited Farc, designated by Washington as a foreign terrorist organisation, and paid off officials in Guinea-Bissau to allow safe passage of the illicit substance.

Then DEA chief Michele Leonhart said, 'These DEA arrests are significant victories against terrorism and international drug-trafficking. Alleged narco-terrorists such as these, who traffic drugs in West Africa and elsewhere, are some of the world's most violent and brutal criminals.'

Then Manhattan US attorney Preet Bharara agreed, and argued that, 'The narco-terrorism conspiracy alleged in these indictments shows the danger that can grow unchecked in faraway places where unfortunate circumstances can allow narcotics traffickers and terrorism supporters to transact unseen at great risk to the United States and its interests.'

The Na Tchuto prosecution resulted in the most high-profile coverage that Guinea-Bissau had received in a long time, and yet my years of investigation since then indicate that the DEA case was ethically problematic, largely futile in terms of its battle against drug-smuggling, and disturbingly revealing about the long reach of Washington in the remotest parts of the globe. The case was sold to the media and general public as a stinging victory in the war on drugs, and yet virtually none of the major players had spoken extensively to journalists before I interviewed them, and many details of the case remained murky. The press had largely accepted the DEA's case.

My reporting reveals that the undercover sting operation and entrapment of these men is a familiar tactic used by the DEA, which often relies on concocting stories around the Farc in Colombia, cocaine, and weapons-smuggling. What went mostly unsaid throughout the entire process was that the DEA created every element of the narrative, the drugs and weapons were never transported, and the accused men had only become involved in the conspiracy after being approached by the undercover agents.

The indictment against Na Tchuto seemed damning. It alleged that he had told undercover DEA agents that the 12 April 2012 coup in Guinea-Bissau meant his country was weak, and that it was therefore an ideal time to traffic cocaine. From August 2012, the US attorney said, Na Tchuto, along with his associates Papis Djeme and Tchamy Yala (a former aide and bodyguard for Na Tchuto who served six months for treason in a Guinea-Bissau prison in 2012), began discussing the importation of tons of cocaine from South America to Guinea-Bissau.

The DEA agents purported to be a cocaine-broker and cocaine-supplier based in South America. These three defendants met regularly with the undercover sources; Na Tchuto met one of them in Senegal in August 2012, and agreed to import 1,000 kilograms of cocaine to Guinea-Bissau. After receipt of the drugs, half was to be sent to the US, and the other half to Portugal. Na Tchuto said that his fee for every 1,000 kilograms of cocaine trafficked was US$1 million. He offered the use of trucks to transport the drugs within Guinea-Bissau from the coast to an underground bunker for storage. He further said that he owned a company that could be used to facilitate the shipment of drugs out of Guinea-Bissau.

They were all arrested on a luxury yacht off the coast of Guinea-Bissau in April 2013 after being asked to meet associates of the deal. After having been initially offered champagne on the boat, they were captured by 50 heavily armed men from the DEA's Foreign-deployed Advisory and Support Team (FAST), a military-style unit that had fanned out across South America and Africa with deadly results. (FAST was shut down in 2017 after involvement in a murderous 2012 raid in remote Honduras.) The government of Guinea-Bissau vigorously opposed the arrests, and accused the DEA of 'kidnapping' the men. The streets of Bissau were tense in the days after the operation. The DEA claimed that the trio had been taken in international waters, but the government of Guinea-Bissau said it was in its territorial waters.

The three men were charged with conspiring to distribute five kilograms of cocaine or more and importing it to the US. They faced life sentences in an American prison. At the time, it was the DEA's most audacious mission against high-level African officials.

The DEA had also tried to entrap Guinea-Bissau's army chief, Antonio Indjai, who had led the 2012 coup, by convincing him to help with the drug shipment and to supply weapons to the Farc. One of his associates said that Indjai would have kept 13 per cent of the drugs as his 'fee' to pay off the Guinea-Bissau government. However, Indjai wasn't caught on the day of the sting due to a series of DEA mishaps. The luxury yacht had had mechanical problems, and the sting was delayed for a month because of it.[27] Na Tchuto was hesitant to travel to the boat, and when he was eventually convinced to go, it was late in the day. The DEA had planned to arrest Na Tchuto first and then attract Indjai to the boat, but Indjai likely believed it was too late to go offshore, and the DEA missed its primary target. Today, Indjai lives as a free man in Guinea-Bissau, though no longer heads the military. He told Reuters in 2015 that he had no involvement in drug-trafficking and just tended his cashew-nut farm.[28]

Reuters reported in 2013 that the DEA decision to pursue Na Tchuto and Indjai had been taken by the US Department of Justice, and not by regional diplomats.[29] The DEA had set up a field office inside the US embassy in Dakar, Senegal, alongside agents across Africa in Egypt, South Africa, Kenya, Ghana, and Nigeria, but hadn't co-ordinated with local US authorities. The DEA was operating as a law unto itself. Washington closed its diplomatic office in Bissau before the sting took place, fearing a backlash against its representatives.

A US official told Reuters after the sting against Na Tchuto, in an anonymous comment, that it was 'an operation that needed to be done just by us. There is a sense in some circles that we've got commandos lurking offshore ready to pounce. I don't think this will become a regular occurrence in Guinea-Bissau. But if they think it is, no harm done there.'[30]

Two other charged defendants, Manuel Mamadi Mane and Saliu Sisse, were both Guinea-Bissau nationals who had pledged to assist in Na Tchuto's trafficking plans, along with supplying surface-to-air missiles and AK-47 assault rifles to the Farc. Their indictment read that these weapons were to have been 'used in the Farc's armed conflict with the United States counter-narcotics forces in Colombia.' The last two defendants, Rafael Antonio Garavito-Garcia and Gustavo

Perez-Garcia, were Colombian nationals and drug-traffickers who had agreed to supply Farc-owned cocaine to their associates in Guinea-Bissau.

The US attorney claimed that many of the conversations between its undercover agents and the defendants had been recorded, but these were never played in an open court and remain hidden from public view. The secrecy of the trials raised suspicions that the government was hiding important details. Just before Na Tchuto's trial was set to begin in June 2013, he pleaded guilty at a hearing on 13 May. The transcript of the hearing was immediately sealed — an occasional procedure when a defendant strikes a deal with authorities — which meant that no details were forthcoming about what Na Tchuto had said, agreed to, or accepted as a deal.

After pleading guilty in 2014, Djeme and Yala were sentenced to prison terms of six-and-a-half years and five years respectively. At his sentencing, Yala told the judge through a translator, 'I made a mistake. Nobody forced me to do what I did, and I did it willingly.'

Manuel Mamadi Mane was deported to Portugal on 1 December 2015 after having pleaded guilty on 22 May and being sentenced to three years in prison. But he reportedly lived as a free man after he arrived in Portugal.[31] Adding to the confusion, the man's real name was a mystery, and US federal agencies couldn't agree on his identity, suggesting his name was either Manuel Mamadi Mane or Malam Mane Sanha.[32] He reportedly had at least ten false identities.

After waiting in US custody for more than three years, 70-year-old Na Tchuto was sentenced to four years in prison in October 2016. US district judge Richard Berman in Manhattan said that Na Tchuto had been co-operating with US officials during his time behind bars; as a result, he was home in Bissau by the end of the month after receiving credit for good behaviour while incarcerated. Upon his return, he was welcomed by President Vaz, and pledged his 'readiness to support the country in any way'. This led to the US, in its 2017 Narcotics

Control Strategy Report, claiming that the government in Bissau was still engaged in drug-trafficking and had done little to change its reputation as a 'narco-state'. President Vaz admitted in 2019 that he was 'afraid' and that his country was still a cocaine-smuggling hub, telling Al Jazeera English, 'We don't have aeroplanes, we don't have boats, we lack the radars that would give us control over our … economic zone.'

I've attempted many times to reach Na Tchuto and speak to him about the charges against him and his time in prison. Since his return to Guinea-Bissau, he has not spoken to any journalists, and I've been unable to reach him directly; however, my fixer, Ali Embalo in Bissau, did briefly speak to him, along with his driver and local lawyer, on the phone in 2018. Na Tchuto told Ali that he had been advised by his lawyers to 'not speak to anyone' about his experiences in the US. The question was why. Rumours in Guinea-Bissau suggested that it was because Na Tchuto had become an undercover US agent and was feeding information to the US. This had reportedly contributed to his relatively short jail sentence. It was impossible to verify this allegation.

This case has always struck me as strange and incomplete. After the US government heralded the capture of Na Tchuto in 2013, it played into the many stereotypes of Guinea-Bissau: drug-addled, corrupt, and in need of outside, namely American, help. There was no public debate about the right of Washington to fight its drug war in West Africa, the US's legal right to operate and arrest suspects in international waters, and the morality of setting people up to face serious jail time when the Western demand for drugs had never been higher. According to a Department of Justice audit released in 2016, more than 18,000 informants or sources were used by the DEA between 2010 and 2015, the majority of whom were criminals hoping to get lenient sentences by co-operating with the government.[33]

This case fitted a disturbing pattern that accelerated after 11 September 2001: the DEA increasingly framed people in plots that it had created, and then celebrated the legal victory of disrupting its own plots. The FBI is guilty of similar behaviour in the last two decades, targeting vulnerable young Muslims in FBI-designed terror plots, and then claiming that the threat of terrorism had been reduced by the agency breaking up the plot.[34] It was nonsensical, and yet it destroyed the lives of countless individuals who spent years or decades in maximum-security prisons. The DEA had curtailed the freedom of many individuals across the world — usually, people who didn't have the voice or power to challenge the long and predatory nature of US justice.

The DEA agent who led the investigation into Na Tchuto and his associates spoke to me in Nairobi, Kenya, in 2015 on the condition of anonymity. 'Greg' had worked with the DEA in Africa since 2007, 'managing' eight countries, and he was a fit man in his fifties. He believed in the US-led drug war, and was a key agent in bringing down Russian arms-dealer Viktor Bout, who was captured in Thailand in 2008 after a sting operation.

Greg worked in Guinea-Bissau between 2011 and 2013, and told me that, 'With influential Guinea-Bissau elites, it was easy to infiltrate them with money. Most pleaded guilty when caught.' His team had wanted to take down the army chief, Antonio Indjai, 'but we couldn't for political reasons. The US state department didn't want any more chaos [in Guinea-Bissau], so there was no attempt to intercept Indjai, even though he was a major drug figure. This is a man who provides drugs and weapons to kill people in South America.'

Greg said that Colombian cartels paid money in cash at the highest levels of vulnerable governments, such as Guinea-Bissau, and 'then cash is never seen again; payment comes in produce like drugs and weapons'.

He supported the DEA's mission, although he was aware of its challenges. 'We are only curbing it [drugs]', he said. 'Unless you teach your kids that drugs are bad, like alcohol, you'll never win this "war". Some people enjoy taking drugs.' He recognised that his work was often 'like a finger in the dyke [of the drug-trade], though I never question what I do in fighting drugs.' He had spent time in Afghanistan, and while he helped Washington arrest and prosecute some Afghan drug-traffickers, he acknowledged the 'futility' of the mission. The country is the world's largest opium-producer.

'The US has good laws against drugs, and they can be used to help Africa', Greg said. 'I'm passionate about my job. I see a lot of good coming out of it. Often there are no hard feelings between us at the DEA and those we're pursuing.' He praised the US government for recognising after 11 September 2001 that there was a 'connection' between drugs and terrorism.

I contacted the DEA to comment on the Na Tchuto case and to ask why, if he had been such a major West African drug kingpin, described as such by the US in 2010, he had only served four years in prison.[35] Spokesman Lawrence Payne emailed that, 'I will let our prior public statements speak for themselves on this case and defer to the prosecutors for comments about sentencing.' Former Manhattan US attorney Preet Bharara, who was fired by President Donald Trump in 2017, declined my request for a comment. When Bharara's book, *Doing Justice: a prosecutor's thoughts on crime, punishment, and the rule of law* was released in 2019, he was celebrated in the media as having been a brave truth-teller during his years as a government employee, ignoring his many cases of prosecutorial overreach, such as with Na Tchuto.

Na Tchuto's US lawyers offered a completely different view, and questioned the entire basis of his prosecution. His court-appointed lawyer for the bulk of his time in the US was federal defender Sabrina Shroff. A New York–based Iranian-born woman, she told me that, because she came from a 'third-world country', she understood the struggles and life realities for a person such as Na Tchuto. She had represented some high-profile clients in the past, including weapons-dealer Viktor Bout, terror suspects, and former CIA employees.

Shroff said that US federal courts were 'ill-prepared' to handle cases such as Na Tchuto's because there was only one interpreter to work with him, who wasn't a certified court-appointed interpreter, and who had another full-time job. I contacted the interpreter, but he refused to speak about the case. Na Tchuto received poor language support, and felt 'genuine incomprehension' about the US justice system as a result. Schroff told me that he had been 'revered' in Guinea-Bissau, but in a US prison he was just another inmate with serious health needs. Doctors' visits were difficult because the interpreter was often unavailable to help him. Na Tchuto was isolated in jail because of his inability to speak English and the trouble he had digesting food.

Officials from the Guinea-Bissau government made representations on Na Tchuto's behalf, but to no avail. Shroff said they believed that she should have got her client released quickly because the US government had failed to capture its main goal, Antonio Indjai, and therefore Na Tchuto was irrelevant to the case.

Shroff said that she had agreed with Na Tchuto's assessment of the indictment against him. 'The whole case was pure entrapment', she said. 'I don't know what was in it for the United States. I couldn't figure any of that out, nor have I figured it out to this day. Why in God's name would they care about Guinea-Bissau?'

She compared the Na Tchuto case to the Viktor Bout experience. The US government was 'after this gun-dealer, and they had trouble arresting him before. The relationship between the United States and Russia wasn't exactly hunky-dory. I may not think it wise or particularly good use of American taxpayer money, but I can understand it. But why Guinea-Bissau? The only thing I could possibly think of is that at some point they had thought Guinea-Bissau to be maybe the new gateway country to drugs to the United States, and they wanted to cut that off.' Shroff said that the only way that Washington could capture both men was through set-ups.

Shroff said that Na Tchuto was 'charismatic', and during his case she learned from fellow Guinea-Bissau citizens that he had 'done [his] country a lot of good' over the decades, helping it gain independence. When Na Tchuto was finally sentenced in 2016 and then released a few days later, she was unsurprised that he went home to Guinea-Bissau so promptly. She told me that this was standard operating procedure in the American justice system, and US district judge Richard Berman had taken into account Na Tchuto's severe medical problems.

I asked Shroff about the curious situation of the US government working around the world to entrap people it claimed were dangerous drug-traffickers, bringing them to the US, and then paying their legal costs. She told me that many of her clients, including Na Tchuto, said to her that they didn't go looking for trouble with Washington. Her clients would say that, 'I may have done other things that are wrong or that the United States doesn't approve of in my own country, but my country hasn't chosen to prosecute me. The US now decides they want to prosecute me. They cannot prosecute me for something they think I really did, so they set me up.'

Shroff said that Na Tchuto didn't want to risk taking his case to trial with a jury because the mandatory minimum if he lost was ten years in jail. She could never find out the identity of the confidential informants against her client. She hoped that a jury would have found in his favour and rejected the government's entrapment case, despite the state having audio recordings of Na Tchuto talking about the drug deal, but it was a big risk and she understood why he refused to take it.

Shroff's immigrant background gave her a unique take on the American government's war on drugs. She didn't defend drug-trafficking, but argued that Washington shouldn't be the 'world's policeman'. DEA global activity showed that 'American exceptionalism is alive and well.' Shroff rejected the idea that the US had the right to dictate to nations what they could and couldn't export; Washington shouldn't be telling Guinea-Bissau that its only allowed export was cashews. 'If you're really a country as poor as Afghanistan or Guinea-Bissau, and the only export you have is a controlled substance, what are you, as the runner [leader] of that country, supposed to do?' she asked.

Near the end of Na Tchuto's US incarceration, he reportedly became frustrated with the lack of resolution in his case, and changed lawyers. He hired New York–based criminal defence attorney Patrick Joyce, who told me that his role, since his client had already pleaded guilty, was to advocate for leniency in sentencing. Joyce said that he convinced the sentencing judge, Richard Berman — after presenting him with a comprehensive brief on the defendant, his struggles in life, and the situation in Guinea-Bissau — that Na Tchuto had already served enough time in prison. Joyce wanted to give the judge a picture of the man beyond merely, *He's another drug-smuggler. Let me just send him to jail for ten years.* A handful of days after his sentencing, Na Tchuto was flown back to Guinea-Bissau in 'decent clothes' that he had insisted on for his arrival home.

I asked Joyce if he thought Na Tchuto should have challenged the entrapment charge soon after his arrest and risked taking the case to a jury. He was sceptical this defence would have worked because 'we have an extremely frightened citizenry', many of whom had accepted the 'war on drugs' rhetoric. 'When the government starts to say stuff like, "We need to do this in order to curb the war on drugs", Joyce said, 'they [juries] don't do a lot of analysis. They think, *We need to do this to curb the war on drugs.*' His experience had taught him that whenever juries heard a defendant admit on tape to trafficking cocaine or boasting about his experience in the drug-trade — both common occurrences in recordings of sting operations — the case was lost.

Joyce was a life-long opponent of the drug war; he believed that drugs should be viewed as a health issue matter rather than through the lens of law enforcement. Like fellow lawyer Sabrina Shroff, he questioned why the US was even active in Guinea-Bissau and the 'ludicrous' amounts of money that the DEA was given to operate with.

The evidence that the Na Tchuto case had helped reduce the influx of drugs into Guinea-Bissau was minimal and anecdotal. When I was in Bissau, I met with one of the western European representatives, who requested anonymity. 'John' thought that drug-smuggling had declined after Na Tchuto was apprehended. 'Before this, local drug-smugglers were brazen and driving around in expensive cars', he said. 'But after his arrest, people became scared. They thought US drones were flying above Guinea-Bissau, looking for drug-smugglers, and they hid beneath trees whenever possible while walking around. There was no evidence that the US was using drones, but this didn't quash the rumours that they were.' US intelligence routinely monitored activity over the South Atlantic, and European governments used surveillance satellites over West Africa. Even if trafficking had reduced slightly in Guinea-Bissau, it had moved to neighbouring countries.

DEA-initiated entrapment had caught countless individuals in its web. Paul Mardirossian, a 50-year-old Swedish citizen who had also been represented by the US lawyer Sabrina Shroff, fitted the bill perfectly. A former owner of popular nightclubs in Stockholm, he fell into an elaborate sting with a remarkable similarity to the Na Tchuto case. After a bad investment of 2.3 million euros in 2008, he desperately needed to retrieve his money. In the process of pursuing the funds from people he thought had stolen his money, he was connected to an undercover DEA agent in 2010 who started suggesting, while audio and video recorded him, that Mardirossian could make serious money if he secured weapons for the Farc in exchange for huge amounts of cocaine.

Mardirossian told me his fantastical story. I'd never been given more intimate details of a DEA-sting operation from the perspective of the victim, and he could certainly be accused of naivety, fear, igno-rance, and greed. But the DEA had to create an elaborate fiction to ensnare him in activities that he would otherwise never have con-sidered. After visits to Barcelona and Panama City, discussing the weapons and seeing at least ten tons of cocaine in an underground bunker, Mardirossian was arrested in Panama City in April 2011 and flown to Guantanamo Bay for a three-day stay on his way to New York. He faced serious 'narco-terrorism' charges. He served nearly four years in prison — the initial deal from the prosecution was 40 years behind bars — after pleading guilty to having conspired to send arms to the Farc. He was released in 2015 and returned to Sweden.

He now had no contact with two of his three children after the trauma of the last decade. He lived with his parents. 'The United States government kidnaps people from other countries [over drug cases] and puts them in jail in New York', Mardirossian said. He was scathing of DEA methods. 'I lost everything I built. I had a good life before.'

The US government claims that its global mission is to disrupt terror plots, curtail drug-smuggling, and take bad people off the streets. Since 11 September 2001, the DEA has said that it's pushing back against one of the pre-eminent threats facing the US, 'narco-terrorism'. But the evidence for this is thin, at best. After the attacks on New York and Washington, the US government moved many of its resources from drug-fighting to terrorism investigations; the DEA's 'narco-terrorism' claims were an attempt by the agency to remain relevant. As a result, its funding for international activities soared by 75 per cent. The DEA pursued cases against what it called a litany of threats and their connections to the illicit drug-trade, including from Hamas, Hizbollah, Al-Qaeda, the Shining Path in Peru, the Taliban, Farc in Colombia, and the Kurdistan Workers' Party.

A comprehensive report in 2015 by one of America's finest jour-nalists on the drug war, Ginger Thompson, offered evidence that challenged the DEA's narrative. The crime of 'narco-terrorism' was only passed into the US Patriot Act in 2006. The effect was that countless men and women were lured into fake DEA plots, caught making incriminating statements on tape supporting drug cartels or terror groups, but rarely if ever committing any crime.

A statute was passed in 2006, pushed by John Mackey, a Republican investigative counsel for the House International Relations Committee, that gave the DEA authority to pursue drug-traffickers anywhere in the world, so long as the agency said it was tied to terrorism. It was deliberately broad, and reinforced the belief that Washington had the right and legal authority to hunt down suspects anywhere and anytime on the planet. Less acknowledged was the US goal of finding reliable, if autocratic, partners to secure regions rich with valuable resources, including oil and gold. West Africa fit the bill.

The DEA spent four years pursuing drug-traffickers in Liberia, working with the country's government to set up Africans in an elaborate sting operation that culminated in many arrests in 2011,[36] but the country was also a prime business opportunity for the American company Exxon, exposed as complicit in a multi-million-dollar oil scandal in 2018.[37] The DEA's agenda often conveniently dovetailed with US corporate interests. The Trump administration said in 2017 that it wanted to deepen the 'long-standing and valuable partnership' with Guinea-Bissau.

The US military also expanded its counter-narcotics operations across Africa in the last decade, under the Africom banner, spending hundreds of millions of dollars in training African armies. The results were desultory: drug-trafficking and militancy soared despite US forces operating in at least 33 out of 54 countries on the continent.[38] In July 2018, Africom admitted that the Guinea-Bissau military could be asked to join in future peacekeeping missions in Africa. Although this wasn't the main reason for Washington pursuing Na Tchuto, forging closer military ties with Bissau was a convenient way for the US to expand its West African reach.

None of this nuance made the corporate media. *The New York Times* reported in 2012 that the Obama administration had 'significantly expanded' its drug war in Africa, akin to Washington's 'earlier escalation of antidrug efforts in Central America'.[39] There was no mention of the apocalyptic violence that these policies had unleashed, but praise for the DEA's 'successful interdictions in Honduras'.

The DEA identified West Africa as early as 2008 as a primary area of focus due to Colombian drug-smugglers who had been arrested in Eastern Europe and had said they'd trafficked cocaine through the Sahara. Na Tchuto was just one of many unlucky citizens in the region who were caught up in the DEA's zeal.

Ginger Thompson examined many cases that the DEA said proved the close ties between terrorism and drug-smuggling, but 'when these cases were prosecuted, the only links between drug-trafficking and terrorism entered into evidence were provided by the DEA, using agents or informants who were paid hundreds of thousands of dollars to lure the targets into staged narco-terrorism conspiracies'.[40]

A former American diplomat who served in West Africa told Thompson that he saw too many examples where 'the DEA provided everything these [suspect] men needed to commit a crime, then said, 'Wow, look what they did.' This wasn't terrorism — this was the manipulation of weak-minded people, in weak countries, in order to pad arrest records.'[41]

After this investigation was published, I asked my DEA contact, 'Greg' in Nairobi, to respond to the allegations that the DEA was deliberately exaggerating the threat of 'narco-terrorism' to secure convictions. He categorically denied this was the case. 'Those links [between drugs and terrorism] can't be shown in court', he wrote, 'because of the nature of the information. We don't just look for anyone to be put in jail. DEA does not do a good job telling the story.'

~

The five-hour journey from Bissau to the Bijagos Islands was on a big and rusty old boat. The beautiful and remote archipelago was advertised as a tourist attraction, but few outsiders ever made the journey. As we approached Bubaque Island, we could see spectacular islands with nobody living on them, others with local villagers in basic shacks, and a handful of bungalows for tourists. Dense, thick, green forests and white sandy beaches framed the horizon. A handful of fishermen passed by on their small wooden boats. This was paradise, but it masked a darker reality.

Bubaque Island was a ramshackle place with no roads, just dirt tracks. The locals were poor, with most people living in mud-brick houses. Pigs and dogs suckled in the street. There were a few upmarket hotels, charging US$50 per night, but they were usually empty, begging the question of how they made enough money to survive. Drug-smuggling was the obvious answer. I was told that many locals who had legitimate jobs still earned too little to live — around US$40 per month — and had to supplement it by working for drug-traffickers.

Leaves, ferns, and trees were taking over the crumbling Portuguese governor's house, which had been abandoned in 1974 when Guinea-Bissau became independent. Young boys, some clothed and others naked, swam and fished on the sea shore. Faded painted signs dotted the paths, including one that read, 'Rue Paris' ['Paris Road']. The humidity was exhausting.

The luxurious Ponta Anchaca Hotel was on the nearby Rubane Island. It was run by a French woman, Solange Morin, in her fifties, who was sporting a severe face-lift and long blonde hair. She wore a short yellow skirt and white tank-top. A handful of older French guests were present, and with only 24 rooms it was hard to see how the hotel remained open. It cost US$110 per night for full board — a huge amount for Guinea-Bissau — and Morin was suspected of running a drug-smuggling operation in the area. She was suspected of managing the nearby airport to bring in the drugs, and of being close to senior members of the Guinea-Bissau government and military. Morin was visibly uncomfortable around me, even though I'd barely said a word, and my fixer, Allen, said it was because she hated journalists asking questions.

The remote airstrip, which was nothing more than a dirt path in the middle of lush, green grass, was near the coast on Bubaque Island. The small terminal featured wooden chairs and a map of the Bijagos Islands, while a three-seater plane sat motionless on the tiny tarmac. The guard on duty told me that it was waiting to take people to Bissau. Palm trees dotted the landscape. A few locals rode their bikes along its track, but it was otherwise empty. A rough track led from the airport to the ocean, making it easy to transport drugs from the airport to a high-speed boat onto Bissau. Allen said we shouldn't loiter in the area, taking photographs and looking curious, because it was certain that there were people watching us.

Allen told me that a few years before, the area was used to import 40 to 50 tons of cocaine annually, but these days it was lower — around 20 tons. This was because the French and the European Union, through the EU's border coast guard, Frontex, had become more effective in disrupting drugs coming from Senegal. However, Frontex's limited resources meant that around-the-clock monitoring was impossible, so drugs inevitably got through. With little to no effective law enforcement in the area, drug-traffickers had free rein. In 2015, the Portuguese government donated two surveillance boats to help monitor the Bijagos Islands.

This shows that law enforcement can slightly affect the flow of drugs in and out of African countries — for a while anyway — but the huge demand for drugs in the West inevitably wins out, and smugglers will find different ways to get illicit substances to those who want it. Principally relying on policing to 'solve' drug use and abuse in the poorest nations such as Guinea-Bissau ignores the suffering of civilians who are caught in the middle, and rarely provides sustainable economic alternatives.

It was an incredibly peaceful area. The ocean was nearby, calm and waveless, and fading sun draped its light on the young men, women, and children eating, drinking, and playing on the beach. It was the picture of beauty, seemingly untouched by the drug-trade, and yet it was one small but essential part of cocaine's route from Africa to Europe.

The inability of the central government to control its remote islands was made clear to me by Djibril Sanha, a 45-year-old member of the Guinea-Bissau army. He told me on Bubaque Island that his main role, as part of the marine control group, was to manage illegal fishing and drug-trafficking. He was one of 13 in his team, which had been formed in 2013. He joined the army in 2006.

'Since we started, we haven't worked at all', he admitted. 'We have no boats, no communication devices, and only our mobile phone. The government barely pays us [around US$90 per month, when the price for 20 kilograms of rice was nearly half that]. I don't understand what I'm doing here. You give us a head and stomach, but no legs.'

He recognised that his role was futile. 'From morning until evening, we do nothing except occasionally help the marine-diversity program here on Bubaque Island as a volunteer. Two times since 2013 I've seen illegal fishing, and I arrested people from Guinea-Conakry. They paid a fine, we took their canoe, and they were released.'

Sanha claimed that he'd barely seen any drug-trafficking activity, a statement that stretched credibility. He said that he'd received information three times in three years that there were drugs in the area. 'Cannabis and cocaine are the drugs here', he told me. 'Many young people on the island smoke cannabis, but they can't afford cocaine. That's for rich people.'

A more honest appraisal of the situation came from Papis Djata, a 45-year-old fast-boats mechanic, fishing guide for tourists, and pilot in the Bijagos Islands. When his mobile phone rang, the ring-tone was Bob Marley's song 'Is This Love'. His frankness was refreshing, because most other people I met in the area were cautious, fearing retribution from smugglers.

'A lot of cocaine is coming in and out of the area three to four times weekly', he said. 'In 2013, I was offered US$25,000 to go to Guinea-Conakry by a Guinea-Bissau businessman to bring in drugs. But I said no, too risky.'

Djata said that drug-smuggling in the Bijagos Islands had declined since the 2013 arrest of Na Tchuto, though other parts of the country were now more vulnerable to traffickers, and locals had nothing to do: 'Young boys used to carry drugs around and make a little money. When these young men used to work for smugglers, I would see them driving around in expensive cars. But when the work stopped, crime suddenly increased.'

To reduce crime, Djata said, the government had to bring employment opportunities to replace the drug-trade. 'The country has good prospects for the future. We must be patient. I want to see the country improve step by step. Drug-smuggling must be stopped.'

~

It was inevitable that the country's position as a major drug-transit country would bleed into locals becoming addicted to drugs. The country's only treatment facility, Quinhamel's Youth Challenge centre, was near Bissau. It was a basic institution run by Pastor Domingoes Te. He was a friendly man with a slight eye twitch. We spoke in his office, a mostly empty room with a poster behind him that spoke of a 'Teen Challenge — Guinea-Bissau: Prevent, Rehabilitate and Re-integration'. He was 48 years old, married with four children, and evangelical.

Driving into the centre, I saw patients milling about in a group. I was told that years ago patients were treated far more harshly, including being locked up and chained. Such treatment of the marginalised wasn't unusual in West Africa — though, thankfully, after public criticism, the pastor didn't engage in this behaviour anymore.[42]

Te told me that his centre rarely had enough food because the funds came only from himself and patient's parents. 'I had a dream when I started this in 2003', he said. 'God told me to help people, not to do propaganda on the radio, so I left being a pastor in a church in Bissau and came to help the marginalised.' He said that drug use soared in the 2000s after Colombian drug-traffickers invaded the country. There were 70 patients when I visited, including only 12 women whose ages ranged between 15 and 60. The pastor said that most had taken hallucinogens, acid, tablets, and alcohol. Around 30 per cent of people relapsed, but the majority stayed clean. Te said he'd treated around 3,800 people.

Te believed that drugs and alcohol should be illegal, and he enforced a strict rehabilitation regime. During the average 12-month stay, patients worked in four areas: religion, spirituality, pedagogy, and social. Patients were involved daily in these classes, and did basic tasks such as cleaning and fetching water.

'A family will contact police because they have a child who is no longer controllable', he said. 'The police bring this person to me, it happens every week, but we simply don't have enough space.' Families paid one euro per day, if they could afford it, but many simply didn't have the money. To keep the facility running, Te sought help from local churches, which sometimes donated rice, money, pens, and copy-books.

The pastor despaired over his government's priorities, though he knew there was a 'cycle of crisis. Our centre is not a top issue. Many public employees are not getting paid, and that's seen as more important.' He told me that drug addiction was getting worse across the nation. It was a trend across West Africa, with rising rates of HIV and the opening of the region's first methadone administrator in Senegal. The UNODC in West and Central Africa estimated that there were 1.8 million cocaine users in 2016, and around one million heroin users in 2015.[43]

I walked around the centre, situated near a swamp, and saw one woman with a blue shawl over her head sitting on her own on the dirty ground. A few dogs and goats wandered the grounds; an open-air meeting room with dirt floor housed nearly all the patients. They sat quietly, on wooden benches and rocks, and a few practised their basic English. I was half expecting some to be aggressive, but they were calm. A few looked at me intently.

One continually cupped his hands. Another man, Nuno, in a yellow football jersey, spoke English. He had lived in Britain, told me that he only smoked cigarettes in Guinea-Bissau, and that 'my mother doesn't like this so that's why she sent me here'. Most of the crowd were dressed in T-shirts and shorts. They seemed docile, even drugged, but I was told that they weren't. The sole woman in the group, wearing a red hoodie top, was all smiles.

~

The challenge for Guinea-Bissau to overcome its status as a 'narco-state' was partly out of its hands. With demand for cocaine and other drugs remaining high in Europe and the US, and increasingly across Africa, nations with weak institutions were vulnerable to ruthless drug cartels. Global interest in Guinea-Bissau would help; this wasn't a 'problem' needing to be fixed, ignoring the vast bulk of the population, but a nation that deserved real independence and economic options to develop. It galled many locals in Guinea-Bissau to be blamed for their country's failings when consumption of cocaine in London, Madrid, and Moscow had fuelled the decay.

A UN official told me in Bissau that, 'It's like the whole country is living in the present, to put food on the table, but history isn't taught in the schools because no one can agree on the past.' When I visited the national radio centre in the centre of the capital, I saw a room filled with decaying audio-tapes; the country's history was withering away. There was no money to maintain this invaluable archive, and the country's recorded history was disappearing.

The drug war, fought by the UN, the US, the EU, African states, and Guinea-Bissau, consumed so much time, energy, and resources that every other issue was pushed aside. It was a tragic way to view poor states that had little control over how they were controlled by cartel forces far bigger than themselves.

CHAPTER THREE

The Philippines

'All of you who are into drugs, you sons of bitches,
I will really kill you.'
PRESIDENT RODRIGO DUTERTE, 2016

Outside the offices of the Philippine Drug Enforcement Agency (PDEA) in the capital, Manila, was a poster with the face of Pope Francis. His message was clear: 'Drugs are evil. No to all types of drugs.'

A police officer stationed at the entrance wore a wristband supporting President Rodrigo Duterte. 'In drugs you lose, achieve change', it read.

The head of the PDEA, Aaron Aquino, was a Duterte ally who had known him for many years. Aquino was completely behind the president's anti-drug crusade, and promised a 'less bloody' war when he was appointed in 2017. In early 2018, his agency released figures that claimed to back up his pledge: only three suspects had been killed during 3,000 operations in Aquino's first 100 days in the job.[1] The PDEA claimed that 4,999 lives had been lost during the drug war between July 2016 and October 2018. The Philippine National Police said that more than 23,000 homicides were under investigation (though they weren't all connected to the war on drugs).

A veteran police chief from Davao City, the commercial city on the island of Mindanao, which Duterte led as mayor for 23 years, Aquino spoke openly about his affection for the nation's president. 'He is a very lucky person', he told me. 'He loves children, and he's very, very compassionate. He loves his country.' He denied that Duterte had any connection to the litany of human-rights abuses that occurred during his time in power in Davao, but acknowledged that some police were corrupt and sold drugs.[2]

During our conversation, Aquino was aware of the international outrage directed at his government's drug war, and aimed to neuter it. He said that he was uncomfortable with some of the violent police methods employed before his time in the position, though, when quizzed, he wouldn't go into detail.

His solution was to tell all police to wear body cameras, and he wanted journalists who accompanied the drug raids to follow suit. 'No executing, no killing, no nothing', Aquino said. 'Let's wear our body cams and co-ordinate with the media to show them that we're doing the right thing.' Authorities understood the propaganda value of media outlets showing brave policemen going after hated drug users. At the time of writing, many police departments had not purchased body cams.

The vast amounts of drugs entering the Philippines was both a reaction to demand and attempts by local and foreign drug cartels from Africa and Mexico to gain a foothold in the market. Aquino principally blamed China for the influx of illicit substances, and as a result he had substantially beefed up monitoring along the country's vast coastlines, and at ports and airports.[3] He had just returned from training in China, and had gained experience from how Beijing tackled illegal drugs.

Aquino didn't distinguish between ecstasy, marijuana, or shabu (the slang term for methamphetamines across Asia), and said that they were all 'equal' and had to be opposed. However, he seemed open to the idea of medical marijuana, 'if the government supported it'. The Philippines moved towards the use and research of medical marijuana, with Duterte's backing, from 2017.

Aquino's ambitions were vast. By 2021, he aimed to eliminate all illegal drugs in the Philippines. When I asked him to clarify what I'd just heard, he said it again. He wanted to create the world's first 'drug-free' country, and believed he could achieve it. When I countered that no other nation in the world had ever done so, he responded that Duterte had addressed drugs in a 'different way' and that was why his goal was obtainable. To achieve his goal, Aquino proposed drug-testing all children from Grade 4 (children of nine to ten years old). A proposed law in 2019 made children as young as nine criminally responsible for their actions, after Duterte condemned the inability of law enforcement to tackle underage offenders tied to drug gangs. Duterte's presidential term ends in 2022.

After the interview, I was shown around the PDEA facilities. The living quarters were called the White House. Many officers and workers lived far away, so they all slept together under one roof. The head of drug operations was Director Levi S. Ortiz, and on his desk the sign said, 'drug buster'. He told me that his team had recently arrested many big drug-traffickers and he hoped that they received long jail sentences.[4] 'Unless they pay somebody off, a real problem here', he said. He was excited about the prospect of using drones to monitor drug cartels. Traffickers already employed them to monitor police activity.

~

The streets of Manila and other cities and provinces have been soaked in blood since Duterte took power. This brash man convinced an electorate that only he could clean up crime-ridden communities across the country. He promised to bring the methods he had employed in Davao City — brute force against drug users and gangsters except the ones he befriended — and spread it widely. As soon as he assumed office in June 2016, he directed the police to target the most vulnerable people in society. The resulting death toll could be at least 30,000, but nobody I met knew the real number. The poor and disenfranchised were powerless, and on some nights dozens of bloodied bodies turned up in the morgues.

International call centres, basic accommodation for menial workers, and overpriced apartments dotted the city's landscape. The US embassy sat alongside Manila Bay, and outside it reeked of sewage.

The face of President Rodrigo Duterte with a Hitler moustache was plastered on a poster by the side of the road. 'Dictator' and 'Fascist' was written below his name. 'Fight!' — a message from the country's bigger labour union — was strong and direct, a sign of resistance. Countless pro-Duterte posters were nearby, and it had become a battle of propaganda messages.

When the 71-year old Duterte assumed the presidency, he was the 16th of the republic and the rare outsider to take the reins of power. Before his presidential campaign took off, he had been largely invisible in the national media. When asked if he had higher political ambitions, Duterte said that he was 'too old, too tired and too poor'. His eventual victory by six million votes appalled the liberal elites, but pleased his legions of followers. Despite making countless gaffes and speeches that demeaned women and his opponents,[5] Duterte demolished the establishment Liberal Party and United Nationalist Alliance.[6]

Duterte's populism was part of a global trend, at a time when US president Donald Trump and some of his European allies were proudly rejecting liberal presumptions about human rights. What this said about Filipino society was uncomfortable for many, but the scars of dictatorship under autocrat Ferdinand Marcos had never really healed. Observers who followed Duterte around the country during the election campaign saw a man who tapped into fiery emotions that lay beneath the surface of many citizens. His spontaneity and grass-roots momentum was genuine, albeit ably assisted by big-money donors and Facebook manipulation. An election strategy document, leaked to *Buzzfeed News*, showed that the Duterte campaign was built on three emotions; anger, hope, and pride.[7]

Filipino sociologist Nicole Curato argued that Duterte both embraced and challenged elite democracy, and that his drug war revealed dark fissures at the centre of it. 'Duterte unsettled dominant assumptions about the extent to which liberal virtues are rooted among the citizenry thirty years after the People Power Revolution that ousted the dictator Marcos', she wrote. 'Duterte's illiberal fantasy, however, has an ironic character. While it rejects the liberals' approach to crime and human rights, his illiberal project is also built on, and perpetuates, the same imperfections that discredited the Philippines' liberal democracy: a corrupt and unprofessional coercive apparatus of the state on which he relies to carry out his war on drugs.'[8]

A self-identified socialist, Duterte unleashed a campaign of terror against his country's destitute population while claiming to rescue it. However, he couldn't have achieved such carnage on his own. This required thousands of police and their online followers to dehumanise drug victims so wholly that killing them felt not only justified but vital to restoring the country's moral health. Like every other drug war I've reported on in this book, the victims were almost all poor while the infrastructure of drug-dealing and -smuggling remained intact. The rich and connected had little to worry about in Duterte's Philippines.[9]

Duterte's drug war was the most explicit I've witnessed, with rhetoric and brutal violence to match. There was nothing phoney about the war's aims or death toll, though the real agenda was arguably less about eradicating drug use and more about controlling the minds and emotions of the country's population.

Internationally, justice was elusive. The Philippines won another three-year term on the United Nations Human Rights Council in

2018 despite its atrocious record. It sat alongside Saudi Arabia, Egypt, and Pakistan, and a host of other abusers. The Philippine foreign secretary, Alan Peter Cayetano, said that, 'We are really greatly honoured, as this is a vindication that fake news and baseless accusations have no place in modern-day human-rights discussions.'

Duterte weaponised history for his own cynical ends, but he was correct to discuss how his country had rarely been truly free from foreign interference. The modern history of the Philippines was scarred by a brutal American occupation that started in 1898, following the ceding of the nation by Spain after the Spanish-American war. The people of the Philippines had already declared independence a few months earlier, but it was ignored. Washington finally recognised the country's independence in 1946, but by then it had overseen years of often bloody rule.

In the early days, hundreds of thousands of villagers were herded into concentration camps where disease, executions, and torture were commonplace.[10] The US waged an ugly insurgency against Filipinos, who fought what US president William McKinley called 'benevolent assimilation'.[11] It was anything but that; the exact death roll remains unknown, although most historians place the figure anywhere between 200,000 and one million people.

Rudyard Kipling dedicated his 1899 poem 'The White Man's Burden' to the US, in support of its conquest of the Philippines. Twenty-six of the 30 US generals in the Philippines had aimed to annihilate Native Americans at home, with one leader, Brigadier General Jacob H. Smith, telling his troops in the Philippines that, 'I want no prisoners. I wish you to kill and burn. The more you kill and burn the better it will please me.'[12]

American writer Mark Twain wrote anti-imperialist texts that are largely unknown today. In 1901, he damned the American occupation of the Philippines and argued in part: 'There must be two Americas: one that sets the captive free, and one that takes captive's new freedom away from him, and picks a quarrel with him with nothing to found it on; then kills him to get his land.'

For decades from the 1900s, interim governments often lacked legitimacy. After the Japanese invasion and occupation during World War II, and the country's eventual liberation by US and Filipino forces, independence was inevitable. Over one million Filipinos died during the war, when major cities, including Manila, were virtually wiped out.

Washington didn't stop interfering in the Philippines, but it did so without assuming any responsibility for its people's welfare. Economic power was embedded with a tiny landowning elite. Journalist Teodoro Locsin wrote in 1950 about this phenomenon: 'While benevolent America was building schools and roads (largely with local taxes), introducing modern sanitation and cutting down disease, imperial America was perpetuating a medieval economic system incompatible with the development of a healthy internal economy.'[13] Too often, according to American attitudes at the time, the Filipino was a 'student' needing to be taught by Washington.

When Marcos rose to power in 1965, the people were initially willing to lap up his message of a nation that had lost its way and needed strong leadership to survive. It was remarkably similar to Duterte's later promises during his election campaign. When he assumed office in 2016, he praised the deceased dictator as a 'hero', allowed him to be buried at the national 'Heroes' Cemetery', and urged the abolition of any moves to recover the stolen Marcos wealth. In late 2018, a court found the dictator's wife, Imelda Marcos, guilty of corruption, in a rare official rebuke. She had stolen US$200 million and sent it to Swiss foundations while governor of Manila in the 1970s.

When Marcos ruled under martial law from 1972 to 1981, his regime murdered thousands, imprisoned and tortured thousands more, and criminalised dissent. He remained leader until his overthrow in the 1986 People Power Revolution. He survived politically so long due to extensive US support and acceptance of US military bases. US president Ronald Reagan bought the lie that Marcos was a reliable partner in the battle against communism. A Reagan aide once said that for the US president, Marcos was like 'a hero on a bubble-gum card he had collected as a kid'.[14] Washington provided military and intelligence support to Marcos in his brutal war against enemies, using anti-communist and counter-insurgency techniques that had been learned during the Cold War.[15] Duterte applied similar vigilante methods in his war against drugs.

The passion, organisation, and grit of those organising opposition to Marcos was inspiring, and President Cory Aquino was his successor. Her husband, Benigno Aquino Junior, was the major opposition figure to Marcos, but he had been murdered on the tarmac at the Manila international airport in 1983 when returning from exile in the US. The manifesto that was released shortly after, signed by Cory Aquino and a range of political parties, specifically mentioned 'the arrogant presence of alien [US] military bases' and pushed for 'a truly democratic and independent' country.[16]

When Aquino took power, she terminated the US bases, claiming that they were an affront to national sovereignty. A US military presence was only re-established in 2014. An onslaught by the militant group Islamic State in Marawi was partly beaten in 2017 with military equipment and intelligence from the US, Australia, and China.[17] Nonetheless, as the Islamic State recedes in the Middle East as a major force, its tentacles continue to grow in the Philippines.

Understanding the rise of Duterte requires a critical analysis of his predecessors and their failings to institute necessary economic and political reforms that benefited the majority.

Countless presidents since Aquino had been far less successful in steering the nation competently. Fidel Ramos and Joseph Estrada, who ruled through much of the 1990s, were experts at cronyism. The president before Duterte was Benigno Aquino III, the son of Cory Aquino. He was a reluctant candidate, even though his six years in office were marked by solid economic growth. This didn't stop the growing concentration of wealth within the country and an obsessive focus, spurred by Washington, on paying back foreign debt.

Many Filipinos were sick and tired of dynastic rule, and Duterte seemed to be the outsider who captured the desire amongst many to build a nation along more independent lines. His appeal, explained Filipino intellectual Walden Bello, was as a 'carino brutal'. This was a 'volatile mix of will to power, a commanding personality and gangster charm that fulfils his followers' deep-seated yearning for a father figure who will finally end what they see as the "national chaos".[18] Duterte was charting an authoritarian future and wholesale rejection of liberal democracy. As a result, Barack Obama cut economic aid to the Philippines at the end of his presidency, even though Washington had continued to send financial support to Filipino police involved in the drug war after Duterte took power.[19]

Capitulation to Washington was a key theme of Duterte's, and he used it often. Duterte rejected the right of the US to criticise his drug war. At a press conference at Davao airport in September 2016, he said that, 'I am a president of a sovereign state. And we have long ceased to be a colony. I do not have any master but the Filipino people.' He was asked if he was worried that US president Obama would condemn his violent anti-drug crusade, and he shot back: 'You must be kidding. Who is he to confront me? America has one too many to answer for the misdeeds in this country ... As a matter of fact, we inherited this problem from the United States. Why? Because they invaded this country and made us their subjugated people.'[20]

More than two years after his election victory, polls showed that around 80 per cent of the population still backed Duterte (though other studies indicated that 90 per cent of Filipinos wanted drug suspects to be captured alive).[21]

Duterte's grip on power was strengthened after his allies won strongly in the 2019 midterm elections. One of the winners was Ronald 'Bato' Dela Rosa, the former chief of the Philippine National Police and Bureau of Correction, who had called for an escalation of the drug war.

Duterte was both accurately describing Washington's paternalistic attitude towards the Philippines over the previous century, but also wilfully deflecting legitimate opposition of his rule. His brutal drug war had generated huge amounts of international outrage; however, domestically, apart from prominent local human-rights groups expressing their disgust, his message resonated deeply with a population that had long-standing, unanswered questions about their place in the world and the role of imperial Washington.[22] They also believed that Duterte would reduce crime and kick out the bad elements within society. Many were struggling. In 2015, the Food Nutrition and Research Institute found that 33 per cent of Filipino children suffered from chronic malnutrition or stunting.

Duterte's fearlessness in speaking his mind resonated with millions. American historian and drug-war expert Alfred McCoy wrote that an overlooked aspect of global populism was 'the role of performative violence in projecting domestic strength and a complementary need for diplomatic success to show international influence.'[23] Drug prohibition was already strong across Asia, but police in Bangladesh, Sri Lanka, and Indonesia were increasingly following the Philippines lead and murdering drug suspects in cold blood. Data released in 2019 by the International Drug Policy Consortium showed that Asian countries that had adopted some of the harshest anti-drug policies in the world had failed to curb drug use or cultivation.

Culturally speaking, the Philippines embraced every form of American pop and food culture, but politically it was a far more uneasy relationship. Duterte's drug war was successfully sold as an indigenous solution to a country-wide problem; the majority of the population deluded themselves into believing that stability and normality would only be restored when every drug user and dealer was eradicated. The policy was almost genocidal in intent, and was executed by an undisciplined group of state-backed killers.

~

The police headquarters in Quezon City were the largest in the Philippines. As I arrived outside the entrance, I saw an armed policeman wearing a full-face mask, with only his eyes visible, climbing onto his motorbike. This anonymity had been a major problem during Duterte's drug war because policemen were killing with impunity without being identified. I later asked Ferdinand Mendoza, chief of the District Drug Enforcement Unit in Quezon City, about this, and he told me that it was a breach of protocol and not allowed. If this happened at the gates of the police headquarters, I could only wonder how common this practice was in protecting police in the dead of night when they barged into homes to attack or kill civilians.

Large letters celebrated the facility: 'Proud to be QCPD' [Quezon City Police Department]. In the main building were signs reminding officers of the values that they should be following. The QCPD band ended its performance, and the assembled media hummed to the song being led by an enthusiastic officer.

A press conference took place, led by police chief superintendent district director Guillermo Lorenzo T. Eleazar, who read an autocue on a TV in front of him and announced the capture on New Year's Eve of four murder suspects. At the end of the media spectacle, the four men were led out to be shown to the cameras. Their faces were covered by towels, and they wore orange prison uniforms. They were handcuffed together. When this concluded, the media were given a complimentary lunch in the hope of ensuring positive coverage.

It was a strange event because, although it wasn't about drugs, it felt rehearsed and largely unquestioned by the assembled all-male media. The news coverage would be a glorified police press release. Large sections of the local media were very supportive of Duterte's drug war.

While waiting to interview Eleazar, I saw copies of the official newsletter of the Philippine National Police. On its cover was a picture of Eleazar in a red Christmas hat handing out gifts to children whose drug-addicted parents had surrendered to authorities.

Eleazar was a big fan of Duterte, no doubt helped by the fact that he had recently received an 80 per cent pay increase. He said that there had been no police abuse of power since he had taken office in mid-2016, local communities supported the greater crackdown on drug users and drug-traffickers, and there was a robust system to investigate any police misbehaviour. 'This government doesn't tolerate any abuses', he said.

He admitted that more than one hundred police personnel were transferred from Quezon City to 'the furthest place' when he took over because of their involvement in protecting drug-traffickers. More than 500 members of the department's anti-drug unit were replaced. Eleazar described this as a 'cancer' that needed to be addressed to gain the 'trust and confidence of the people'.

Two senior police told Reuters in 2017 that police were paid US$200 specifically for killing drug suspects, rapists, gang members, and other 'troublemakers'.[24] Police often carried bibles and rosaries while visiting drug suspects' homes in an attempt to generate public support for Duterte's drug war.

Eleazar rejected accusations that his police force solely used violence to tackle the reported 1.8 million drug users in the Philippines. The total population is over 106 million. Eleazor said that his officers often visited the houses where occupants were drug addicts, and 'asked them to mend their ways'. They were encouraged to go into rehabilitation. If they refused, the police executed a search warrant, the so-called 'upper barrel' approach. Many citizens feared Oplan

Tokhang — the government's operation against illegal drugs that had police knocking on poor people's homes and that often led to death. The police established secret death squads to 'neutralise' suspected drug users or dealers.[25]

There were many Scientology books translated into the local language sitting on the police department press office bookshelf. A list of cases from the last 24 hours showed that many related to the drug shabu. It listed names and personal details left for anybody, including reporters, to peruse.

Thanks to Eleazar's support, we were given a private tour of the department's drug-enforcement unit. A photo of Quezon City's mayor, a baby-faced celebrity, was placed on a wall above a collection of weapons. Outside was a small, narrow locked area for arrested and alleged drug-traffickers. Families stood outside talking to them, looking distressed.

Ferdinand Mendoza, chief of the District Drug Enforcement Unit in Quezon City and a self-described Freemason, told me in his office that he had been in his position for one year. His job was to arrest and 'neutralise' the drug threat and users 'within the limits of the law'.

'Since I arrived here, there have only been three interactions with drug personalities', he said. 'Suspects opened fire on our undercover agent. The agent survived because he had been given tactical techniques. Two drug dealers were killed. We arrest many people for drug-dealing, being runners and look-outs.'

Mendoza was pleased about life imprisonment for drug-traffickers. If a citizen was arrested in possession of ten grams of illegal drugs, no bail was possible. Possession of over 50 grams of marijuana also meant that no bail would be granted. Marijuana remained illegal, but the state now saw it less seriously than other illegal drugs.

'I'm against legalising marijuana like in the US', he said. 'The character of Filipinos are addicts. More people would use the drug here if legal.' His team had never received any US funding or training, but he was keen to get US embassy and DEA 'knowledge and world experience'.

Mendoza gathered eight men and women from his drug team, sat them in a room, brought out their guns and bullet-proof vests, and explained on a whiteboard how he would instruct them to seize drugs in a neighbourhood. It was a show for me, and impossible to validate, but he stressed to them all that violence was never to be used, except in self-defence.

Some of the police officers in this drug unit — not the most violent ones causing the vast bulk of deaths under Duterte's rule — told me that they spent their own money to attend drug hearings for suspects. Their salary was too low to support the most rudimentary of police tasks.

Spending time with friendly police officers was disarming, knowing the damage some of them had caused. Foreign media and critical local media were loathed within the government, so for whatever reason I was given a positive PR experience. I didn't buy the spin, always asking about the countless cases of police brutality against civilians, but the supposed evils of drugs were used as both a justification of Duterte's drug war and a defence against any potential excesses. These were Duterte's people, without whom he couldn't have won an election.

~

Since the first days of Duterte's drug war, photojournalists became known as 'nightcrawlers' for chasing the dead bodies into the early hours of the morning. I wanted to experience this camaraderie in the face of horror, and spent a few nights waiting around with a group of predominantly male photographers. We were in the media section of the Quezon City police station, a strange place to congregate so close to those responsible for the murders.

From late afternoon, around ten journalists sat, read, smoked, and chatted, waiting for news on a killing or a police action. The reporters spent huge amounts of time together, day and night, talking about and documenting the bloody Duterte era. Whoever was around cooked, and everybody ate around a large table. I bought chicken, pork, and soft drinks, and we all shared a meal with white rice. One freelance photographer told me that he worked more than full time for the mayor of Quezon City, but earned so little money that he wanted to know if there was any work in Australia, including physical labour. His wife was a domestic worker in Hong Kong.

It felt like a relatively quiet night — the drug-war killings had slowed down in the months before I arrived — but everybody had heard that it would likely begin again in earnest soon. We watched the evening TV news, and one veteran journalist, wearing a Duterte wristband, wanted to know what I thought of the country's president. He seemed disappointed when I said I was 'critical' of him.

Waiting for a murder to occur was a strange and surreal feeling. Journalists and photographers wanted to document the killings, in all their gory detail, but it felt voyeuristic.

Just before 8.00pm, a journalist came in and said he'd heard there was a shooting nearby. My fixer, Bernard, and I jumped into our car to investigate, even though we didn't have the exact address or any details of what had happened. Close to the final location, we saw a police car making its way slowly through the heavy traffic.

The blue-and-red flashing lights stopped, so we parked our car and walked towards a small crowd. Lying on the ground, in almost darkness, was a lifeless body. Dressed in trainers, shorts, and short-sleeve shirt, the man was in front of his scrap-metal shop. The man's two dogs sat relatively still at the entrance of the business, occasionally barking. Locals and children stood and stared. The police had erected some rope to stop people walking right up to the body, but it was still possible to come within a few metres of him. Many took photos with their mobile phones. Photographers and journalists gathered, speaking to witnesses and taking pictures of the crime scene.

It was the first dead body I had ever seen, apart from that of a deceased relative. I felt fascinated and sickened, wondering if I was a vulture for taking so many photos. Then, I thought, I was a journalist documenting the drug war. This was what it looked like.

Staff from the Philippine National Police Crime Laboratory arrived, wearing gloves, and started looking around the body for evidence. They took photos of the crime scene. They seemed to be doing a competent job, but it was impossible to know because police were likely culprits in the murder. A large and growing pool of blood flowed from the victim's head.

A stretcher arrived, and the dead man was lifted and placed on it. It was the first time I had seen his bloodied and bloated face. He was stripped to his underwear, a bandana placed on his face, and his belongings put beside him. A few metres away, a female family member appeared, weeping and slamming her hand on her heart.

With the body moved from its position of death, a young man appeared and lit a candle in its place beside the pool of blood. It was a poignant moment, lighting up the concealed red of the man's blood.

I didn't learn the name of the deceased until the following morning. According to the initial police report, Manny 'Buddy' Wagan had been gunned down by motorcycle riders in tandem, a common method of execution killings in the Philippines. They were likely either police or police-backed vigilantes. According to a witness, who was across the street when he heard two gunshots, a man in a helmet and woman in a white cap fled the crime scene.

The assailants walked about five metres towards Wagan while he was talking to a couple. He was shot twice, although none of the other bystanders were harmed. One witness claimed that Wagan was a former barangay [neighbourhood] leader and had no known enemies. The police said that the case was a 'death under investigation'.

Four months after Wagan's murder, I asked my fixer, Bernard, to contact the police in Manila to see if there were any updates to its investigation. There was not, apart from speculation as to the motive behind the assassination. Wagan's case would likely forever remain unsolved.

~

Unlike vast parts of Manila, where extra-judicial killings against suspected drug users were common, often daily, occurrences, Makati City was an oasis of generic calm. The streets were clean, the traffic moved — in the rest of the city it took hours to drive a few kilometres — and high-rise buildings touched the clouds. It reminded me of an American city, even around Wall Street, and had few traits that made it particularly Filipino. Makati was in the middle of Manila, but it felt like a foreign country.

The human-rights advocacy and law group Centre for International Law (Centrelaw) was based there, one of the few legal firms representing drug-war victims and publicly pushing for justice. It was risky work — its lawyers feared for their lives, and they changed their routes to work daily and watched their backs. Lawyers were regularly targeted. At least 34 had been murdered since Duterte came to power.

'We know that 99.9 per cent of cases from the drug war won't go to court', Centrelaw lawyer Gil Anthony Aquino said. 'Centrelaw and all of us are scared of this government. We don't personally attack Duterte, and don't call for his ouster. We skirt around the issues, and try to get accountability from the police.' Aquino had faith in the Philippines' legal system, with all its faults, because the 'courts have been the most independent of all three branches of the state'.[26] The group had a rare legal win in 2019 after the Supreme Court ordered the government to release documents related to the thousands of drug-war killings.

Centrelaw was working on just five cases through the courts related to the drug war. Aquino was frustrated that so few cases were being pursued by the victims' families, but fear was a major factor. He said that nobody knew the exact death toll since Duterte had been elected, but he believed it could be as high as 17,000 or even more.

'You can have gross human-rights abuses in a democratic country', Centrelaw lawyer Gilbert Andres said. For Andres, this fight was personal. His father had been killed by a drug addict in Manila in 1989, and that was a key reason he was built for this moment: not to demonise drug users while understanding the factors that created them.

One of the founders of Centrelaw was Duterte presidential spokesman Harry Roque, a man who now stood on the opposite side of the moral divide in the Philippines. He told me that international human-rights groups should not simply criticise Duterte in numerous reports, but financially support Filipino citizens and local lawyers who wanted justice through the courts. It seemed like a reasonable suggestion, though Roque didn't accept that his government had made many mistakes (and presumed that local courts could deliver justice) or killed many civilians, so he was asking international groups to investigate murders caused by his leader's rule.

I put Roque's comments to Andres, and he said they had merit. 'International NGOs should support local NGOs through general funding and by investing in local lawyers', he said. 'At the end of the day, it's the local lawyers who do actual litigation that will carry the burden for human rights.'

Aquino said that the government had to do a better job of investigating its own crimes. He worried that more international funding for local litigation would be wasted, 'given how time-consuming and costly it is.' Because there was not a culture of litigation in the Philippines around the drug war, 'we should try and develop a more court-based approach to help solve the human-rights disaster currently happening'.

Andres explained that there was a public perception that, 'If you're a drug suspect, you don't deserve rights. If you're an advocate for human rights, you're an enemy of the state.'

Both Andres and Aquino were critical of other Filipino law firms for being so tentative in a time of crisis. Many human-rights groups collected evidence of drug killings for the historical record, but Centrelaw wanted to stop the killings now. 'There's too much emphasis on press releases', Andres said, though he quickly noted how important it was to the struggle to collate evidence. Local journalists were reluctant to file cases if they were in danger, because they said their sources would dry up. The state-backed Commission on Human Rights had its budget slashed after being a constant critic of the drug war.

Victims of the drug war were understandably scared of taking on the regime. Centrelaw only had one person they represented who lived in a safe house; the rest resided in the communities or houses where the murders took place.

Centrelaw had a novel way of challenging Duterte's killing machine. In 2017, they filed a 'writ of amparo', a legal procedure used in many Spanish-speaking countries, against the police. It was a legal remedy available to any citizen whose right to security, liberty, and life was threatened or violated by an unlawful act committed by a public employee. The writ aimed to protect 26 communities across Manila. The country's solicitor-general led a comical opposition to the case, claiming it would set a 'dangerous precedent' because 'drug personalities' could use the legal device to 'fish for evidence' in the name of human rights.

Francisco H. Blanco Junior was one of Centrelaw's clients. His brother, Emiliano Blanco, also known as Jack Lord, was killed by police on 30 November 2016. Francisco was transgender, born a man but living as a woman. He was 45 years old, and was often called Joel. He arrived with Emiliano's seven-year-old son, Franco Blanco, who had red, blotchy skin. Joel lived on Mercurio Street in San Andres, Manila, an area that had seen countless drug-war assassinations.

Joel was part of Centrelaw's 'writ of amparo' claim in 2017, one of 47 petitioners who claimed that there had been 35 'drug-related deaths in the area' in the preceding 13 months, and demanded all anti-drug activity cease without the presence or co-ordination of legitimate witnesses.

Emiliano's partner, Marie Tamaya, and boarders in their house had all been taken to prison by police before Emiliano was killed. Young Franco had been playing outside and hadn't seen any violence, but now knew what had happened to his father.

On the fateful night, Emiliano was left alone in the house while uniformed police waited outside and watched for witnesses. Five plainclothes police were inside the house, a common tactic in slums where drug killings took place. Emiliano was a drug user, and he'd surrendered to police in mid-2016 before being released.

He was a big man and asleep when police woke him, held him down, and stomped on his arms. His bruised body proved these injuries. One policeman shot him, and four others watched while their colleagues cordoned off the area and shut down all shops to remove witnesses. Police claimed Emiliano had a gun and tried to fight back. Joel denied this, and said police planted a gun, shabu, and grenade on his brother.

'It's hard for me', Joel said. 'He never hurt anybody. He was a good father. I want police to go to jail and [for me to] get financial compensation. I'm scared. I pray to God to protect us.'

Joel now lived in fear of losing his life. 'If I was there on the night of the murder, I would have been killed for sure. When my brother was in the morgue, I was told to leave for my own protection. I was told I'd be next. I went to the countryside with his boy, Franco, for a while. Relatives in the country said I looked guilty because we'd fled, so we came back to the city.'

Joel recounted how the police continually harassed him, starting a few months after his brother's death. One night, authorities came to his house, stole expensive perfume, and replaced it with a cheaper brand. They took 60,000 pesos (US$1,125) and a friend's bag. It happened again in March 2017, even though he wasn't on any official police list. 'One policeman made a violent gesture, mimicking a knife cutting my throat, and said, "Do you want the same fate as your brother? I will do the same to you as I did to him." I recognised his face, and I knew that was my brother's killer.'

As in many poor areas decimated by the drug war, police regularly patrolled the streets looking for trouble. So-called 'catwalks' in the area were a ubiquitous feature where authorities harassed residents. Joel knew of many cases where police didn't bother investigating when other police committed crimes. 'I was told they've likely been instructed to ignore requests for help from anybody connected to deaths in the drug war', he told me.

I admired Joel. He was softly spoken, but defiant and scared. At times, he looked on the verge of tears when describing his brother's death and tough life. He was powerless, and his words and gestures confirmed that he knew it. Despite this, he wanted justice. It was a massive risk seeking legal help and refusing to capitulate to police threats.

Another Centrelaw client was Marilyn Malimbam. Her partner, Jessie Cule, was murdered by police on 21 August 2016, along with three other garbage collectors. She was quiet, and faced constant pressure from local authorities for daring to speak out, as did the relatives of the other survivors. Dead bodies were dumped by police or vigilantes near their homes as a warning. During Jessie's funeral, Marilyn saw suspicious people walking around.

A few days after the incident, Marilyn went to police headquarters and discovered that Efren Morillo, a vegetable seller, was a survivor from the night of the murders. He had been shot in the chest, but had crawled away. She feared the police 'would finish what they started' and target him in hospital. Morillo was transferred to a safe house organised by Centrelaw. He rarely saw his two young children anymore, felt lonely, and needed counselling.

'All I want is justice', Marilyn, 43 years old, told me. 'Jessie was my live-in partner. [She described him this way because they weren't married.] I'm still afraid today. I choose paths where there are few vehicles, worried somebody could pop out of a car and kill me.'

Marilyn had recurring images about the night of the murders. A child witness had recounted that Jessie was on his knees, holding the policeman's legs and begging for his life, but he was shot dead. Marilyn sobbed while telling this story.

Autopsy reports of all four men found that they had been killed at point-blank range, despite police claiming it was a shoot-out. Police also alleged the men were drug suspects, but no credible evidence was produced to support this claim.

'Life must go on until I get justice', Marilyn said. She told me that Centrelaw knew who killed Jessie and the other four men, but this police officer had inexplicaby disappeared.

~

Not all drug users were killed in cold blood. Renewal was possible, but you had to accept Jesus Christ as your saviour. The San Roque De Manila Parish ran a community-based Catholic rehabilitation program for drug takers.[27] Shabu was regularly traded in the area. Beyond the dingy entrance stood statues of Christ in the half-darkness. In a devoutly Catholic country, this program was designed to avoid the violence unleashed by police during Duterte's drug war.[28]

Police senior inspector Ana Lourence Simbajon was a petite woman who had been working on the program in the area for one-and-a-half years. Her job was to manage 'drug surrenderers' (in her words). A drug watchlist had existed for a long time, she told me, well before Duterte. It was drafted by barangay leaders, and allowed drug users to be identified.[29] This list in the Duterte era, unavailable to the public, had up to one million names of suspected drug suspects, and included politicians and police. Duterte publicly named officials he claimed were corrupt and connected to the drug-trade, and some were killed as a result. Simbajon said that shabu and marijuana were the primary drugs of choice for the mostly poor and homeless people who were addicted.

'We ask drug users to admit their drug use', she said. It was 80 per cent men aged between 25 and 40 years old. 'Users have never said no when asked to admit their drug taking.' The threat of death that hung over them was surely a motivating factor.

This was a rehabilitation program that emphasised religion, Jesus, and God. It lasted for six months, and included random drug testing. Participants regularly visited doctors and psychiatrists for a weekly evaluation. Four failed drug tests meant that a person wouldn't pass the course and get a certificate, but they could keep going until they succeeded.

Simbajon was a Duterte fan and sensed that I wasn't 100 per cent on-board with his agenda. 'We are asking the public and media to focus on this positive program and not just the violent activities', she said. 'Users have been reformed and drug syndicates closed. Give Duterte a chance.'

In the church basement sat a group of former drug users undergoing their daily classes. Heavily influenced by lessons about God and Jesus — 'God is a perfect being' was one PowerPoint slide — the men and a few women sat quietly. Occasionally, they stood up to sing songs praising Jesus. On some days, they did Zumba and learned about spirituality, life skills, sports, arts, and culture. 'Five stages towards love' read the whiteboard. At the end of the session, police officer Simbajon handed out food in a polystyrene container to the group.

George was a 50-year-old metal worker who spoke glowingly of the program. He had many missing teeth. He used to take shabu and marijuana, and for ten years he'd taken drugs due to peer-group pressure and family problems. He told me that he wanted to stop because of his five-year-old daughter, Michelle.

'I was on a government drug list during the rise of Duterte', he said. 'I was seen by the community and identified. I was scared of police and vigilante groups.' He was nervous giving too many personal details, and remained frightened of being targeted by both groups. Informants were everywhere.

'I volunteered to surrender. My girlfriend knew I took drugs, and she wanted me to stop. My daughter never saw me high. I moved to a different neighbourhood to avoid bad influences.' He said that prayers had cleared his mind, and he now volunteered at the church. George proudly showed me his drug-testing report, which detailed negative results for shabu.

He was philosophical about his prospects of living a long life. 'I don't know if I'll die from illness [he complained of arthritis in his knees, and wondered if it was due to drug withdrawal] or bullets.'

Near the church was a barangay where many former drug users were being rehabilitated and lived. 'Support the drug war', one sign read in the spacious area on a basketball court in the middle of the facility. 'To achieve our goal towards a drug free world, community and a well-develop [sic] country', read another.

Veronica Sevilla was one of the lucky ones. She was 45 years old, and proficient in English. With barely any teeth, she had a hearty laugh. The rehabilitation program had likely saved her life. She had eight children ranging in age from two to 28 with four different men. She first married in 1992, and it was her husband who introduced her to shabu. It was a physically abusive marriage, and they often took drugs. In 2006, she left the Philippines for the first time and went to Indonesia with her three children.

'I had hatred in my heart years ago', she said. 'I wanted revenge on my first husband. I was good looking, and I used my good looks to lure men and get shabu.' This angered her husband, who wanted her back; he was jealous, but she was not interested. 'My son was a porter, and I decided that I wanted a better life for my family.' Back then, Jesus guided her, but she was no longer religious.

Sevilla moved back to the Philippines and had another baby, but started taking drugs again in 2013. She was sleeping on the streets, and homeless. Her youngest child lived with her mother out of town.

'I started taking drugs again in 2013 because something was missing', she said. 'I didn't have love.' She had been drug-free since mid-2016.

'The life I destroyed when taking drugs, I had to get trust back. My mother supported me throughout, crying when she saw me. My oldest son was angry with me, but now I communicate with all my children on Facebook. I don't want them to come here yet [to see me]. When I graduate [from the drug-rehabilitation course], they could come. Life is the only gift I can give.'

Her partner, Jose Mari Beslig, with whom she had twins (but who lived with her mother), was also a former shabu user. In his forties, he had struggled to give up his addiction, but the welcoming environment in the barangay and Sevilla's love had transformed him.

Savilla showed me the living area she shared with her boyfriend. A mattress sat under a shelf, and they slept in a small space with no real privacy. There was a fan and some clothes on a hook. After years of unhappiness, she kept on stressing that this small community had given her what nobody else ever had: comfort and stability. She said she didn't miss drugs and the lifestyle that went with it. She had travelled to many countries — including Indonesia, the US, and Europe — and was more worldly than anybody else I met.

'I live in a small space, but I'm happy and content with my life', she told me. 'I'm surrounded in the barangay with love.'

Outside the central square in the barangay sat Halloween toys: a bloody, severed head and teddy bear. Men were sitting nearby alongside caged fighting cocks.

The chairwoman of the barangay and 'mother' of everybody living there was Victoria Grande. She was compassionate towards people who were willing to change; she had taken in Sevilla and her boyfriend from the streets and pledged to help them. With one boy and two girls of her own, she told me that she was a 'public servant'. The rehabilitation program in the barangay had started in September 2016 and targeted shabu users, marijuana smokers, and abusers of cough syrup.

'My personal mission is to help other people', she said. 'They need hope and spiritual formation through the church to get them off drugs.' She thought that people followed her because she was 'sincere'. She aimed to help everybody, but acknowledged that some cases had eluded her due to 'weak personalities or family problems'. I saw her crying in the church earlier in the day. She said it was because three people had failed their drug tests and were back smoking shabu.

Grande was an enthusiastic supporter of Duterte, and dismissed any criticisms of him. 'I support Duterte's war on drugs to bring back trust and progress in our country. I don't believe EJK [extra-judicial killings] are happening by police. Critics want to damage our dear president. The people should believe that change is happening. Drug users must be saved. Our president is doing his best. I see him as a model, following the drug campaign.'

Like many Filipinos that I met, she wasn't opposed to all drug use, and backed medical marijuana. 'The drug is already used illegally and privately for pain relief today', she said.

In her small office filled with folders detailing all participants in the program, a photo of Duterte was proudly hanging on the wall. She gave tough love to her flock, and chose to ignore and deny the violence unleashed by the president. It wasn't her method — she told me she opposed violence and preferred her strategies of rehabilitation — and yet she was able to fully back Duterte, despite knowing that thousands had been killed. She blamed drug users and dealers for refusing what she viewed as benevolent visits by the police.

People like Grande were like many others in the Philippines; they weren't bloodthirsty, and had no interest in seeing or hearing the details of the carnage, but were content to allow it to happen in the dark alleys around them while they slept. They believed the government's rhetoric that cleaning up the streets would be messy and time-consuming. They'd also seen the devastating effects of widespread shabu use and the breakdown of families. It wasn't overly surprising that they then supported a man who pledged to make the Philippines great again, recreating a mythical past of peace and tranquillity that never existed.

During my time with Grande, I regularly wanted to challenge her on why she supported Duterte, and to explain the human cost of his policies. But I had to restrain myself, as that wasn't my job. I'm a journalist, not a preacher. Besides, she lived amongst the people who suffered the most from drug abuse, so who was I to judge harshly? At moments like this, my role as an advocate for the marginalised had to be suspended. I could fully oppose Duterte's drug war, and I told people in the Philippines if they asked, but my responsibility was listening and not berating.

The real problems were far greater. The South-East Asian underworld produces around two billion methamphetamine speed tablets a year, making the drug increasingly more popular in the region than heroin and marijuana. Washington's silence or complicity in backing the Philippines and other nearby nations fighting a violent drug war is making the regional carnage worse.

Near the barangay was a small funeral home that had seen huge amounts of business since Duterte came to power. I visited it with my fixer, Bernard, but there were no bodies when we arrived. One family was waiting for the delivery of their dead relative, who had been killed by a gunshot wound, but we couldn't get confirmation it was drug-related. In the manager's office was a sign that read, in English, 'Autopsy is free of charge' and an annual calendar for 'Casino', ethyl alcohol. A pretty woman was holding the product alongside the message, 'Germ-friendly, skin friendly.' There was something grimly humorous about this advertisement, because it was the product used to clean the hands of workers after touching and preparing dead bodies.

Next door, a family sat with their deceased relative in an open casket.

One of the funeral parlour employees walked with a slight limp, and said that in 2017 they received at least ten bodies per day due to the drug war. It was now more like five bodies per week.

~

The shocking death toll from Duterte's drug war rightly garnered international headlines, and yet they weren't giving the full picture. The government made halting efforts to rehabilitate drug users, though the country needed far more clinics, in facilities that received far less attention. It was a deliberate strategy: scare users into surrendering or face death.[30] However, I heard multiple allegations that many addicts were willing to be arrested by police but were murdered nonetheless.

One of the biggest facilities is the Department of Health Treatment and Rehabilitation Centre in Bicutan, close to the centre of Manila and run by Alfonso Villaroman as its chief health program officer. It was one of the first drug-treatment sites in the Philippines. Situated in a large police camp, the sound of an active shooting range was always within earshot. Police were living, training, and working near people they might otherwise be killing on raids.

Villaroman was a jolly man, fluent in English, having lived and studied in the US, and travelled widely. He was 54 years old, a trained surgeon, and an expert in psychiatry and psychology. His left leg had been amputated below the knee, and he was obsessed with motorcycles. He repaired old bikes with his patients as a form of therapy.

Villaroman told me that in the early 1970s, the idea in the country was to punish people as a treatment for drug abuse. Back then, it was marijuana and opioids. Many people died during treatment, traumatised by the experience. By the late 1980s, shabu had become the major drug.

'I restore old motorcycles with my patients', he said. 'I tell them that it's not junk, one little piece repaired at a time, and this can be like you. I give them the book *Zen and the Art of Motorcycle Maintenance*.'

Bicutan was a speciality hospital, a treatment facility for drug dependence. It had nurses, doctors, surgeons, and a rehabilitation team. Some patients had mental-health disorders, schizophrenia, psychosis, and HIV. There were 600 patients when I visited — young boys, men, and some women — and Villaroman said that this number had decreased during the Duterte era. It had 2,000 patients when he took power in 2016, with a capacity of 550, but Villaroman started training doctors in communities around the country, and they sent patients to other locations. He knew that more than 30 patients had left this facility — 'Addiction is a disease, it's chronic and relapsing' — and been killed in the drug war.

He was cautious when talking about Duterte; he was a government employee, but he was clear in his opposition to the violence. Nonetheless, 'Many people affected by meth are aggressive, and this could explain at least some of the violent encounters between them and police.'

'The government is not killing our patients', he said. 'Police are not out to kill addicts. I like to believe they're following the law. It's not perfect here. Law is made by humans. I like to think that deaths in the drug war are collateral damage.' I sensed that he didn't really believe what he was telling me, but felt constrained as to what he could say in front of a journalist.

Local and foreign patients stayed between six and twelve months, and were given vocational training, including in mobile-phone repairs and job placements when they left. The youngest-ever patient was a seven-year-old boy with his mother, both addicted to shabu. The teenagers went to school nearby before and after their daily treatment. Violence used to be common between patients — many arrived with anger-management problems — but this had radically reduced (though metal forks and spoons weren't allowed inside).[31] Villaroman said that he had a 70 per cent success rate.

Villaroman was a doctor and activist, advocating for a more humane government approach to drug addiction. The current law in the Philippines meant that anybody who was admitted for drug-treatment more than twice would be prosecuted. He was talking to politicians to get this changed. He welcomed a visit from the president. 'If Duterte came here, I'd say that addicts have hope. Recovery should be fun and pleasurable. Love is the best catalyst to ease pain and fear.'

Treatment wasn't free. After the US$85 admission fee, patients and their families had to pay at least US$50 per month. For some patients, Villaroman said, 'Paying makes them feel like this is not welfare.'

A harsh prohibition against drugs in the country was a key reason the drug war was so publicly popular. Many citizens claimed that they just wanted the laws to be upheld. Villaroman said he supported only parts of Portugal's decriminalisation of all drugs — namely, the marijuana part — but argued that Filipinos 'lacked maturity' for any major changes to the nation's drug laws. He believed legalisation would happen one day in the far future.

In a large indoor basketball court, patients sat and waited for their families to visit, in what was a fortnightly opportunity. Western music played, including 'Hot in Herre' by Nelly, as background texture to visiting hours. The patients were all wearing white T-shirts and shorts.

Ahron R. (I was asked not to use his last name) was 42 years old, muscly, married, and with only five teeth. He had a 12-year-old girl and six-year-old boy, and spoke proficient English. His brother was also a former drug user and had just left the facility after his fourth attempt.

'My wife convinced me to come', he told me. 'I was on shabu at 21; my cousin introduced me. This is my sixth visit here — 1999 was my first time. I kept on coming because I wanted to change for my children, but when I get out, my extended family discriminate against me. I'd like them to not be so negative, to help me.'

He said that the temptation with shabu was its cheap price. It was less than US$2 for a bag. He explained that the drug made him 'feel strong in the short term, but then I need more drugs'. He used to be a barangay investigator, but they no longer trusted him, and he lost his job. He desperately wanted to move to a different area, to change his environment.

Ahron's wife visited him regularly, but he didn't want his children to see him. 'I tell them I'm working and studying', he said. 'I worry they won't respect me. I'm worried that my son will take drugs when he's older. My daughter wants to be a nun. I'm not afraid of coming out [of rehabilitation]. I'm not a hardened criminal, thank God.'

Despite his drug-troubles, Ahron loved Duterte. 'I'm thankful Duterte is doing his war on drugs', he said. 'Not sure who is killing all the people — police or vigilantes — but I voted for him. Duterte's critics have sour grapes. The main goal of the president is to protect our country and people.'

Ahron was likeable and talkative. He was clearly struggling with years of addiction, and yet his wife had thankfully stuck by him. His support for Duterte surprised me, but perhaps it shouldn't have. He was a potential victim of the drug war — regular shabu users were routinely killed — but he separated himself from the people who had been murdered. Perhaps Duterte represented his ideal view of society, devoid of drugs and addiction.

His hope that his children didn't know about his drug addiction and treatment seemed like wishful thinking, certainly for the 12-year-old daughter, but maybe he had to believe that his offspring weren't tainted by the same problems that had impacted him.

Around the basketball court were other patients sitting and eating with their families. The sound of gunshots was a constant background noise, with police training nearby.

Mohammed (not his real name), 43 years old with slicked black hair, sat with his wife and 12-year-old daughter. It was his first time in rehab after smoking shabu for two years. He and his wife were luggage makers.

'I wanted to rehabilitate outside, but my wife said it would be easier in the facility', he told me. 'I have twin sons [from a previous marriage] who were taking shabu and dealing it, and I got involved in drugs to help them, but I got addicted myself. I sent the twins to Mindanao to my father to get clean, and they are.'

He praised the facility. He received three meals a day. 'I've put on weight. Before, I was thin when taking drugs.' It was a rigorous daily schedule, with a 5.00am rising time and 9.00pm bedtime, with no access to media or the internet except some TV on the weekends, but Mohammed welcomed the discipline.

Both his wife and daughter were cautiously optimistic that rehab was the best and only way to transform Mohammed. 'I miss him because of the business and as a wife', she said. 'I hope he won't do drugs again. I've done my part. Before he was thin and dirty when on shabu, but now he's handsome.'

Mohammed's daughter, with long black hair, black jeans, and black-and-white trainers, told me that she didn't know her father was doing drugs when he lived at home. She wanted to be a doctor when she was older to help people like him. 'I found out he was on drugs when he came to treatment', she said. 'I was angry and sad. Now I'm happy because my dad is happy and has muscles. When he's out, I hope he doesn't go back to drugs.'

I asked the family if they believed, after their own experiences with shabu, that drugs should be decriminalised or even legalised. They expressed shock when I told them that Portugal had decriminalised all drugs for personal use in 2001. Until we parted, they couldn't stop talking about it, asking me questions about how Portuguese society viewed people who consumed drugs. The idea that a society could handle illicit substances in a less draconian way — that didn't threaten death by police or vigilantes — was a foreign concept in much of the Philippines.

~

Duterte's massive appeal didn't happen overnight, and it required constant government vigilance to keep his support base satisfied while the drug war was unleashed. This was achieved through a savvy use of Facebook and its complicity in building the Duterte brand. The president and his online team created troll armies to both direct and stifle debate.

Facebook has faced justified criticism for allowing its platform to be used to spread genocidal comments against Rohingya Muslims in Myanmar: voluminous amounts of hate speech pollutes the site in that country, and Facebook has done little to address it.[32] Mark Zuckerberg's company admitted allowing Russian-aligned pro–Donald Trump accounts to target voters in the 2016 US presidential election, though its impact on the final result was debatable, and the corporation was dogged by evidence that it contributed to the corruption of democratic debate in Cambodia.[33] Facebook has faced similar charges in Sri Lanka.

The company has a global government and politics team that claims to be neutral by working with virtually any political party or group aiming for power around the world. The exact number of staff in this department is unclear, but Bloomberg reported in 2018 that it had the capacity to send hundreds of people into the heat of an election campaign from its legal, policy, and information-security teams.[34]

Headed from Washington, DC, by former Republican digital strategist Katie Harbath, the team sent out its employees to become de-facto campaign workers from India to Britain. Her team worked closely with Facebook advertising staff to find new markets to monetise. When a party won government, Facebook was able to exercise huge influence over its officials, including by advocating for less regulation.

The secretive Facebook team helped Germany's far-right anti-refugee party, Alternative for Germany (AfD), win seats in the Bundestag in 2017. Facebook boosted Duterte's election campaign in 2016 by training its staff how to best use the platform, including by targeting overseas Filipino workers, amidst evidence that opponents of the candidate were smeared on the site, a trend that only increased after he won.[35]

When questioned by Bloomberg about helping parties that benefited from spreading false information or hate speech, Harbath said, 'We take our responsibility to prevent abuse of our platform extremely seriously.'[36] Facebook has admitted that it is struggling to cope with the growing proliferation of trolling on its platform.

The Philippines under Duterte perfected a textbook example of 'patriotic trolling' — organised online hate mobs designed to silence critics of the regime — and the effect radically skewed what the public understood about their society. An extensive investigation by *Buzzfeed News* into the prevalence of Facebook in the Philippines found that the company had been wilfully negligent in removing false or defamatory information since the rise of Duterte. This mattered greatly because for millions of citizens — two-thirds of the population — Facebook was the only place they received information.[37] With only 15,000 content reviewers globally, Facebook was incapable of tackling the epidemic of fake news and hate speech that pervaded its site.

The CEO of the independent Philippines news outlet *Rappler*, Maria Ressa, told a 2018 Senate hearing in Manila that there was 'a sock-puppet network of 26 fake accounts' in the country that could 'influence about three million accounts'. She warned that 'what you're seeing in our country is a campaign machinery that's become weaponised'. Ressa had collated a vast collection of Facebook accounts — at least 12 million — that distributed fake news or pro-Duterte propaganda. With 97 per cent of Filipinos using social media and spending huge amounts of time online, people were vulnerable to manipulation.[38]

The Duterte regime was increasingly targeting independent journalists and media outlets, including *Rappler*, for daring to question its rule. During my time in the Philippines, the government initiated proceedings to shut down *Rappler* for spurious reasons. I attended a rally in the heart of Manila to support the outlet; it was loud and passionate, but small, comprising around 300 people. Protestors held signs opposing the reintroduction of martial law, a move threatened by Duterte, and advocated for free speech. An Al Jazeera English journalist told me that the situation in the Philippines would need to get much worse before the masses poured onto the streets. In late 2018, *Rappler* and Ressa were charged with tax-evasion charges that looked politically motivated. Ressa was the joint winner of *Time Magazine*'s 2018 'Persons of the Year'. In 2019, the state launched another case against her, for supposed defamation in a 2012 article, and briefly arrested her for 'cyber libel'.

Lorraine Marie T. Badoy, the government's undersecretary of the Presidential Communications Operations Office, led Duterte's online strategy. She was a true believer in her leader. 'I love the president', she told me. 'I fully support him.' She admired Duterte for helping the poor. Badoy said that Duterte was the first leader of the Philippines who was willing to adjust its relationship with Washington, which many Filipinos welcomed. The nation used to be the 'whipping boy of America. We're now not kowtowing to anyone.'

Although she had some 'concerns' about the war on drugs, such as the huge amount of violence it entailed, it wasn't enough to detract from her affection for Duterte. Badoy claimed that her department was simply 'telling the truth' about the 'good news' being done by the government. She said that her office didn't use social media to spread propaganda; rather, it conveyed useful information to the masses.

Badoy dismissed most criticism of the president as sour grapes from opposition figures. She claimed that there was no regular relationship between Facebook and her office, and suggested that the head of Facebook Philippines was sympathetic to the opposition Liberal Party.[39]

She said that the foreign media always gave Duterte's government a hard time because they didn't know the realities of its achievements. She denied that there was a troll army of Duterte's followers, and said that his opponents routinely used anonymous accounts to attack Duterte and his backers.[40] She claimed her office didn't pay any bloggers to support Duterte; many Filipinos just loved the president, and were happy to back him without pay.

Despite Badoy's denials, Duterte has run an effective troll army to promote his message and attempt to silence his critics. Mocha Uson, made famous by dancing and singing in the Mocha Girls band in central Manila, was appointed as presidential communications assistant secretary, and with her large online following had become a key figure in disseminating fake news and pro-Duterte information, and in attacking critics.

After my interview with Badoy, a high-level official from the government's communications departments told me, off the record, that Mocha was 'terrible' and didn't do her 'due diligence. She doesn't check details.' I asked her why Mocha still had a job if she was so incompetent, and she said it was because Duterte liked her. She explained that it was hard in the Philippines to fire somebody if the president would lose face over it.

Duterte attracted fierce loyalists who helped craft his tough-guy image. I interviewed three of his closest advisors, and they all claimed that any local or international opposition to the president came from frustration over his popularity. I requested an interview with Duterte, but it was refused.

Martin Andanar, who was his presidential communications secretary, told me that he followed Duterte because before his leadership the Philippines was consumed by drugs, crime, and corruption. He praised the drug war because the prices of illegal drugs had risen since Duterte's election win, apparently making it harder for users to get drugs, and suggested that many of the deaths since 2016 were due to gangsters killing each other.

Presidential spokesman Harry Roque was more aggressive in his support for Duterte. He used the populist playbook employed by US president Donald Trump and Hungarian prime minister Viktor Orban, and blamed international human-rights groups for stirring up trouble. He named US billionaire George Soros as a key culprit in demonising Duterte — because he had given Human Rights Watch US$100 million in 2010 to be spent over ten years. This supposedly meant that Soros was to blame for 'besmirching this administration' — and defended his boss in his extreme choice of words against drug users, women, and minorities.

Roque stressed his leader's desire to end the 'neo-colonialism' experienced by the Philippines for over one hundred years. By not being so closely aligned with Washington, and befriending India, China, and Russia, his nation now had an 'independent foreign policy'.[41]

Most government officials didn't want to engage in a robust discussion on the drug war. I craved an engaged conversation about Duterte's anti-drugs policies, but most of his backers resorted to slogans. It was far easier for them to ignore or dismiss the vast numbers of civilians killed, and instead repeat government talking points.

The presidential advisor on the peace process, Jesus Dureza, was a notable exception. He was tasked to negotiate with Muslim and communist rebels around the country, but as a long-time friend of Duterte from his days in Davao City, Dureza had known the president since they were both in high school.[42] Dureza supported US president Donald Trump's methods of threatening enemies, and said Duterte acted similarly.

During the 2016 presidential election campaign, Trump said that beating the militant group Islamic State would require 'taking out their families'. With this statement, Trump had threatened to commit a war crime, and Duterte had found a natural ally: both he and Trump had successfully combined show business and politics. In October 2016, Duterte compared himself to Adolf Hitler, and said he would be 'happy to slaughter' millions of drug users.

During a phone conversation between Duterte and Trump in April 2017, Trump said that the president was a 'good man. Keep up the good work. You are doing an amazing job.'[43] When Trump visited Manila in November 2017, Duterte serenaded the US president with a Filipino love song.

Dureza said that to deal with 'bad guys' in the Philippines, 'you have to threaten them. You have to do unconventional means.' When I pushed him on how exactly he believed the state should behave towards drug dealers or suspected terrorists, he said that 'the threat will say, if you kill my children, I will kill you. You don't deal with good language for the bad guys. You have to threaten them too, right?' Dureza said that 'carrying out the threats' was another issue entirely, but he supported Duterte's position of providing lawyers for policemen who were accused of murdering civilians. In late 2018, three policemen were the first to be found guilty of an extrajudicial killing of a civilian since Duterte's drug war began.

Kill or be killed was the Dureza mantra, all explained with a smile. He claimed that many victims of the drug war didn't complain publicly because they knew that their relatives were involved in drugs. He said that Duterte had no choice but to pursue these policies within the law because the country's drug problems were so great. At some indeterminate point in the future, Dureza argued that 'people will start complying with the law. People will stop manufacturing shabu. People will stop taking people for ransom, kidnapping for ransom, shooting or ambushing.'

This was the most honest appraisal of the drug war that I'd heard. Fear would convince the Filipino population that authoritarian rules had worked, and they'd either comply or face death.

~

The areas in Manila most affected by Duterte's drug war, suffering the highest number of killings, were always the poorest: police didn't just target drug suspects, but also thousands of people drinking in public and loitering.[44]

The Binondo district sits alongside the Pasig River. With the assistance of Catherine Peralta, who volunteered in barangay 275, which was situated under a bridge and major road, I was shown around. Her son was a policeman in a nearby suburb.

Peralta told me that over 1,000 people had been killed in Binondo since Duterte had won office. Many were murdered for using drugs and running drug dens. Despite this, Peralta backed the president.

'I support Duterte because it's now much safer to walk the streets day and night', she said. Before it was very dangerous'.

This was a common sentiment that I heard widely across Manila, and was based on fact: the crime rate had fallen in many parts of the city. However, the violence unleashed by the drug war had brought instability and uncertainty for millions of residents. In the end, Filipinos' perspectives on Duterte depended on whether they believed his rhetoric about the necessity of so many deaths.

As we walked around Binondo, one local approached me and said that many citizens in the area took drugs to simply get through the day. 'People work hard, long hours, and use drugs to help them work harder and carry more goods. They're the victims', he said.

The area was desperately poor. Unemployment was high. Many women played bingo, waiting for their husbands to return from work at the nearby market or port. A few children ran around naked, and others looked dirty. There were no toilets, so people urinated and defecated below their houses into the Pasig River.

Children and teenage boys played computer games and Facebook in darkened rooms hooked up to the internet. Rubbish covered the sides of the road. It had rained earlier in the day, and some streets were flooded with water nearly running into makeshift homes. During the rainy season, the Pasig River would overflow, leaving countless homes, all made of tin, submerged. They would be rebuilt, only to face the same cycle every year.

Children were playing basketball, and others joked with a puppy. A group of men watched TV in a poorly built wooden box owned by a friend. One man, with a bushy grey moustache, sat almost motionless in the outdoors while behind him, amongst rubbish, a solitary pot was cooking on a small fire. A blackened wall rose behind it. Behind the flimsy homes sat empty shipping containers four storeys high. Pogi's Barber Shop was filled with a family watching TV, waiting for business. A printed sign asked residents to call a police hotline to report drug activity. My fixer, Bernard, said that he wouldn't go there alone at night, even though security had reportedly improved.

Another day, I visited Payatas, an area with high numbers of drug killings. I heard nobody express support for Duterte — they were just civilians who had been left desperate after a loved one was murdered. The streets became narrower and more uneven as we drove closer to our destination. Houses on the side of the road were rickety, and the smell of rubbish filled the air. Men and women were foraging in garbage dumps. Violent police and vigilante groups operated freely. It reminded me of the shadier parts of Honduras.

The Mother of Promised Land Parish church was a refuge where drug-war victims were supported. A dirty baby Jesus lay near the entrance in a pile of rubbish.

Pearl Helene (not her real name) had five children, and was estranged from her husband. She ran a mobile food business walking the neighbourhood streets. We sat in an empty room with a photo of Pope Francis on a door in the corner.

Her 37-year-old half-brother, Bryan Infante Avistado (not his real name), was killed on 19 May 2017. The police accused him and an accomplice of stealing money, but Pearl said that this was untrue. For days after the killing, she was not told where his body was being stored or what had happened to him. Five days later, the police told her to go to a local funeral home, owned by a policeman, to see his body.

There was no body. Instead, an employee showed her photos on a mobile phone of her deceased half-brother. His face was swollen and damaged. She was crying as she recounted the story, and I was almost in tears myself. Her brother had tattoos on his stomach and upper chest, which was how she recognised his body.

His body was in a different funeral home. The body had no ID, and the other funeral-home owner said he was about to dispose of it. He asked Pearl to identify it after showing her five bodies on his mobile phone. The body was finally delivered to her house 11 days after his death. It had been cleaned up, but had deteriorated so badly that skin was peeling off his face.

Pearl's story was tragic, but typical. As she told me, she had 'one trauma after another', but had to suppress the pain to cope. She was given no comfort or respect by the police or government authorities. She was invisible and powerless, and therefore could be ignored.

When the owner of her house discovered that her brother had been killed, he kicked her family out.

In typical Filipino style, Bryan's mourning period lasted more than a month. Every three days, Pearl had to pay the funeral home 3,500 pesos (US$65) to inject embalming fluid into her brother's body to keep it looking presentable. Her family collected 65,000 pesos for the injections, mostly raised from two churches. However, during the month, fluids leaked out of his body, so they had to close the casket and cover his head with a cloth. It's traditional in the Philippines for the casket to be open at the funeral and wake.

'Before he was buried, I wanted my children to kiss my brother goodbye, but I was worried they would get sick', Pearl said. 'My brother had been tortured on his hands. They were covered with gloves in the casket. Wire had been placed across his neck.'

Pearl still didn't know what had befallen her brother. She claimed that he had never taken drugs. It was possible he was a drug dealer or somehow involved with drugs, but this didn't justify his execution by police or vigilantes. The police report said they'd found a bag of shabu on Bryan, but she said that this had been planted. She now feared that his killers would come after her.

~

Duterte won the 2016 election against weak opponents. Although it was an exaggeration to say that this represented the death of Filipino democracy, the future of the Philippines as a country accountable to its own citizens was in doubt. Duterte was the latest leader to promise renewal through the barrel of the gun, and many millions bought his message. 'Your concern is human rights; mine is human lives', Duterte accused international-rights advocates in 2018. The danger remains that the Philippines becomes a model for other nations that are tackling drug use. As many parts of the world embraced more enlightened and fact-based drug policies, Duterte showed that fear and extreme violence was still an effective tool in demonising the most marginalised citizens in society.

CHAPTER FOUR

The United States

'In many ways, the imagery doesn't sit right. You know, here are white men poised to run big marijuana businesses, dreaming of cashing in big — big money, big businesses selling weed — after 40 years of impoverished black kids getting prison time for selling weed, and their families and futures destroyed. Now, white men are planning to get rich doing precisely the same thing.'

MICHELLE ALEXANDER, ASSOCIATE PROFESSOR OF LAW AT
OHIO STATE UNIVERSITY AND AUTHOR OF *THE NEW JIM CROW*[1]

Alan Amsterdam took his bar mitzvah money and grew cannabis away from his mother's prying eyes. 'My room smelled like a marijuana factory', he told me at his home in Washington, DC. She never called the police on her son, but he was forced to take the drugs to a friend. Even before his bar mitzvah at the age of 13, Amsterdam had a love of weed and had been involved in the industry since 1980.

There was a waft of marijuana on the ground floor of Amsterdam's apartment building, though he lived a few storeys up. He had long blond hair, loved heavy-metal music, and was the first American to own a pot coffee shop in the city of Amsterdam in the 1990s. He spoke with passion and intensity about his love for cannabis. After he had spent decades advocating a change in drug laws, politics was finally catching up to his vision, but it was far from complete.

The suburb where we met, Adams Morgan, was a haven for post-graduates — it hosted one of the highest concentrations of holders of master's degrees and doctorates in the US — and was declared by *High Times* magazine readers to be the area in which most consumers of weed in the state lived.

Amsterdam grew marijuana in his house for sale, perfecting the Green Love Potion buds, and ran the Capital Hemp shop in Washington with his business partner, cannabis advocate Adam Eidinger (though he sold his stake in December 2017). Amsterdam had a small number of plants in his home that he gave to sick friends, and he smoked regularly when he woke up and during the day. He stressed that he didn't want to 'sit on the couch and eat Doritos', so he smoked pot, which gave him energy.

When I arrived, his friend Josh was sitting in the living room in front of a bunch of sweet-smelling cannabis — 'It'll give you a great high', he said — and cutting buds from the stems. They opposed the over-commercialisation of the drug, and feared that the US was moving towards a system that would exclude the smaller pot growers such as themselves.

Amsterdam's house was messy and crowded. He proudly showed me a framed picture from 1962 when the state certified the People's Drug Store in Washington. At the bottom, it said that the shop sold 'opium, coca leaves, marijuana etc'. He marvelled that it was possible so recently in American history for these drugs to have been sold openly in a shop. He longed for those days again.

Eidinger, Josh, and Amsterdam constantly told me how much they loved cannabis and wanted all drugs to be legalised and regulated. For them, it wasn't just about getting high, but about the delicate art of growing the plant, tending and loving it. 'Freedom' was mentioned on many occasions — the idea that individuals had the right to do what they wanted with their own bodies. During our conversation, Amsterdam took occasional hits on a joint between drawing breaths.

Amsterdam and Eidinger were trailblazers for legalised marijuana in their state. After failing in their attempts to have Proposition 19 in California accepted — a 2010 ballot initiative that would have legalised cannabis — their Capital Hemp shop was raided by police in 2011 for allegedly selling marijuana paraphernalia, and it was eventually shut down in 2012. This galvanised them into mobilising local activists to change marijuana laws, and after years of lobbying and shifts in public opinion, Initiative 71 succeeded in 2014 in legalising cannabis in Washington.

The law went into effect in February 2015. There was immense satisfaction that a liberal state, the home of the US Congress — a body that led, funded, and directed a drug war domestically and globally for decades — had accepted the once-illegal drug. In the first year of legal weed, Washington state took in an extra US$65 million in tax revenue (though many states that have legalised cannabis are seeing less revenue every year due to the falling price of the drug).

However, in 2019, one year after the start of California legalising cannabis, the promises of huge tax revenues and a reduction in the black market were yet to be realised. Legal sales declined in 2018 amidst a robust illegal market.[2] Law enforcement still arrested and prosecuted illicit marijuana producers, often in minority communities, questioning the state's commitment to addressing the historical racial wrongs associated with the drug war.[3] It was a delicate balancing act between police taking down business owners who worked illegally and abused their employees, while at the same time not repeating the mistakes of the past.

Washington was unlike the 50 other US states, thanks to a strange clause in the constitution that allowed Congress to attach riders to bills passed by the city council, even though federal politicians had the ability to influence laws for residents in an area that they largely didn't represent. This brought inevitable conflict when a liberal state clashed with a conservative justice department.[4]

Amsterdam's desire for legal changes was fuelled by both his personal desire to be around cannabis every day of his life and to rectify an historical injustice that had been wrought on African-Americans and minorities by the drug war. He believed that cultivating cannabis at home, learning the skills to create delectable marijuana, was the best way for these groups to gain knowledge, power, and then work. 'That's how the peaceful revolution starts', he told me.

He imagined his city becoming the centre of pot tourism, with parents bringing their children to see museums, and then 'Mummy and Daddy can go to that special place [and smoke].' Amsterdam didn't want big companies monopolising the market — cigarette-multinational, Philip Morris–type firms — but he worried that the corporatisation of cannabis was inevitable.[5]

As early as 2013, one of the country's leading advocates for legalisation, Ethan Nadelmann, executive director of the Drug Policy Alliance, warned that big business had the potential to ruin the then-nascent cannabis industry. 'Give me my choice — I want the microbrewery or vineyard model', he said. 'I'm not fighting for the Marlboro-isation of marijuana.'[6]

A range of new cannabis businesses, such as edibles, as well as cannabis beer and wine, were either already available or on the horizon. There were encouraging clinical tests showing that cannabis helped war veterans to manage their PTSD, and the elderly were finding that cannabis oil treated acute pain. Where some only saw dollar signs, others saw the opportunity to use the drug for good. Although there is strong evidence that excessive use of cannabis can cause mental harm in some individuals — especially young people — prohibition and the assured violence around its use is inarguably more damaging. Nonetheless, caution around legalisation is warranted. One 2019 study showed increased rates of hospitalisation in the emergency room in Colorado, five years after legalisation, due to the excessive use of edibles and inhaled cannabis.

Eidinger was worried about Washington, DC, becoming known for the wrong reasons. He told me that pot tourism could create too many consumers who came to the city just for the drug, like what happened in Amsterdam, Holland, and that the city would become 'the epicentre for drug culture'. Eidinger wanted cannabis to be normal, just a healthy part of life — not highlighted or exploited solely for financial gain.

Amsterdam saw himself as a necessary watch on out-of-control consumerism. 'Adam and I, we're the culture', he said. 'We're the ones fighting for the culture. We're not fighting for money, because this initiative is not about money. This initiative is about freedom. Everyone else wants profit. We want profit, too, but we want to work through the system. We want everyone to have a fair shake.'

Eidinger said that the legalisation campaign had been successful because 'we made a civil-rights argument. We talked about the racial disparities first and foremost between blacks and whites when it came to these laws. And we said that they are racist laws. That they can never be enforced fairly.' It was a fair concern even after the drug was legalised. *Buzzfeed News* reported in 2016 that only 1 per cent of the 3,600 marijuana dispensaries across the US were owned by black people, largely due to laws banning convicted felons from entering the business and the prohibitive cost of funding an enterprise.[7]

In practice, Amsterdam wanted it to be like getting a liquor licence and opening a bar. 'We don't want it to be only the rich dudes who are politically connected with its closed systems.' He was hopeful that, in the end, 'the best marijuana wins' and that people would flock to it. 'People are going to want boutique [weed]. They're going to want people that make new strains. They're going to want people who care about the plant, that grow organically.'

Eidinger had a similar vision. In 2013, he co-founded DCMJ (DC Marijuana Justice), a group pushing for equal rights for Washington weed users, growers, and families. Its key aim was to pressure politicians to allow a voter ballot to legalise the drug, and Initiative 71 was the successful result. Eidinger framed his fight as a human-rights battle, angry that people of colour were disproportionally being arrested for the possession of cannabis.

He lived on prominent Massachusetts Avenue, adjacent to foreign embassy missions. Outside his house was a large cage sitting in the driveway, a prop that had been used to signify repressive drug laws in the US. *The New York Times* reported in 2017 that since 2010 there had been at least 20 deadly SWAT raids on marijuana dealers across the nation. The drug didn't kill anybody, but law enforcement did.[8]

Police still discriminated against minority groups after Initiative 71 took effect. It was legal to grow a small amount of marijuana at your house, smoke in private, and carry less than 57 grams in public, but it remained illegal to smoke it in public, carry too much, or sell it.[9] Marijuana-related arrests soared 186 per cent between 2015 to 2017, and 86 per cent of those arrested were black. 'As the proposer of the initiative, this is not what we intended,' Eidinger told a local news network. 'We never intended for low-income people to continually be targeted.'

A measure passed by local lawmakers in 2018 aimed to help minorities and women get better access to the industry.[10] In March 2018, statistics showed that none of the licences issued for cannabis businesses had been given to a black owner in Maryland, despite one-third of the state's population being black. Some progressive lawmakers advocated for drug-war reparations, which included removing criminal records for all cannabis-related offences.[11] Prosecutors in San Francisco started doing so in 2018 when the district attorney announced that he would retroactively apply California's recreational marijuana-legalisation policy to thousands of cases going back decades, and either reduce or dismiss many cannabis-related convictions.[12]

Eidinger was in his mid-forties, Jewish, and had once served in the Israeli army, but now identified as an anti-Zionist. He was the social-action director for Dr Bronner's Magic Soaps, an organic, hemp, and fair trade company. He moved to Maryland in 2018 to fight Republican Andy Harris, who was vehemently against the total legalisation of recreational marijuana.

Eidinger's home was filled with signs, posters, and advocacy material from a life dedicated to cannabis. There was a photo of President Barack Obama and his successful 2008 presidential campaign team; they were all smoking joints (thanks to Photoshop). 'Choom Gang 2016' was emblazoned across the image. Choom means pot in Hawaiian, and Obama was part of a Choom Gang in his youth. Before our interview began, Eidinger pulled out a joint, lit it, and asked if I wanted to take a hit. I declined, wanting to stay focused on the conversation, though perhaps it would have been enhanced.

Eidinger had been arrested nearly two dozen times, held a sit-in outside the White House with a 51-foot replica of a joint, and was involved with a campaign to hand out 5,500 joints before US president Donald Trump's inauguration in January 2018. It was a form of non-violent civil disobedience against what Eidinger and his colleagues viewed as repressive cannabis laws across the country.

Washington, DC, still lacked a suitable tax and regulatory framework for cannabis, stymied by reluctant politicians. This was why Eidinger helped organise free joints and cannabis seeds for city council members in March 2018 to push them into action.

~

The rapid acceptance of marijuana by vast swathes of the American population has radically shifted public attitudes to the natural plant. There's now a widespread belief that it should be a legitimate part of modern life. The demonisation of marijuana, along with police and judicial attitudes that disproportionally targeted minority groups for decades, was always illogical and based on fear and ignorance. But it worked for years, and destroyed the lives of millions of people who were imprisoned, lost job opportunities, had families torn apart, or were killed. That racially tinged ignorance has not disappeared in the Donald Trump era. If anything, it has been reinvigorated.[13]

Shifting attitudes towards cannabis should be compared to Americans now embracing same-sex marriage, another social campaign for which it had long been impossible to raise majority support. Something that was once a taboo, outside the bounds of mainstream society, has become widely accepted and even normal — mostly uncontroversial, except amongst a tiny minority. The Pew Research Centre found in 2001 that 57 per cent of respondents opposed same-sex marriage, but by 2017, 62 per cent supported it. The US Supreme Court made it legal in 2015.

According to Pew Research Centre polling released in early 2018, 61 per cent of Americans supported marijuana legalisation, reflecting a steady rise in the preceding decade. (By the end of 2018, Pew found that 66 per cent backed legalisation.) More Democrats than Republicans backed the change, and support was strong amongst the young and old. It was a long way from attitudes held at the height of the Vietnam War: in 1969, Pew found that 84 per cent of Americans thought that cannabis should remain illegal. The legal marijuana market in North America was expected to grow from US$9.2 billion in 2017 to US$47.3 billion in 2027. Globally, that figure rises to US$57 billion in legal cannabis sales by 2027.[14] Hipster magazines promoting marijuana and the lifestyle around it started popping up, promoted in *The New York Times*, with names such as 'High Quality' and 'Broccoli'.[15]

A Quinnipiac University Poll in April 2018 found that 63 per cent of Americans backed marijuana legalisation, and a huge majority — 70 per cent — opposed federal encroachment on states that had legalised the drug. Significantly, 61 per cent of voters did not view cannabis as a 'gateway drug', an argument of prohibitionists from the 1900s until today, and a majority believed that legalised weed would have little impact on the widespread use and abuse of opioids.

In 2019, media outlet *Politico* summed up the shift in attitudes in a headline: 'Why 2019 could be marijuana's biggest year yet: a green tide in Congress raises hope that pot could be legal under federal law by year's end.' The World Health Organisation announced in 2019 that cannabis should be rescheduled to a less draconian category (although it didn't advocate full legalisation of the drug).

Historically speaking, marijuana has only relatively recently been seen as a menace. As far back as 1619, the Virginia Assembly passed legislation requiring every farmer to grow hemp. Hemp was a legitimate form of legal tender in a number of states. Before the Civil War in the later 1800s, cannabis was openly sold in pharmacies and used for medical purposes.

It wasn't until the 1900s, with the influx of many Mexican migrants and recreational marijuana, that the drug was viewed suspiciously as a Trojan horse that apparently caused violence, sexual assault, and murder. It set a pattern for the entire century, with minorities, African-Americans, and Hispanics accused of destroying the moral fabric of the nation by smoking weed and using other drugs, including alcohol. A *New York Times* headline in 1914 referred to 'Negro cocaine fiends' as a 'new southern menace'. Facts didn't matter, but creating a moral panic worked. A 1944 report issued by the New York Academy of Medicine found that marijuana was not a gateway drug and didn't lead to insanity, sexual violence, or killing. The authorities ignored it.

Seventy years later, in a 2017 report published in *The Economic Journal*, it was shown that the US states on the borders of Mexico that had legalised medical marijuana had experienced reduced violence. Local US farmers could grow cannabis, and Mexican cartels were involved in far less smuggling as a result.[16] It was a message that was more readily received in the 21st century than decades earlier.

Washington's modern battle against illicit substances had a tawdry history. After president Richard Nixon declared a 'war on drugs' in 1971, weed became the government's public enemy to be exposed and controlled. It failed to dent the popularity of cannabis, but hugely increased the incarceration rate and demonisation of users. Nixon crafted a message that drug takers were morally inferior individuals who had to be punished and isolated. The private prison industry benefited handsomely from the 1980s after an explosion of inmates.

President Jimmy Carter supported the decriminalisation of marijuana, arguing that possession of less than 28 grams should not be a criminal offence. He backed full treatment for addicts and softer attitudes towards cocaine, but remained opposed to heroin. He told Congress in 1977 that jails full of young people who posed no threat to society were counter-productive, and that 'penalties against possession of a drug should not be more damaging to an individual than the use of the drug itself'. His ideas were opposed by vocal parents' organisations and Republicans, including ex-governor of California and future president Ronald Reagan. Congress eventually ignored Carter's pleas, despite a poll in 1978 that found 53 per cent of college freshmen backing legalised cannabis.[17]

Many states decriminalised marijuana during the 1970s, though what this meant for citizens living there differed, depending on who ran the state politically; usually, it allowed small amounts of the drug for personal use, not for sale, and being caught with the substance incurred only a small fine. Oregon was the first state in 1973 to decriminalise weed. After Nebraska decriminalised cannabis in 1978, it took more than 20 years for other states to follow suit.

By the late 1970s, some legislators in New York thought that they had a solution to the problem. Nixon's drug war had caused carnage across college campuses, and countless reputations had been ruined over the simple possession of cannabis. Many white and black parents were outraged that their children were being stigmatised for life by a minor infraction. In 1977, lawmakers designed a bill that would result in anybody found with a small supply of marijuana being given a ticket by police instead of a criminal record. Republicans were only convinced to support the legislation when an exception was created that stipulated it would still be illegal to carry marijuana 'open to public view'.[18]

The numbers of arrests for cannabis possession fell until the 1990s, but then more aggressive policing methods became the norm. Authors of the original bill in 1977 had hoped to eradicate mass arrests for marijuana forever, but it failed. Less than 15 years later, police were tasked to routinely pursue New Yorkers to empty their pockets in questionable attempts to reduce crime. Since African-Americans and Hispanics were the focus of racially targeted policing, these were the groups that suffered huge numbers of arrest for cannabis possession.

This was how the bill's intention was abused: when the police stopped and frisked people, and demanded that they empty their pockets, marijuana would suddenly fall to the ground and become 'open to public view'. White New Yorkers were much less affected by this absurd reading of the law. The problem became so serious that the New York police commissioner, Raymond Kelly, reminded his officers in 2011 not to arrest people who had marijuana in their pockets.[19] In 2016, more than 22,000 New Yorkers — 80 per cent of whom were Latino or black — were arrested for possession of tiny amounts of cannabis. In early 2018, 93 per cent of New Yorkers arrested for cannabis were people of colour.[20] Cannabis possession still led to nearly 6 per cent of arrests across the country in 2016, according to the FBI, with 40 per cent of all arrests in some counties for marijuana alone.

At least one judge fought back. A 96-year-old federal judge in Brooklyn, Jack B. Weinstein, promised in 2018 that he would no longer re-imprison people simply for smoking cannabis, expressing regret for having done so over many years. Another form of resistance was the country's first scientifically based harm-reduction classes offered from 2018 to teenagers at a school in Manhattan. Organised by the Drug Policy Alliance, students were shown how drugs work on the body.

Criminalising vast swathes of the population who took drugs was never an impediment for American politicians in their pursuit of votes. The numbers of citizens who were viewed as criminal by their choices or addictions were staggering. In 1988, with a nation-wide population of around 244 million people, federal figures indicated that about 18 million people used marijuana at least once a month; 5.8 million used cocaine at least once a month; 500,000 took heroin; and 113 million drank alcohol at least monthly.[21]

Millions of Americans take illicit drugs in their own time, and yet fear of adverse judgements about drug consumption is embedded in the country's fabric as a puritanical nation. It's wrongly viewed as a sign of societal breakdown. This is ably assisted by cautious and sometimes ignorant politicians, a rabid tabloid press, religious conservatism, and a desire to control maligned groups. According to Charles Whitebread, a former professor at the University of Southern California Law School, a constant theme of US drug policy was that 'prohibitions are always enacted by *us*, to govern the concept of *them*'.[22]

The Reagan years saw an explosion of anti-drug initiatives. During the 1980 presidential campaign, Reagan called marijuana 'probably the most dangerous drug in the United States today'. His eight years in power oversaw a suite of policies that reflected a fanatical and irrational hatred of drugs. But this wasn't about reducing drug use — the prevalence and trafficking of most drugs increased during the Reagan era — so much as about creating a moral and racially charged narrative that targeted minority groups who couldn't fight back. Reagan's senior political operatives knew that the billions of dollars spent were being wasted — attorney-general Edwin Meese III acknowledged that 'the gap between the amount of drugs seized and the amount imported and consumed is growing annually' — and Reagan himself in 1986 said that, 'All the confiscation and law enforcement in the world will not cure this plague.'

But this didn't stop his administration worsening the problems that drug prohibition inevitably created. Nancy Reagan's 'Just Say No' campaign, focusing on teenagers to stop taking drugs entirely, was a public-relations campaign designed by New York advertising executives in the early 1980s. It didn't work. Reagan's anti-cannabis policies involved using the military, foreign policy, the navy, and other aggressive tactics to stop the smuggling of marijuana. The US navy engaged in a 'pot war' that targeted drug-traffickers in international waters. The budget for these activities soared from US$4 million in 1981 to over US$1 billion by 1989.

In 1981, US officials admitted that despite many drug busts, the supply lines for bringing marijuana, cocaine, and heroin into the US were mostly intact. The Drug Enforcement Administration's (DEA's) solution was to convince — or, more accurately, strong-arm — Colombia to spray the herbicide paraquat on its cannabis crops, despite the serious health risks of using the poison. It had been previously sprayed in Mexico to attack marijuana plants, but as *The New York Times* explained in 1978, 'Paraquat has become, for many young Americans, a symbol of governmental malversation as emotionally charged as napalm was for an earlier generation.'[23]

US funding for Mexican spraying was halted because of serious health risks from the sprayed marijuana that included deadly lung disease for US consumers of the drug. None of the media reports at the time mentioned the deleterious effect on Mexican farmers and civilians who inhaled the pesticide (and Washington later also used it on its domestic marijuana fields).

This policy had an effect, but perhaps not what was intended. Despite Reagan targeting the supply, distribution, and transportation of illicit drugs, the amount of most drugs entering the US didn't decline. Instead, 'Drugs got enormously cheaper so users didn't have to hit as many old ladies over the head and steal their pocketbooks', author Travis Wendel, an anthropologist at John Jay College in Manhattan, wrote in 2011. Whenever the prices of cocaine and heroin fell, assault and murder rates did, too. If prices increased, like they did again in the early 1990s, crime rose.[24]

When I conducted research for this book in the US, the availability of drugs and their prices were subjects constantly brought up in interviews. An illegal drug market automatically created a hierarchy of needs and power. Many people I met either complained that drugs were too cheap, therefore making them too attractive, or too expensive and out of reach for daily use. Legalisation and regulation would partly solve these problems because drug cartels would have less power and would need to find alternative sources of income. This was not an impossibility, as some Mexican cartels expanded their empires to include stealing fuel, kidnapping, extortion, and piracy. Washington's drug war, from the Nixon era onwards, guaranteed violence, because there were always new and cleverer trafficking groups who believed only they had the solution to maximising profit.

'The franchising of criminal brands', writes Tom Wainwright in *Narconomics: how to run a drug cartel*, 'has been a successful strategy for drug cartels … It has allowed a few criminal organisations to expand very rapidly, while diversifying their revenue stream from simply drug-trafficking into a whole spectrum of illegal activity.'[25] This wasn't a secret during the Reagan years, with authorities playing favourites domestically and globally, befriending cartels from which they could get useful intelligence, and destroying others who were deemed expendable. This was what the drug war meant in practice: colluding with the very individuals you claimed were destroying society.

This was never admitted publicly, of course. All drug cartels were created equally bad, according to successive US administrations, but that wasn't how the DEA fought the war. The rhetorical flourishes of the war on drugs clashed with reality. The Reagan years saw increased violence against civilians domestically and internationally, but also rising government and media propaganda in support of tougher prohibition. The war was real and bloody, but the ideologues who backed it knew that it successfully targeted only the groups that were deemed troublesome (whether African-Americans at home or Latinos in Central America).

Reagan's drug war did affect the ability of marijuana traffickers to bring their product into the US (although cannabis consumption remained high). Subsequently, many Colombian farmers switched to the coca plant. Heroin production spiked in central Asia, and South American cartels found new ways to penetrate the US market. Cocaine and heroin were both easier to transport and far more profitable. Subsequently, prices in the West fell, a reality that exists to this day.[26]

The prevalence of mass incarceration soared. Reagan continued Nixon's obsession with law-and-order tactics to fight drugs by locking people up for often-minor drug offences, thereby disproportionately affecting African-Americans, Hispanics, and other minorities. Reagan also pushed for the privatisation of prisons, and his corporate friends were satisfied. By creating a false sense of fear around drugs — before the Reagan era, the majority of Americans didn't view drugs as a major threat to society — the president was able to present his 'solutions' to the problem.

This included paying TV networks to insert anti-drug propaganda in their programming. This was never disclosed to the viewing public, and it continued well into the Bill Clinton era. Many of the most prominent programs of the day — including *ER*, *Beverly Hills 90210*, *Chicago Hope*, *The Drew Carey Show*, and *7th Heaven* — were filled with anti-drug messages featuring overdoses, drug-testing at work, and undercover police. The White House viewed scripts and inserted lines that they wanted, and the TV networks and the government's drug czar office decided on the messages to be inserted into shows, often not telling the producers and writers involved in the programs. In return, the networks received valuable advertising income.[27]

Reagan also removed probation and parole for some offences, and sent police into schools under the guise of fighting drugs and alcohol; the principal targets were black and Latino children.[28]

In 1986, Reagan signed the Anti-Drug Abuse Act that created mandatory minimum penalties for drug offences. Because there were differences in sentencing between crack and powder cocaine — crack was cheaper, and its users were mostly from lower-income groups — it was an attempt to institutionalise vast swathes of America's underclass. It succeeded in devastating the black population. Department of Justice statistics proved that these criminal-justice changes caused the national prisoner population to grow from 740,000 in 1985 to 1.6 million in 1995.[29] The US has never recovered from this profound shift in sentencing and incarceration.

Marijuana remained a demonised drug well into the Clinton years. Despite giving speeches that suggested a softening of the drug war, in practice he and his administration continued the Reagan agenda. Clinton rejected a Sentencing Commission recommendation to stop the disparity between crack and powder cocaine sentences. In 1994, Clinton signed into law the Violent Crime Control and Law Enforcement Act, which was the biggest piece of crime legislation in US history.

Pledging US$30 billion, Washington introduced a 'three strikes' mandatory life sentence for repeat offenders, the hiring of 100,000 more police officers, nearly US$10 billion for prisons, and largely punitive measures for troubled drug users. Clinton claimed the law was required due to a surge in violent crime across the country, and that it came at the request of black leaders who saw their communities being decimated by gun crime, but his government did little to offer economic opportunities for low-income areas.

When Clinton left office, the number of people behind bars was over two million. He had come into office with the figure at 1.3 million. Although Bill, supported publicly by his wife, Hillary, championed mass incarceration, he actively pursued legislation that reduced regulations on banks with the Riegle-Neal interstate banking bill.[30] He loosened rules for the rich while punishing the poor.

The same president who joked that he had never inhaled when smoking marijuana while studying in Britain in the late 1960s deepened the government's war on cannabis. Prisons expanded, police confiscated property from tens of thousands of people for the smallest of drug infractions, and medical-marijuana users were prosecuted. *High Times* magazine was unsurprisingly scathing of these policies, writing in early 2001 that, 'Teen use of drugs is substantially higher than it was when he entered office. Heroin and cocaine are cheaper and purer than they've been since they were outlawed in 1914. And Clinton has overseen it all with a smile.'[31] A month before leaving office, Clinton said he believed that marijuana should be decriminalised, and questioned the high rate of imprisonment.

It wasn't until 1996 that California became the first state to legalise cannabis for medical use. Alaska, Washington, Oregon, Nevada, Colorado, and Maine followed soon after. Public opinion was shifting rapidly, although the George W. Bush administration ignored this sentiment entirely. From 2001, a new Republican government focused obsessively on cannabis in futile attempts to control it. After a Supreme Court decision in 2005 that gave federal authorities permission to crack down on medical marijuana, the DEA raided clinics in California.

Bush's drug czar, John Walters, gave speeches that had echoes of the 1970s under Nixon. Cannabis was a 'gateway drug', he said, and

launched TV advertisements that accused citizens who bought marijuana of indirectly supporting the terror group Al-Qaeda. Despite
Walters' best efforts, the number of young people and adults smoking
weed remained steady: around one-third in the first category, and one
in seven individuals over 35 years old in the second. Like during the
Reagan and Clinton years, Bush advocated zero tolerance for drug
use in the student population, and pushed for random drug-testing.
Many states refused to comply.

There was an inherent contradiction at the heart of the Bush
strategy. While public polling found growing numbers of the population believed that strict prohibition didn't work and should change,
successive administrations charged ahead regardless, imprisoning
growing numbers of people. In 2005, the Sentencing Project found
that arrests for marijuana since 1992 had increased from 300,000
to 700,000 per year. Bush spent around US$4 billion annually on
arresting and prosecuting cannabis violations; many of the resulting
inmates in state prisons were non-violent without any risk to the
community.

Police were encouraged to arrest their way out of the drug
problem, with cities across the country seeing huge increases in cannabis busts.[32] By the time Bush left office in 2009, there were around
40,000 paramilitary-type SWAT raids being conducted on Americans
annually, often for non-violent drug offences.[33]

Supply was never a problem, with the justice department reporting
that in the mid-2000s 19,000 tons of pot were harvested each year.[34]
While marijuana was an obsession of the authorities, other drugs such
as cocaine and methamphetamines continued to be widely available,
with the latter causing huge problems in rural communities. Federal
funds to address this crisis dropped during the two Bush terms.

The failure of the federal government to change its drug-war tactics forced the hand of many states. Politicians also stopped fearing
acknowledging their own past drug use. Barack Obama openly

admitted using cocaine and marijuana. 'When I was a kid, I inhaled frequently', he said. 'That was the point.'

President Obama's eight years as president were both the most progressive and disappointing for the cause of serious drug reform. Despite Obama's softer rhetoric towards some drugs, police continued to arrest huge numbers of people for often minor drug crimes. There were 1,572,579 drug arrests in 2016, roughly one arrest every 20 seconds. This was 5.6 per cent higher than the year before (though less overall than when Obama took office in 2009). Seven hundred thousand people were still being arrested annually for marijuana possession.

According to figures released by Human Rights Watch and the American Civil Liberties Union, law-enforcement bodies arrested more than 574,640 people for small cannabis offences in 2015, while fewer citizens — 505,681 — were arrested in the same year for violent crimes that included rape and murder. The state still wielded the immense power to present marijuana as being more dangerous than sexual assault.

During Obama's first term, according to a 2013 report issued by Americans for Safe Access, the DEA raided 270 medical-marijuana facilities — 12 more than had been undertaken in the previous 12 years combined. The report found that Obama had spent US$300 million 'interfering' with states' medical-marijuana laws since he took office, while the George W. Bush administration had spent US$100 million less.[35] Nonetheless, Obama's drug czar, Gil Kerlikowske, admitted in 2010 that the drug war had failed. 'Forty years later [after Nixon and spending more than US$1 trillion], the concern about drugs and drug problems is, if anything, magnified, intensified', he said.

At the end of his presidency, Obama told *Rolling Stone* that he believed cannabis should be treated 'as a public-health issue, the same way we do with cigarettes or alcohol'. He blamed the DEA for not moving with the times and for being stuck in a prohibitionist mindset. Marijuana remained a schedule-one drug, the most serious clarification for an illicit substance. Many drug-reform activists damned Obama for not pushing back harder against the DEA and not advocating for marijuana to be removed from the schedule-one drug list.[36] Michael Collins, the deputy director of the Drug Policy Alliance in Washington, DC, told me that he understood the president 'didn't lean on anyone' at the DEA, so the status quo remained.

Nonetheless, during his eight years in office, Obama instituted a range of policies to reduce the number of prisoners serving time for drug offences, and he didn't stand in the way of eight states — including Colorado, Alaska, California, and Washington, DC — legalising recreational cannabis.[37] Arrests for marijuana dropped in states that had legalised the drug. Colorado gave US$230 million to the state's department of education between 2015 and 2017 to support school construction, prevent bullying, and back early literacy. Washington dedicated 25 per cent earned from legal cannabis to support education, prevention, and substance-use disorders.

Despite these changes, most banks refused to accept funds related to cannabis transactions, fearing federal prosecution. This left a nascent industry forced to store money under its pillows (sometimes literally); it had to operate in a grey market. Regardless, the first cannabis company, Cronos Group, listed on the New York stock exchange in February 2018.

The numbers of Americans who admitted smoking cannabis also soared. Figures released in 2016 by the British medical journal *Lancet Psychiatry* found that around 31.9 million Americans admitted to smoking at least once in the previous year. In 2002, the figure was 21.9 million.[38] Addiction to marijuana was a growing problem: in national surveys, one in ten people said that they had problems after smoking, but this did little to subdue the legalisation movement.[39] Synthetic marijuana, far more dangerous than cannabis and sometimes laced with rat poison, was causing increasing problems.

One of Obama's most important acts was the Cole memo, a justice department directive to the states, telling them that the federal government would not intervene in their marijuana affairs if they followed some basic rules, such as not allowing cannabis to fall into the hands of children. The Trump administration overturned the memo (although Trump's second attorney-general, William Barr, pledged not to go after states that had legalised cannabis, despite being personally against the drug and the legalisation).

Obama's legacy was keenly discussed by virtually every person I met in the US. Most expressed disappointment that he hadn't gone further on drug reform, believing that it simply wasn't his administration's priority. Others applauded his moves to release non-violent prisoners who were languishing in prison on drug convictions. Yet it was hard not to sense a feeling that Obama had missed a unique opportunity to profoundly shift the country's stance on illicit substances.

I secretly dreamed of what he could have done. Imagine if the US president had outlined a vision to decriminalise all drugs within five years because the evidence from Portugal, a nation that had decriminalised drugs in 2001, had overwhelmingly shown that problems associated with drugs had declined. North America could have followed, and led the world in ending the drug war once and for all. Although legalisation and regulation was the better option than decriminalisation, Obama could have taken a significant step down the path.

However, as with many contentious issues, such as same-sex marriage, Obama wasn't a leader but a follower. He read the polls: Gallup found that only 44 per cent of citizens supported marijuana legalisation in 2009, but that rose to 60 per cent in 2016. He acted cautiously as a result. Obama remained a contradiction on drug policy, afraid to push for many major changes until the end of his second term while also being stymied by a recalcitrant Congress.

Regardless, he undeniably acted at times with a conviction that affected thousands of citizens positively. He pumped substantial money into treating the opioid and heroin epidemic. He wanted to reduce the country's world-beating prison population from a record high of 2.3 million. This was achieved through a number of measures, including the Fair Sentencing Act of 2010, which changed the sentencing disparity between powder cocaine and crack cocaine, a long-standing racial disparity that, as we have seen, negatively affected blacks. The independent Sentencing Commission recommended that judges give more lenient sentences for drug offences. When Obama took office in 2009, there were close to 209,000 federal inmates. By early 2017, there were fewer than 190,000.[40]

These achievements were threatened by President Trump. During the 2016 election campaign, he said that he was in 'favour of medical marijuana 100 per cent' and questioned the legalisation of recreational cannabis, but pledged to leave the states to decide their own policies. During a conversation with Mexican president Enrique Pena Nieto in early 2017, he said that, 'I won New Hampshire because New Hampshire is a drug-infested den.' He advocated the death penalty for drug dealers, echoing his admiration for China and the Philippines. He pledged to build a higher and stronger wall between Mexico and the US, claiming it would stop drugs entering the country.[41] History showed that smuggling heroin would not be curtailed by the construction of a barrier.

Trump's first attorney-general, Jeff Sessions, was one of the country's most vociferous war-on-drugs supporters; he was a lifetime believer in incarcerating the country out of its drug problems, opposed immigration, used the 'n' word, and in 1986 joked about the Ku Klux Klan, with colleagues saying that he thought they were 'okay, until he learned that they smoked marijuana'.

Sessions was one of Trump's earliest supporters, and it didn't take long for him to ramp up the failed policies of the past. In 2016, Sessions stated that the federal government should utilise its law-enforcement capabilities to send a message that 'good people don't smoke marijuana'. Sessions issued a memo that instructed prosecutors to charge even low-level offenders — often Latinos and blacks — with drug offences. Sessions made it easier for police to seize property and profits, called civil asset forfeiture, claiming it reduced drug-related criminal activity. However, evidence proved that it often affected innocent people when police abused their powers, and took property and cash.

Despite Trump declaring the opioid crisis a 'health emergency' in 2017, he offered no more funds to support it. This fitted into the Sessions worldview: the attorney-general blamed Americans for failing to 'say no' to drugs. He was 'astonished' that some argued medical marijuana could be a cure for opioid addiction (despite evidence of fewer overdoses in states that had legalised medical cannabis).[42] He told police officers in 2017 that the way to end the opioid and heroin crisis was through tougher enforcement. He pushed for prosecutors to seek the death penalty in drug cases. Homeland Security chief John Kelly announced in 2017 that immigrants would be deported for marijuana possession.

Sessions was an old-time preacher of Nixon's message, oblivious of the fact that the previous 40 years had proven him wrong (unless he believed that mass incarceration was the way to redeem America's soul). 'I realise this may be an unfashionable belief in a time of growing tolerance of drug use', Sessions stated. 'But too many lives are at stake to worry about being fashionable. I reject the idea that America will be a better place if marijuana is sold in every corner store. And I am astonished to hear people suggest that we can solve our heroin crisis by legalising marijuana — so people can trade one life-wrecking dependency [on opioids] for another that's only slightly less awful [cannabis]. Our nation needs to say clearly once again that using drugs will destroy your life.' Sessions was fired by Trump in late 2018.

Trump's administration was filled with drug-war warriors.[43] Soon after he took office, in February 2017, Trump's first press secretary, Sean Spicer, dishonestly linked the country's opioid crisis to the rise in recreational marijuana. 'When you see something like the opioid addiction crisis blossoming in so many states around this country,' Spicer said, 'the last thing we should be doing is encouraging people. There's a federal law that we need to abide by when it comes to recreational marijuana and other drugs of that nature.' Despite his claims, there is no evidence that cannabis is a gateway drug, it is established fact that opioids are far more addictive and dangerous, and opioids were (and still are) killing people by the thousands while weed did not.

The era of Sessions and Trump galvanised opposition to its draconian positions. In 2017, the Marijuana Justice Act was introduced into Congress by New York Democrat Cory Booker. It aimed to end the federal prohibition on cannabis, prevent deportations related to marijuana offences, and cut funding to states that disproportionately arrested or incarcerated people of colour or low-income individuals on cannabis charges. Just as significantly, the bill would design a process to expunge marijuana offences at the federal level and create a 'community reinvestment fund' of US$500 million to support communities that had been most directly impacted by the 'war on drugs'. This included job training and community centres to help people re-enter society after years behind bars for low-level drug offences.[44]

By 2018, many prominent Democrats, including 2016 and 2020 presidential candidate Bernie Sanders, had signalled support for the act. After decades of being fearful of speaking out in support of legal marijuana, increasing numbers of Democrats and Republicans realised that the American public was ready to embrace the legalisation of cannabis and to oppose punishment for using or selling it.[45] Native American communities are now actively exploring the possibility of entering the marijuana industry to grow, process, and dispense the drug. It would be one way to support a community that has been demonised and isolated for a long time.

Thankfully, the goalposts of politically acceptable positions on drugs and criminal justice reform had shifted. Take Kamala Harris, one of the 2020 Democratic presidential candidates, who once opposed marijuana legalisation and whose record as attorney-general of California from 2004 until 2011 included countless examples of indifference and callousness towards the poor.[46] She finally signed on to the Marijuana Justice Act in 2018, endorsed legalised cannabis, and admitted that she had once smoked the drug herself.

It was now common for former supporters of mass incarceration and tough sentencing of drug users to acknowledge that they were wrong. Trump's second attorney-general, William Barr, had held the same job during the Republican presidency of George H.W. Bush in the early 1990s. During his first time in office, he pushed for higher prison numbers. By 2019, he said, 'I think that the heavy drug penalties, especially on crack and other things, have harmed the black community.'[47]

But Trump's war on weed continued. *Buzzfeed News* uncovered details in August 2018 of the administration's Marijuana Policy Coordination Committee telling 14 federal agencies and the DEA to find 'data demonstrating the most significant negative trends' about marijuana and the 'threats' it created for the country. Only negative stories about cannabis could be included, regardless of the facts. Turning public opinion around on cannabis was an impossible task, but Trump officials tried nonetheless.[48] Trump's opioid drug czar, Kellyanne Conway, falsely alleged in 2019 that marijuana was being laced with deadly fentanyl.

The Trump administration was a sobering reminder that there was nothing inevitable about a more progressive drug policy. Obama himself said after his loss to Trump in 2016 that, 'History doesn't move in a straight line. It zigs and zags. Sometimes goes forward, sometimes moves back. Sideways.' Although public attitudes towards drugs had undoubtedly shifted in the last decades, it was conceivable that Trump and his media backers (or any future president) could create a Reagan-style blitzkrieg that demonised the poor and minorities, and argued that only tough-on-crime responses were appropriate. It had worked before and it could work again; the Trump administration seemed committed to it.

Old-style drug-war propaganda never dies. A former senior White House aide to Trump, Cliff Sims, wrote in his book that the president wanted a graphic TV ad to scare children away from opioids. 'We need people dying in a ditch. I want bodies stacked on top of bodies', he told Sims. 'Do it like they did with cigarettes. They had body bags piled all over the streets and ugly people with giant holes in their faces and necks.'[49]

Intriguingly, the Trump administration initiated major criminal-justice reform in late 2018. Some of the proposals included reducing mandatory minimum sentences for some drug offences, changing the 'three strikes' penalty from life imprisonment to 25 years in jail, and giving judges more leeway when sentencing.[50] These changes would possibly reduce the incarceration rate and help rebuild lives on the outside.[51] They were, wrote *The New York Times*, 'the most substantial changes in a generation to the tough-on-crime prison and sentencing laws'. Within months of the new law coming into effect, more than 1000 federal inmates had their sentences reduced for offences related to crack cocaine.

~

As marijuana became a more socially accepted drug, the opioid crisis consumed the entire country, though mostly in white communities. This last detail was important, because it dictated how authorities reacted to the crisis. A *New York Times* story in 2015 was headlined, 'In heroin crisis, white families seek gentler war on drugs.'[52] The figures were startling, and reached epidemic proportions. One hundred and seventy-five people were dying daily due to drug overdoses, including from heroin, prescription painkillers, and synthetic fentanyl, which was up to 50 times stronger than heroin and 100 times stronger than morphine. Deaths from cocaine laced with fentanyl, often coming from China, soared, along with meth-related overdoses. Illicit substances that were untested and dangerous — the reality when drugs were illegal and trafficked by cartels — guaranteed deaths. The Chinese regime pledged in 2019 to ban fentanyl, making good on a promise it had made to Trump in 2018.

The Obama administration missed many opportunities to tackle the fentanyl crisis, including in 2016 when national health experts privately urged the government to declare the drug a 'public health emergency' and to address the growing epidemic. The request was denied. Fentanyl was never taken seriously until it was too late, and is now killing tens of thousands of Americans annually. It is inarguably the deadliest drug crisis in US history.

In a study published in *Medical Care* with 2013 figures, the 'economic burden' of the problem cost the country $78.5 billion every year due to the involvement of the criminal-justice system, healthcare costs, and addiction treatment. Another study from 2016 put the figure at US$95 billion. The Obama White House said in 2015 that the annual cost to the economy of opioid addiction was US$500 billion.

But this didn't paint the entire grim picture. According to the Institute of Medicine, nearly 100 million Americans lived daily with chronic pain, in a total population in 2017 of 325.7 million. The death toll from opioid overdoses and suicides was so serious that life expectancy fell for Americans in their twenties and thirties, according to figures released in 2018 by the *British Medical Journal*. The opioid crisis was blamed for this by researchers. It was increasingly easy to order the strongest opioids on the market through dark-net drug markets. The US surgeon-general, Jerome Adams, issued a rare, nationwide advisory in 2018 for more citizens to access the overdose-reversing drug naloxone.

The problem was so vast that it almost defied belief. A study published in *Science* magazine in 2018 found that 600,000 people had died from unintentional overdoses between 1979 and 2016, and, on current trends, deaths would double every eight years for the foreseeable future.[53] The easy availability of deadly drugs coincided with economic decline in the richest planet on earth, and the result was a death toll that rivalled the numbers from full-blown wars. The epidemic caused mainstream media outlets to publish stories that advocated prescription heroin and supervised consumption sites — controversial suggestions in the US, but normal across Canada and Europe.[54]

As with marijuana, treatment and social attitudes were affected by the colour of a person's skin. A 2018 study at Yale University discovered that black veterans who were prescribed opioids were more likely than their white counterparts to have their medication discontinued if they tested positive for the drug. The effect of this could be serious because more deadly alternatives such as heroin and fentanyl might be used. Although the number of people dying from opioids hit a record high in 2017 of 72,000, states that had prioritised addiction treatment and public-health campaigns experienced a reduction in overdoses.

One hospital in Massachusetts took matters into its own hands due to the seriousness of the crisis. It obtained waivers for doctors to prescribe the opioid buprenorphine, sometimes called Suboxone, as a way to immediately start treating addiction. This was instead of the usual treatment for addiction, which involved a rehab facility and a bed at a detox facility. Amazingly, many emergency doctors don't learn about tackling addiction during their training, but being on the frontline of the opioid crisis has forced many of them to find innovative ways to cope.[55]

The opioid earthquake didn't happen without the medical profession and drug manufacturers working together to hook an entire generation on highly addictive drugs. One of the biggest opioid products is OxyContin, made by the Purdue Pharma company and owned by the Sackler family, doyens of the philanthropic scene across the US. The complicity of Purdue was explained by Andrew Kolodny, co-director of the Opioid Policy Research Collaborative at Brandeis University, who told *The New Yorker* that prescribing trends changed from 1996. 'It's not a coincidence', he said. 'That was the year Purdue launched a multifaceted campaign that misinformed the medical community about the risks.' He blamed Purdue for the 'lion's share' of today's public health emergency.[56] Purdue even discussed internally in 2014 whether the company could financially capitalise on the mass addiction to its products.[57] By 2019, the company was in the crosshairs of federal authorities, and faced multiple legal cases for its complicity in the opioid crisis. Oklahoma was the first state to reach a US$270 million settlement with the company, resolving a lawsuit that accused the corporation of contributing to the deaths of locals, downplaying the drug's risks, and exaggerating its benefits.

Information was disclosed in the JAMA *Internal Medicine* publication in 2018 that proved a direct link between doctors' (over) prescribing opioids and the financial benefits they received. If a drug company, such as Insys Therapeutics or Purdue, bought doctors more meals or gave them other benefits — free travel and accommodation, 'education programs', and consulting fees — they saw a rise in how many of their drugs were given to patients.[58]

Purdue lied about the effectiveness of its opioid for years, claiming that pain relief lasted for 12 hours, when it was far less; many doctors took the company's claims at face value, no doubt helped to do so by financial inducements. A study by CNN and Harvard University released in 2018 found that opioid makers paid huge amounts of money to doctors in 2014 and 2015, and that the doctors earned more money the more drugs they prescribed.[59]

Unlike the crack epidemic in the 1980s and 1990s, when presidents, police, and officials said that the US could arrest its way out of the problem, this was not how the opioid crisis was managed. Why? Crack was predominantly a drug used by blacks in poor inner-city neighbourhoods. This population was public enemy number one, ably assisted by leering and exaggerated media reporting by the (mostly white) corporate press, and they had to be controlled and incarcerated. The approach fitted neatly into the country's anti-drug war narrative: people of colour were dangerous drug users and had to be taught a harsh lesson; meanwhile, the white, often rural, population were victims and deserved sympathy. Economic decline and depression were two factors behind the opioid epidemic, but so was the easy availability of dangerous drugs that could be misused with deadly results. Latino and African-American communities are also affected by opioid abuse and deaths, all at rising rates, and yet media coverage of this epidemic is far less common than of fatal overdoses amongst the white population.

Dr Kolodny told National Public Radio in 2017 that many doctors, either consciously or otherwise, prescribed far fewer opioids for their black patients. He said that the doctors were 'more concerned about the [black] patient becoming addicted, or maybe they're more concerned about the patient selling their pills, or maybe they are less concerned about pain in that population'. For this reason, black patients were less likely to become addicted. 'Racial stereotyping is having a protective effect on non-white populations', Kolodny said.[60]

He was pleased that policy-makers and politicians weren't looking to punish white populations for getting addicted to the drugs, but wished that the same level of understanding had been shown decades earlier to black citizens. Kolodny urged federal and state authorities to better fund outpatient facilities where treatment could be easily accessed to deal with the sickness experienced by people who were unable to get opioids. If these services weren't available, heroin or fentanyl were often the dangerous alternatives.

~

At the 2007 sentencing hearing in Maryland for Evans Ray Jr, judge Alexander Williams Jr told the defendant that he didn't want to give him the legally mandated life sentence. 'I believe that the circumstances justify a sentence shorter than life', he said. 'I further believe that there is some disproportionality between what you've done and the sentence of life.'

But Evans, an African-American man then in his mid-forties, was sent to jail with the likely prospect that he would die there in old age. After two previous drug convictions, he was initially reluctant to get back into drug dealing, but eventually became a middleman for a transaction. A person he thought was a friend turned out to be a government informant. He made no money from the deal — he ran a barber shop at the time — and the other two defendants received shorter sentences. He was going down on drug charges and for having guns in the house. The judge pushed for a 27-year sentence, but this was appealed by prosecutors. The result was a so-called third strike, introduced by President Clinton in 1994 to ensure that a third felony would guarantee a mandatory life sentence — which in Evans's case meant life behind bars. Evans was given a life sentence plus ten years.

Evans thanked the judge after the sentencing, despite the crushing decision. 'I have to own up to my own responsibility', he said. 'The law says life. I'm not in agreement with it, not at all, and I know you weren't. But I just want to thank you and the courts for at least trying.' He spent part of his time at a rough prison in Kentucky where violence was common and white-supremacist inmates wielded their power.

President Obama changed Evans's life in 2016 by commuting his sentence. A long-time opponent of mandatory minimums, Obama commuted the sentences of 1,715 people by the time he left office in early 2017.[61] Evans had gathered evidence for his clemency application with assistance from a Maryland federal public defender, Sapna Mirchandani. One of the prosecutors in his case, Del Wright Jr, thought that the sentence was unfair, but told *The Washington Post* that because Evans had declined a plea deal and was found guilty at trial, prosecutors had little choice but to demand a mandatory life sentence.[62]

One supporting statement in the clemency application came from his sentencing judge, Alexander Williams Jr. 'As I stated at the time of sentencing, and as I believe even more strongly today', he wrote, 'imposing a life sentence on Mr. Ray for the single sale of 60 grams of cocaine base ... amounted to cruel and unusual punishment.'

Obama's letter granting clemency was dated 3 August 2016, and when it was received at the prison Evans was so nervous that he asked a fellow inmate to read it aloud to him. It said in part, 'I am granting your application because you have demonstrated the potential to turn your life around. Now it is up to you to make the most of this opportunity. It will not be easy and you will confront many who doubt people with criminal records can change ... I believe in your ability to prove the doubters wrong, and change your life for the better. So good luck, and God speed.'

I wanted to understand how Evans, now 57 years old, was coping with life on the outside. He picked me up in Washington, DC, and we were joined by his brother Mark, who had just been released from jail after serving seven years for violent assault with a weapon. Evans told me that Mark used to have a drinking problem, but no more, and in the last month he'd moved to a halfway house.

Mark told me that this facility was privately run, in terrible shape and dangerous, with a constant risk of stabbings and shootings, and people doing all kinds of drugs. He kept his head down, found a job working in a nearby sports store, and arranged a driver's licence. Mark wore a black beanie, black-leather jacket, and blue jeans. He embraced his newfound freedom, pleased to be out of jail and able to re-connect with his daughter.

As we drove to their mother's house in nearby Maryland, we made a slight detour to a cemetery where their sister, Kimberly, was buried. She had died in a car crash in 1993 while driving to visit Evans in prison, during his time inside for a previous drug sentence. He told me that he felt responsible to this day because she was coming to see him.

The cemetery was stark, with wide-open spaces, in which ground-level graves sat amongst the off-green grass. Neither Mark nor Evans had visited the cemetery together for years. It was the first time they could share the moment. I felt like I shouldn't have been around during such an intimate reunion, but they both said they were happy to have me there.

Around 45 minutes from Washington, DC, Evans and I arrived at his mother's house in Maryland. She had had a mastectomy, and his stepfather had lost both legs to diabetes. He sat in a wheelchair in the kitchen watching a cooking show on TV. The family home was kitschy and spacious, situated in an area with many two-storey houses. Evans had four children, and wanted to re-connect with them after years of separation.

His mother said that she loved having both her sons back at home and out of prison. Although she acknowledged that Evans should have done some jail time for his crimes, she believed it was 'inhumane' sentencing him to life and death in prison.

When I asked how Evans viewed his years away from his family and what he was trying to achieve today, he answered like a man who didn't want to think about all his years spent incarcerated. 'You can't catch up', he lamented. 'Don't ever forget this one. Don't ever try to catch up, just keep up. That's gone. The past is just what it is. I'll never forget it, but I'll never revisit it either. I'm not doing that again. I'm not being taken away from my mom, my dad, my kids, my family. It's not worth it.'

With a greying moustache and wearing a blue-and-red plaid shirt done up to the neck, Evans spoke with me outside on the back deck.

It was a surprisingly mild winter day with sunshine and blue skies. Next door, children bounced on a trampoline. He joked that his hair had greyed like Obama's.

Evans told me that he had been brought up as a Jehovah's Witness, and still loved the religion for giving him a sense of who he was. He explained that he had first started dabbling in dealing crack cocaine in the late 1980s. He served five years in prison in the 1990s on drugs and weapons charges. Evan said that his gambling obsession likely caused him to get greedy. 'If you hang around the barber shop long enough, you gonna get a haircut', he said. He meant that even though his friends were 'grown men', peer pressure led him and others to deal drugs.

He was eventually set up by an old friend with whom he had shared many special moments over the years. This man was likely pressured by the authorities in exchange for a more lenient sentence. This was a common way for the DEA and police to entrap drug suspects, but, as we've seen, it's a much-criticised form of law enforcement. Like the DEA entrapping individuals around the world — with the agency creating plots in attempts to ensnare the vulnerable or greedy — similar tactics were used across the US.

Evans was another victim in a long line of victims. He later discovered that the DEA had known that they couldn't put him away with 62 grams of powder cocaine; it had to be crack, because the law at that time viewed the drugs differently, and being found in possession of crack would guarantee a life sentence.

When Evans was sentenced to life, he said, 'All the life left out of me. I just remember, just staring. But I didn't feel bad. I remember looking back at my family and I was like, *Life? Where you start that [sentence]?* I have no violence in my past. Not a shooting, not a stabbing, not nothing. I am not a violent guy. Not even a fight.'

On his first day at the Kentucky prison, nicknamed 'Killer Mountain', he saw a black man stab another black man right in front of him, before the attacker was shot by prison guards. The facility was racially segregated with tables for blacks, whites, skinheads, and Aryan Brothers. He had to carry a knife for protection. Evans only spent a year there before being moved, but he tried to focus on reading law books and finding a legal loophole that could get him released. All his co-defendants had been black, and Evans learned in jail that the 'three-strike' laws disproportionally affected the black population.

'The prosecutors didn't want me to come home', he said. 'They wanted me to die in prison because I wouldn't be an informant. *We're gonna fuck you.*'

The day that Obama won the presidency in 2008 was the 'happiest day of my life'. He was in prison, and Evans had no idea that the president would play such a pivotal role in his case years later, but he couldn't believe that a black man had assumed the highest office in the country. However, the optimism didn't last long. His appeal was rejected, and by 2011 his marriage had disintegrated. Evans said that when he went to jail he had told his wife that he understood she needed to live her life and be with other men, but asked her not to be with their friends. He said that she didn't comply.

He told his children during the long years behind bars to stand tall despite their father's predicament. 'It ain't like Dad is locked up for killing somebody, or raping somebody, or some paedophile shit', he said. 'I'm incarcerated for a small amount of drugs and two pistols in the house.'

Families against Mandatory Minimums (FAMM), a non-profit group that opposes mandatory sentences, had helped Evans for a long time, offering guidance and legal support. FAMM's president, Kevin Ring, told me that he backed Obama's efforts to commute sentences, but feared that Trump had successfully framed himself as 'Daddy is here to make you safe' and believed in harsh prison terms. FAMM's focus wasn't on the crime an individual committed, but on the capacity of a judge to issue an appropriate sentence after a guilty verdict had been reached. Mandatory minimums made discretion impossible, which FAMM believed was inherently unfair and racially discriminatory.

Ring celebrated the cultural shift around drugs— the fact that treatment was now more popular than deterrence, and that, when Ring and his colleagues visited politicians in Congress, including Republicans, it was a now a minority view to support increased penalties for criminal violations.[63] Because the country had built a new prison every ten days between 1980 and 2013, when mass incarceration became an American way of life, FAMM's challenge was immense.[64] However, FAMM found that 35 states had removed or amended their mandatory-minimum laws in the previous 15 years.

During the Obama years, the group worked with other organisations to help the administration find prisoners who could be eligible for commutation. Working for free, over 3,000 lawyers got together and received over 36,000 applications from inmates, all drug-related: they had to be inside for non-violent crimes, be low-level participants, and be able to convincingly argue that, were their cases heard today, their sentences would have been much lower than what they had received, due to legal or political changes since then. It was one of the biggest pro-bono efforts in the nation's history, and yet Obama's clemency operation still left thousands of worthy recipients imprisoned, with no explanation for the government's refusal.[65]

Evans fitted the bill perfectly. He wrote to Obama in 2016 in the hope that the president would consider his case. He was a model prisoner, ran rehabilitation programs in prison, and had no violent record. Part of his letter was an appreciation of Obama's work. 'You and your wife have helped all races', Evans said he wrote. 'Black, white, Hispanic, everybody. And I just want to tell you thanks. And I appreciate you.'

When the news of his release came through, Evans said he thanked God. 'I got in my cell, shut the door, got on my knees, and I prayed and cried. I just thanked God. I thanked him, man.'

Over a long conversation with me lasting many hours, Evans spoke passionately, sometimes crying, when explaining his remarkable life. Until relatively recently, he was facing the real prospect of dying in prison. I liked his humour and honesty. I sensed that he couldn't believe his luck being pardoned by Obama (though, when I met him, Evans still faced a ten-year parole period, something his lawyer hoped to remove after he'd been out of prison for a year). He proudly showed me the framed letters he'd received from president Obama, one in response to his 2016 letter requesting commutation, and then another one that formally announced the president's decision. Evans wanted to personally meet Obama, to thank him, and Oprah Winfrey.

Today he cherished the moments of seeing his children grow up. 'To be able to watch my son play basketball, to listen to my daughter when she got something going on and to my oldest daughters, my 18- and 19-year-olds, telling me they got a boyfriend and they're scared to meet me.' He said he was happy that both his children and their friends viewed him as somebody they could 'trust'.

Evans drove his girlfriend, DeShonne Martino, and me back to Washington, DC. DeShonne had been a 'lover' of Evans's many years ago — I presumed when he was married to his now ex-wife — and they had kept in contact during his years in prison. She had a 21-year-son who she and Evans both said needed more motivation to get going in life. She had braids in her hair and braces.

I took them both out for lunch to show my appreciation of their time. I watched them hold hands and look at each other with affection. During lunch, he joked, to her slight embarrassment, that he loved being able to touch DeShonne again.

She told me that they were good friends and that she had encouraged him to seek psychological assistance for his acknowledged PTSD. They had spoken on the phone and written letters to each other during his period in jail. DeShonne said that they had agreed that she had to continue living her life while he was incarcerated. I took this to mean that she would be with other men, though it wasn't clear if they'd spoken about who these men were.

Evans had conservative values. He opposed Obama's embrace of gay marriage, and disliked the growing legalisation of recreational marijuana, including in his state (though he backed medical marijuana). He worked with young children from the inner cities on a government program aimed at giving them skills to get a job. He mentored many of them. Tragically, he was diagnosed with colorectal cancer in 2017, but at the time of writing he had successfully fought back the disease.

He was sceptical of legalised cannabis because he believed it was a trap to disenfranchise black people. He worried that they would be caught out with a positive urine test and not be able to gain decent work because of it. Evans feared that the easy availability of marijuana would only increase the chances that other African-Americans would make the same mistakes as him.

Evans's life had taught him not to trust the government. Legal cannabis was setting black people to 'fail', he argued. 'That's what they want you to do. You're gonna be another statistic. A black person that couldn't say no, and you can't go nowhere.'

~

Dinah Ortiz was 14 years old when she started using drugs. She liked powder cocaine socially at parties. Despite this, she told me that she was a 'responsible, productive member of society'. She lived in her own apartment at 16, had a job, and was paying her own bills. She was one of nine children. Her mother died when she was 13, and drugs filled a void in her life. During these years, she bounced around between New York and Florida.

Ortiz said that her youth spun out of control when she started using heroin after she got married at 26. She didn't realise that her husband was an active heroin user until it was too late. She recalled being traumatised as a child from seeing the effects after one of her older brothers was shooting up. His hands were swollen. 'I'm never going to use that', she remembered thinking.

Her husband successfully hid his heroin use from her for years, but one day she noticed that he was nodding off constantly. She confronted him and he admitted everything, including that he sold drugs from their house. By now, they had a child together, but in her rage she snorted heroin for the first time from her husband's stash and liked it. 'I didn't know that you couldn't do heroin like you do cocaine', she told me, 'so I pretty much did the entire little bag of heroin. I was just knocked on my ass that very first time.' Soon after, she became obsessed with it. 'It was almost like my lover', she said. Then she hid her own use from her husband. It was 'just insanity' during this period.

Ortiz needed money to support her addiction, so she robbed and stole from drug dealers. When she was pregnant with her fourth child, she knew that her life had to change. Wanting to go on a methadone program, she visited a doctor for advice, but, instead of offering her support, he screamed at her. 'You're a bad mom, and you should have just stayed on heroin', he said. 'Methadone is the same thing.' Ortiz was angry, but went cold turkey, hoping to save her unborn daughter. When she went into labour, her sister-in-law offered her Xanax, a mild tranquilliser, to manage the anxiety. She took it, but her baby was born with the drug in her system. Thankfully, she survived, and she's now a healthy 13-year-old girl.

During this difficult stage of her life, Ortiz was constantly visited by child-protective officers who threatened to take away her children. She spent two years in prison, and only saw her newborn daughter once. After being released, she was faced with another crisis. 'I came home to adoption proceedings', she told the National Interdisciplinary Parent Representation Conference in 2018. 'I was not afforded an attorney, and I represented myself on the most important decision anyone would ever make about my life. The daughter I had always prayed for, that I had always longed for, was now being snatched from me because I couldn't be around for the first two years of her life.'[66]

These searing experiences led her to the job she currently occupied and the reason I wanted to meet her. She worked as a parent advocate supervisor at the Bronx Defenders, a public-defence non-profit that supported low-income people in the justice system. Because the drug war negatively affected this community more than any other, Ortiz and her team were on the frontline for individuals whom a majority of society dismissed or ignored. She helped formerly incarcerated mothers and fathers dealing with addiction, and educated lawyers and social workers in child welfare to be far more sympathetic to those struggling with drugs.

Drug courts exist in New York state — studies suggest that they can help to reduce recidivism and re-conviction — and are far less draconian than locking up people in prisons for years and burdening them with criminal convictions. A judge in Rochester, New York state, Jack Elliott, estimated in 2018 that eight out of ten defendants before his drug court were addicted to opioids.[67]

As Ortiz told the National Interdisciplinary Parent Representation Conference, the best parent representation in the courts 'shouldn't be based on your wallet size, and very similarly to the mass-incarceration movement, it shouldn't be based on the colour of your skin ... I deserved the same opportunities afforded to those parents who use [drugs] in the comfort of their home, while they sit behind their laptops and blog about it.'

I met Ortiz in Harlem at the office of New York Harm Reduction Educators (NYHRE), a non-profit organisation committed to helping marginalised drug users in the city. The facility housed sections for holistic treatment, acupuncture, and massage to treat drug addiction. It was bustling, full of users — some slumped and sleeping on seats, others wandering around, some shouting into mobile phones, and others talking loudly to staff. It was chaotic, but a vital hub for people that the government had forgotten.

'We don't promote, condemn, or endorse drug use', NYHRE's outreach and advocacy program manager Terrell Jones told me. 'Our thing is to keep people alive.' Jones believed, as a former user and dealer himself, that the community had to change the harsh ways in which it viewed people who chose to take drugs.

Homelessness in New York had reached the highest level since the 1930s' Great Depression. This shocking fact was directly related to the number of citizens who were being punished by the state for the inevitable effects of severe mental-health and drug problems. Poverty was a major reason that drugs were abused. New York police routinely used undercover agents to entrap often homeless drug users to buy substances from dealers, and then arrested them for drug-dealing. The dealers were not arrested. The city's narcotics team was investing huge amounts of effort into arresting low-level drug addicts.[68]

The Coalition for the Homeless found that in July 2018 there were 61,697 homeless people in New York — which included 15,032 homeless families with 22,384 children — many of whom slept in the city's shelter system. An unknown number of people slept in public places without any support. African-Americans and Latinos constituted the highest percentage of homeless people, and these were the very groups that received the roughest treatment at the hands of law enforcement and the courts if they were drug users. The rates of HIV infection and overdoses were skyrocketing. The Bronx Defenders often assisted individuals who from birth lived with disadvantages because of their skin colour, parents' behaviour, or institutional racism.

Ortiz wasn't endorsing drug use or making judgements about people who snorted, injected, or smoked illegal substances; but she believed, based on her experiences, that everybody deserved respect and fairness. The current system did not provide this. The Bronx Defenders were backers of harm reduction, didn't preach to recipients of its services that they had to stop using drugs, and opposed abstinence programs because they argued that too many people using them ended up relapsing.

Ortiz wanted to change the mainstream perceptions of drug use and to prick the hypocrisies of largely white-made popular culture. 'Tell me how many times you see these white bougie [bourgeois] women on TV talking about, "Oh, when I get home I'm going to have a tall glass of wine." So what's wrong with going home and having a joint? What's wrong with going home and having a line [of cocaine]? What's the difference? It's just so crazy to me that it's okay for you to go home and drink a tall glass of wine because it's legal.'

She was worried about the Trump administration and its draconian attitudes towards the marginalised. But Ortiz told me that the Obama years were disappointing, too. 'I don't think he was a president for us, not for our community', she lamented. 'And just because he was black didn't mean that he helped his people at all.'

~

After decades of fighting a drug war domestically and globally, US government agencies are now caught in a bind. Their rhetoric has changed little since Reagan's war on drugs — an oft-stated belief that drug-trafficking and abuse can be stopped by spending more money on more effective enforcement — and they vigorously oppose state-run initiatives across the US to legalise and regulate marijuana. But this gives them a credibility problem when arguing for tough policies internationally; it's hard for US officials to make the case for complete opposition to drugs when millions of Americans smoke weed legally, and governments make money from it.

The drug-legalisation debate has been around for decades — a

1988 article in *The New York Times* was headlined, 'The Unspeakable Is Debated: Should Drugs Be Legalized? — but it was only during the Obama era that public opinion fundamentally shifted.[69]

Alternative voices are increasingly heard when policy hypocrisy is so strong. Open Society Foundations (OSF) is an international network of civil society groups backed by billionaire George Soros. Its global drug-policy program advocates an end to the drug war through a range of measures, including decriminalising the possession of all drugs. Its policy officer, Diego García-Devis, told me that the rhetoric and reality of US government bodies tasked to fight drugs had shifted, but little had changed on the ground.

Take the state department's Bureau of International Narcotics and Law Enforcement Affairs (INL). Designed to counter drugs coming into the US as well as to manage law-enforcement training programs in drug-war hot spots such as Afghanistan and Colombia, the INL had a mixed record at best. In Afghanistan, the INL claimed to be helping the US-backed government tackle drugs, but opium production had never been higher — making the country the world's biggest supplier. In the Trump era, the INL's deputy assistant secretary, James Walsh, wrote in January 2018 that his team was working to stop the flow of heroin, opioids, and fentanyl into the country, especially from Mexico and China, but he mostly spoke in the language of old, unwilling to accept that war-fighting against drugs had not and would not stop the traffic in illicit substances.

Nonetheless, García-Devis said that the INL was no longer fighting a war on drugs — that was an outdated concept — but instead claimed it was battling organised crime. Walsh mentioned this regularly in his 2018 comments. On the ground in nations where the US's drug war was being most keenly fought, such as Colombia, the INL and the local forces with whom they operated had changed little, despite the high levels of violence that were unleashed by these partnerships. Civilians were still suffering and dying on a massive scale.

García-Devis explained that since 11 September 2001, the US-led war on drugs and the war on terror had merged in ways that worsened violence. In Colombia, Washington aimed to combat the Farc insurgency while battling drug cartels. 'It's the same people and the same funding that goes directly to strip farmers of their livelihoods by forcefully eradicating coca or militarizing the citizens and security in cities like Rio de Janeiro or Mexico', he said. The results were the same: the US might have changed its public narrative about the drug war, but this didn't matter to those being killed because of it.

Kasia Malinowska was director of OSF's drug program — she'd spent 18 years with the organisation — and she'd noticed some important changes since the early 2000s at the international body tasked to manage drugs, the United Nations Office on Drugs and Crime (UNODC). In the early part of the 21st century, she said, 'It was incredible to hear government representatives speak with such disdain [at UNODC headquarters in Vienna] about people who were drug users. There was zero accountability. They would fly into Vienna, say awful things, pass awful resolutions, and go home. Then those resolutions and discussions provided the guidance to the UN as the global institution that failed with drugs.' Civil society engaged far more with the UN these days, but Malinowska wasn't sure it had made much tangible difference.

Progress is slow, but perhaps the pressure is working. In 2019, all the UN bodies unanimously agreed to support the decriminalisation of drug possession for personal use. Nonetheless, the UN has had a largely abysmal record on drug reform, regularly pledging in the last 50 years to eradicate globally all illicit production of coca, opium, and marijuana, despite knowing such a program would inevitably fail.

Although the UNODC now said that drugs were a health issue and not a criminal problem, the global body still believed in a punitive and abstinence-only response. The OSF's Daniel Wolfe, director of the International Harm Reduction Development Program, condemned the tens of thousands of forced-treatment centres in South-East Asia and Latin America, where people were subjected to private, often religious, rehabilitation, and told me that they involved treatment, forced feeding, forced labour, and humiliation. Although it was better than people being executed, it was hardly praiseworthy progress.

Nonetheless, Washington was no longer the loudest voice at the UNODC pushing for the punishment of drug takers. Russia, Egypt, Iran, Pakistan, China, and the Philippines were leading the charge.[70] During the 2016 UN General Assembly's Special Session on Drugs (UNGASS) — the first since 1998, and only the third in history — Russia insisted that the words 'harm reduction' not be included in the outcome document. Despite the fact that needle exchanges, and the use of methadone and other techniques were generally accepted as productive ways to tackle drug use, Moscow wouldn't budge. While there were and still are legitimate criticisms of methadone, Russia's position was based more on its fundamental belief that drug users should be punished. Domestically, its HIV-infected population had ballooned under President Vladimir Putin, but Russian officials remained in denial about the problem.[71]

Back in 1998, the US had been at the forefront of the UNGASS mission statement and motto, 'A Drug Free World — We Can Do It'. The UN had pushed to eliminate or reduce cannabis, opium, and coca in Colombia, Bolivia, Peru, Myanmar, Laos, Vietnam, Afghanistan, and Pakistan, but a study four years later found that these goals had failed. Latin American leaders, whose countries had borne the brunt of US-backed anti-drug policies, hoped that the 2016 UNGASS would herald a more progressive understanding of drugs and would reject the past prohibitionist mindset, but it was not to be. Although the 2016 UNGASS took place during the Obama administration, and countless US states had legalised marijuana, Washington was still unwilling to adopt initiatives on the table such as decriminalisation, drug-consumption rooms, and the regulation of coca in Bolivia.[72]

However, the Obama years created a space for other countries to experiment with drug policy and not receive a rebuke from Washington for doing so. This was unprecedented. Colombia moved towards legalised medical marijuana; Chile followed suit; Mexico moved in a similar direction (including moving down the path towards legalising and regulating all cannabis); and Uruguay became the first nation on earth to legalise cannabis in 2013 (although the drug didn't become legally available until 2017). These developments didn't happen because of Obama, but the usual foreign-policy pressure and threats from the US were absent.

Trump aimed to reverse this. At the 2018 UN General Assembly meeting, the Trump administration cajoled 129 nations to sign up to a non-negotiable one-page document called the Global Call to Action on the Drug Problem. Trump spoke to delegates, and pledged to 'deliver a drug-free future for all of our children'. The statement said that Washington was 'collaborating' with Saudi Arabia, Singapore, and China, amongst many others — nations with severe drug policies, which executed drug offenders.[73]

It was all very reminiscent of the George W. Bush era, when Mexico under president Vicente Fox was rebuked by the US in 2006 for daring to propose the decriminalisation of possession of small amounts of marijuana, cocaine, methamphetamine, and other drugs.[74] The proposal was shelved until 2009, when Mexican president Felipe Calderon moved ahead. It was a strange policy decision in many ways, despite its sensible underpinnings, because Mexico under successive leaders had been waging an extremely violent war on drugs against certain drug cartels, killing hundreds of thousands of people in the process. But Calderon and the bill's supporters argued that it was important to distinguish between big-time dealers and personal users.[75]

~

While conducting research for this book across the country, I regularly heard Americans who had some relationship with marijuana say that the time had finally arrived both for a natural plant to be publicly appreciated by millions and for the government's right to control its use to be rejected. Used properly, weed brought fun, relaxation, and relief (notwithstanding the dangers of excess).[76] The personal-freedom ethos that ruled much of the US — the idea that an individual had the right to do what he or she wanted if it didn't harm anybody else — had mainstreamed marijuana.

This was a huge change from a decade ago, and it should be celebrated — and yet the opioid crisis, mass incarceration, and racial disparities in policing rightly claims many of the headlines. The country that created and designed the global drug war isn't willing to let it go any time soon (despite the seeming inevitability of marijuana becoming legal across the nation). It serves too many powerful interests and Trump administration preoccupations, but it is now at least imaginable that heroin, cocaine, and a range of other drugs could one day be viewed like cannabis is today, deserving of legalisation and regulation.

CHAPTER FIVE

Britain

'They're [Washington] making the rules, and we're [Britain]
the children doing as we're told. For a country which
has spent hundreds of years developing an empire, we
should have realised that we'd be sleepwalking into moral
imperialism. The collective and political judgement which
is our drug policy is not British at all. It's a successful
invasion by American thoughts and ideals. That special
relationship is not equal.'

FORMER BRITISH UNDERCOVER POLICEMAN NEIL WOODS[1]

Donna Marie had lived her entire life in the same council estate in
Newcastle in north-east Britain. Centred around a grassy square,
four-storey flats had been her surroundings as a child and adult.
Her parents lived a few doors down from her own place. Her son,
Grayson, had been taken away by social services due to her drug use.
She had a few more months to prove that she was free from drugs;
otherwise, he would be placed in permanent foster care.

Donna, 31 years old and wearing fluffy white slippers, black jeans,
and a black top, was jittery when I met her in her apartment, and the
conversation quickly turned to matters of life and death.

'I stabbed a man in the face under the influence of alcohol,
Valium, and [psychoactive drug] benzos', she told me. He survived,

and soon after her release from prison in 2014 she fell pregnant after a brief affair. She had thought she was infertile due to sexual abuse as a child, and had initially planned to have an abortion, but her parents convinced her to keep the baby. 'This may be the one chance you'll ever get', they said. Grayson was born in July 2015.

Donna's apartment was spotless, with photos of her son and father displayed prominently. With chipped red paint on her entry steps, and a tidy green lawn outside her flat, Donna gave the impression that she was trying to manage her chaotic life. While sitting down, walking around, and constantly licking and playing with her lips, Donna was clearly anxious, and cried when imagining losing her child.

She explained the abuse that she had suffered as a child from her father, mother, and sister. Her father was a football hooligan who viciously beat her mother, and her brother followed in his father's footsteps. She was sexually assaulted in a flat in the council estate when a drug- and drink-addled man brutally used a hammer to attack her, injuring her vagina and anus. She said that these reasons were probably why she started using heroin. Her life was defined by struggle, boredom, and drugs.

She stayed off drugs during the bulk of her pregnancy. 'I ate healthy', she said. 'The only thing I didn't do was stop smoking ciga-rettes. I decorated my full house, everything. I was doing absolutely brilliant. It was the best time of my life. Then I hit eight months preg-nant, I started getting in with the wrong crowd, and this other girl was pregnant. She was only six months pregnant and I was eight, she was taking heroin, and I ended up taking some Valium again and benzos.'

Donna's probation officer suspected that she was taking drugs again, so Donna admitted everything. She was ashamed that she hadn't remained drug-free. Her friend lost her baby after she had placental abruption due to excessive drug taking. 'I blame myself for that because I knew my friend was using during her pregnancy', Donna said. Both women were on a methadone program during pregnancy, and her friend needed clean urine for court dates. Donna gave her own urine, but after using Valium again, her urine was no longer viable. It was a messy situation, and Donna severed ties with the woman.

Donna had a history of drug taking. She started smoking cannabis at the age of 13, and when she hit high school she was using ecstasy and heroin, and sniffing glue. 'I took Valium and mixed alcohol', she said. 'I was a walking charge sheet. If I was to take benzos and alcohol, there was a 90 per cent chance I was going to end up killing somebody, somebody killing me, or getting arrested. Before I went to prison I was injecting, my God, up to 50 pounds of heroin. That shit will last people a week. I think the most I ever did was 60 pounds of heroin in one session. How I never killed myself I'll never, ever know.'

Donna loved being a mother, proudly telling me that she had a maternal instinct, but social workers never trusted her around Grayson. At one point, her parents took her son because they thought, due to her weight loss, that she was using drugs again. Her sister took custody of her son at one stage. When I met Donna, she was being allowed supervised visits with Grayson while he lived at her parents' house. She knew that this was her last chance to finally get free from drugs for good, or forever lose her son to foster care.

Throughout my time in Britain and Australia, I often heard criticisms of methadone, the substitute drug given to people with a heroin addiction, on the grounds that addicts simply became conditioned to methadone. Donna was scathing about the drug, and wanted the government to ban it. She preferred Subutex, a drug used to treat withdrawal symptoms for addiction to narcotics. Donna knew of many people who 'wanted the methadone because they couldn't afford the heroin for that day, and methadone was there as a substitute. It's the best thing I ever could have done, getting on Subutex. If anything, I feel like I've wasted eight years of my life going on methadone, heroin, methadone, heroin, methadone and heroin.'

The counsellors with whom I visited Donna said that a caring government response to her situation would be to provide at least temporary accommodation and support in another part of Newcastle where she would finally see a different reality away from the over-familiar red-brick council estate. They believed that she would need constant encouragement to survive, but it would be an improvement on her current circumstances; as things stood, it almost felt like her life wasn't seen as important to authorities.

Donna's story was tragic but sadly familiar in Newcastle. The north-east of the country had the highest rates of death from drug use in Britain, rising 90 per cent from 2007 to 2017, with pure cocaine, heroin, the synthetic cannabinoid spice, and crack being the main culprits. Drug use caused 532 deaths in the area between 2014 and 2016, compared to 283 deaths between 2004 and 2006.

The three-hour train trip from London was flat, through green farmland and endless mist. The image of Northern England is often grim, but picturesque Durham with its ancient buildings and winding roads dispelled that stereotype. Nevertheless, parts of Newcastle, with their boarded-up shops and endless frozen-food supermarkets, conformed to my expectations of a deindustrialised city. While the centre of Newcastle looked like a healthy, vibrant place, not far away were small towns whose main streets were nearly empty at 11.00am. Industry had largely died in the area, killed by prime minister Margaret Thatcher in the 1980s, and nothing had replaced it. Economic deprivation was endemic, ignored by most politicians in Westminster. There were now lost generations of youth who had no jobs or prospects. In these circumstances, drug use was unsurprising.

Newcastle felt like a city falling apart. I visited a high-rise council building on the outskirts of town. A shopping centre was on the ground floor, and yet virtually every shop was desolate. A restaurant had empty tables. It was eerily quiet, with nobody around in the middle of the day. Urine sat in small puddles in the elevator, the smell overwhelming. On the third floor was a dirty window that over-looked the city in the distance. It was an apt image, this filthy window through which people saw their city.

Every major city had grim council estates, but more than half of children in some areas of Newcastle were growing up in poverty, according to a report by End Child Poverty Coalition in 2018. The city council was struggling to cope with the number of children at risk of harm from homelessness, drug abuse, or domestic violence. Years of extreme austerity, designed by the conservative party in Westminster, had caused a huge social crisis across the country. The biggest food bank in Britain was in Newcastle, and it often ran low on essential supplies. It was the working poor, not the homeless, who often used it. The use of anti-depressants soared across the country during the austerity period, and in 2018 alone there were more than 70 million prescriptions written for the drugs, according to the National Health Service. This was nearly double the amount of a decade earlier.

I met a Greek woman, Despina, in her third-floor apartment. Her daughter, Natalie, had been using heroin for at least two decades. Despina told me a desperately sad story of her child, who lived in misery, addiction, and secrecy. Despina was dedicated to caring for her 38-year-old daughter. Despina had seen things a mother should never have to: Natalie bloodied with puncture marks on her neck. Despina felt helpless. At times during our conversation, she cried, stood up to fetch water, and took a breather. Despina knew who to blame for the nation's economic woes. 'That Thatcher woman, she destroyed England totally', she said. 'She sold everything we had.'

Sadness permeated the Newcastle landscape. Jamie Bell, 38 years old, lived in a modest house, and a large but friendly dog roamed the halls. When we met, Jamie was Helen, and later told me that they'd always felt uncomfortable with traditional female identity. Non-binary orientation gave comfort (and I was asked to use non-binary pronouns to describe them).

Jamie drank from a mug with 'Drama Queen' written on it. Their rooms were full of children's toys. Friendly and constantly smiling, their life had been marked by sexual abuse from a young age by their mother, father, and sister. At the age of five, they burned themselves with hot water in the bath, which soon developed into putting out matches on their skin. Eating disorders began. They were groomed at 14 by older men for sex. They lost their virginity while being raped. 'I put myself in vulnerable situations', they said. 'I didn't have self-care or boundaries.' They reported their abuse at the hands of their family to authorities when they were 27. 'I couldn't catch a break from the people who were meant to support me', they lamented.

Raped multiple times as a young adult and assaulted by their ex-female partner, who was their support worker for ten years and faced few legal ramifications for the abuse, they had two young girls conceived with a sperm donor. I had rarely heard a story of such depravity, and yet they spoke with relative confidence.

For Jamie, alcohol and cocaine were their 'saviour'. They said that because 'control and power were taken away from me from such a young age, I needed to get that back in some way'. They started taking speed at 15, and by the time they went to university they were spending £200 (US$263) on marijuana every week (ironically, they used money from their abusive parents). They took ecstasy, ketamine, and cocaine.

Months before we met, Jamie had decided to try to turn their life around, because they needed healthy relationships. 'I wanted a relationship with myself', they said, 'and I didn't have that. I'd existed and existed and existed, but I'd never actually been able to feel because of PTSD.'

Jamie put on a brave face. Articulate, considered, and recently free from drugs, they were determined. They said that they often judged character badly — their life experiences gave them few skills to know how to build trust with people — but they were trying. They recounted the horrors of their life with calmness. They wanted to start

an NGO for women who'd been abused by women to better explain
this largely hidden crime to law enforcement.

Jamie was a damaged person. Their parents had provided financial
support in the past, but they'd recently established strict boundaries
with Jamie, and didn't want to see them. Jamie volunteered overnight with a suicide-prevention hotline. Their positive demeanour
was disarming considering their life's experiences, and it was more
impressive because of it.

Many cities contained people like Jamie, but Newcastle had
greater problems than most. According to figures released in 2016,
the city and its surrounding areas had one of the highest rates of
drug-related crimes in the country. Public Health England found
that the Newcastle region had the highest rates of youth drinking and
alcohol-related hospital admissions in the nation.

What this meant for young people on the ground in Newcastle
was explained in visceral detail by Mark Tunney, the co-founder of
Jigsaw Recovery Project, a group that helped young people transitioning to the outside world after being in foster care. They may have
suffered sexual or violent abuse or drug addiction. Tunney explained
that the community spirit that used to exist in his area was dead.
'Nothing's replaced it', he said.

People were scared of drugs, gangs, and violence. Young people
with guns worked for local families and controlled the drug-trade. 'It
does my fucking head in', he said. 'Especially because it's the area I live
in. I know all the families; I used to sell drugs to their families. And
now it's the kids. It breaks my heart.'

Having grown up in Newcastle, in a poor part of the city, he said
that the situation had never been worse. The government and social
services didn't even 'scratch the surface' of the huge drug-abuse
problem. He said he'd called ambulances on multiple occasions after
finding men overdosed on fentanyl outside his office building. Many
in positions of authority in the area either denied there was a major

drug problem, or refused to invest in enough services to help the growing numbers of people suffering from alcohol and drug abuse. The number of young Britons who drank heavily or to excess had fallen since the early 2000s — 25 per cent of 16–24-year-olds in a 2018 study classified themselves as non-drinkers — although overall numbers for some older populations continued to increase.

Governments and local councils had slashed their budgets in recent years. According to the BBC, £162 million had been cut from treatment budgets since 2013–2014. The UK Addiction Treatment Centres said that these cuts were killing people, because long-term residential facilities were being replaced with cheaper community-based services. The BBC found that councils that had reduced support for drug and alcohol treatment experienced a rise in drug-related deaths.[2] Nearly 60 per cent of local authorities slashed budgets for alcohol-related services in 2018 and 2019 due to government cuts. Release, Britain's only charity that provides a free legal and advice service to drug users, released figures in 2019 showing that local authorities in the country had only supplied take-home naloxone to 34 per cent of opioid users in 2017 and 2018. (Naloxone can reverse a deadly opioid overdose.) The other 66 per cent's lives were deemed expendable.

Austerity policies led to a massive slashing of public services, with devastating effects. The *British Medical Journal* assessed in 2017 that severe cuts since 2010 had led to 120,000 excess deaths, mostly in the over-sixties and home-care communities, largely due to reductions in nursing numbers. By 2019, life expectancy for men and women had dropped by six months in England and Wales. The United Nations special rapporteur for extreme poverty and human rights, Philip Alston, released a report in 2018 that found austerity had entrenched 'high levels of poverty' and inflicted 'unnecessary misery in one of the richest countries in the world'.

Mark Tunney had a colourful past himself, and a tough look, with tattoos on both arms, and a crew cut. He had taken and dealt drugs from a young age. At the time, he wore it as a badge of honour — 'because of the environment I was living in, which was quite a deprived area, it was very much an ego boost. I'm one of the guys now, I've got a criminal record' — but the effect on his life had been horrific. He had been unable to get any work that wasn't connected to the field of recovery because of a long charge sheet that included drug dealing, assault, and shoplifting. 'Every single crime I ever did was related to drugs', he told me. He was now 48 years old, and his last 13 years had been free of any drugs or alcohol. From the age of 13 until he was 34, he had taken anything he could get his hands on.

In Jigsaw's common room, open every day of the week, at-risk youth relaxed, received lessons in finding work by applying on the internet-connected computer (where only porn was blocked), played computer games, and hung out in a safe space. On the whiteboard was a piece of paper headed 'King Baby', explaining a common personality type that included people who sought 'approval of others and sacrificed their own identity'.

Tunney was overwhelmed with the problems his city faced, but he knew who to blame. 'I think the biggest problem we have in this country at the moment, and they've had it for a very long time, is that we punish people who use drugs', he said. He argued that the *Misuse of Drugs Act 1971* should be abolished, because it had led to the needless arresting and stigmatising of generations of people for possessing or using drugs. 'It's really killing people', Tunney said. 'Out of the seven people I grew up using with, I'm the only one that's still left alive.' The rest had died from heroin overdoses.

He despaired at the way in which British society spoke to young people about illicit substances, sending mixed messages to them. 'We don't tell our young people to stop using drugs', he said. 'You're going to need to be able to work and have a relationship. You're going to need to be able to cook your kids a meal. Instead of making drugs your life, make drugs part of your life.'

The most confronting stories I heard were from two sex workers, Jill and Patricia, both in their thirties, who worked in the industry to fund their serious heroin use. Although they received support from local authorities, the economic crisis in the area worsened both their personal situations and their need for drugs. The meeting was organised by Nicola Quarnby, Durham police's 'dedicated liaison officer' in adult sexual exploitation.

Every city and town had sex workers — it wasn't unique to Newcastle — but the north-east of Britain was especially positioned to suffer because of a dramatic decline in support services to it over the last years. In this way, the drug war found new victims whose backgrounds, poor families, and economic positions increased the likelihood of them suffering trauma from drug abuse. The area was also hit with a major sex-grooming network that operated between 2007 and 2015, where 700 girls and women were abused and raped. The gang targeted the most deprived areas of Newcastle.

Jill used heroin daily, wore heavy make-up and a black Nike tracksuit, and told me how her son had been taken away from her many years before. He lived with her mother, although she saw him weekly. She said she couldn't give up heroin, though it didn't produce the buzz it used to years ago, as it got her through the day. She slept with many men, but didn't want to; she had to get money to score from dealers, who were often violent. She had recently overdosed, had aneurysms on her back, and said that she 'nearly lost limbs' due to her drug taking. Both women were likely high when we met — they said they used heroin multiple times daily — but we had a cogent conversation.

Jill had been using heroin for ten years; her child's father had got her hooked, but she thought that her male clients didn't know that she was a drug user. 'I think if they found out that they were funding my drug use, it would absolutely stop', she said. 'Because I'm using that much, I've got such a high tolerance to it now. What it's really doing is just stopping me from feeling unwell rather than making us high. I would have to take an awful lot now for it to get the effect I ever had when I first took it.'

Jill's view of men was unsurprisingly negative — 'A lot of them treat women like the olden days, like second-class citizens' — and she said that she was uninterested in having a boyfriend and believed that no man would accept her work. She was a qualified dental nurse, but told me that after being sexually abused when working in that profession many years before, she quit and started dancing in a club. Sex work came later. The financial realities of living near Newcastle meant that she could dance on the weekend and triple the money she made working a nine-to-five job during the week. For her, the decision was easy.

The day after we met, Nicola, the local police officer, messaged to give me more details about Jill and Patricia, and filled in what they had left out:

> What I am sure of, as we were talking and laughing and they hid it well, is that they actually hate what they do and hate themselves for doing it. I have seen in particular Jill take calls from clients be really nice on the phone and then break down, loathing that she does this to feed her addiction. The only way I can describe it is that they take calls from people whom they do not know, make the appointment, mostly have unprotected sex as 'bareback' is preferred and they can get more money, then move onto the next appointment.
>
> Can you imagine having some stranger inside you who you don't fancy, or like, 8–15 times a day? It is brutal. Equally when we were discussing the victim's side of the drugs, some of the girls steal from elderly clients. Knowing that this is a hidden subject, most of the sex workers are victims of serious physical rapes and beatings and do not report this to police. I can say

that most of the people I work with all have elements of trauma, mental health, and addiction.

~

Britain eventually fell victim to the prohibitionist mindset that devoured so many other allies of Washington. In the 19th century, drugs had been widely available and used with little controversy. Opium, cocaine, and arsenic were available at pharmacies, and beer in pubs could be laced with opium to protect customers against malaria. Queen Victoria liked opium, and used cocaine gum with a young Winston Churchill. Opium dens existed in London — although they were more often the creation of imaginative writers — and while the Pharmacy Act of 1868 attempted to restrict opium, it had little effect on its use.[3]

The rigid class system was never far away from public attitudes towards mind-altering substances. Marek Kohn, author of *Dope Girls: the birth of the British drug underground*, explained that opium became known as a 'downer' drug, but cocaine was an 'upper', explaining why the Sherlock Holmes character injected cocaine. This, Kohn wrote, was because, at the time, cocaine was for 'brainy, highly strung people' who required constant stimulation.[4] Implicit in such stories were ideas around the kind of people who took and could afford the drug.

It wasn't until the 20th century that serious attempts were made to control and stigmatise drug users and the drugs themselves. Cocaine and opium were still legal in Britain when World War I began, but soon after its end, the country introduced the *Dangerous Drugs Act 1920*. Alcohol, widely consumed by the population from all classes, was viewed as harmful, and restrictions were placed on it (although it arguably did little to change the nation's drinking culture).

The media started introducing a moralising tone to its coverage of drugs, akin to what was happening in the US and Australia in the same period. This began a long campaign of constantly evolving panics over drugs and what they were doing to the minds and bodies of the young, especially white women. As in Australia, the Chinese were blamed for entrapping young women and forcing them to take cocaine. Once again, in the public imagination, white women were given no agency and supposedly had no ability to resist.

This was a convenient myth about ethnic minorities, and helped propel a dangerous stereotype that lasted into the 21st century. The police watchdog, Her Majesty's Inspectorate of Constabulary and Fire and Rescue Services, released a report in 2017 that black people were less likely to be found with drugs on them than white people, though were more than eight times more likely to be stopped and searched.[5]

Although there was never really a drug scene in Britain until the 1960s — it was largely used by a select few in London — the media and politicians created an impression of degenerate celebrities divorced from reality and shunning the proper morals of the day. The 1960s changed the equation entirely, with masses of young people using cannabis, LSD, cocaine, and heroin. Washington pressured Britain to try to restrict the exploding drug scene and forced Westminster to enact the *Drugs (Regulation of Misuse) Act 1964*, which soon gave police the power to search people for illicit drugs and to make them subject to criminal sentences.

The *Misuse of Drugs Act 1971* was 'the stupidest and most ineffective ever passed by Parliament', wrote British journalist Simon Jenkins in 2013. The act criminalised heroin and 'handed the queue and Britain's entire drugs trade over to the world's racketeers, crooks, and desperadoes. It was the greatest-ever act of denationalisation. The drugs market soared, and untold human misery with it.'[6]

The law remains in place, despite the overwhelming evidence of its failure to control the flow and use of drugs. But that was never the real intention. The act split drugs into three categories, and designated penalties for possessing or supplying various drugs from heroin to cannabis. Following Washington's lead, Britain wanted to find ways to control society — largely the underclass, the economically vulnerable, and minorities — under the guise of keeping the population safe. Using that flawed definition, Britain could claim success.

A 1973 cover story in the *Observer* magazine aimed to reveal the reality of drugs, explaining to its readers that the bulk of users, who took cannabis, heroin, methadone, and morphine, were 'mainly young, mainly male, mainly white, mainly working-class'. It went on using words that could have been written today: 'For the lonely or inadequate, another basis of addiction is the need to belong … In their moments of truth, 99 per cent of dependents would admit they want to be part of our world, not stuck with their own.'[7]

By the 1980s, heroin use had soared, as had HIV infections. Needle-exchange programs became widespread and helped stop a major epidemic. This was the decade when Britain's party culture went mainstream, with ecstasy becoming the drug of choice in the country's burgeoning club scene. Governments of both major stripes, Labour and the Conservatives, pursued politics that talked about increased treatment of problem drug users. Funding did increase from the 1990s to the late 2000s, but the language of law enforcement was ubiquitous in seeking to crack down on what officials claimed was an epidemic of drug-related crime related to the party scene. The tabloid media happily played along, despite many of their own readers (and journalists) consuming illegal substances. Hypocrisy was never an impediment to front-page outrage.

Britain fought its drug war with a combination of aggression and caution. While it was no longer an imperial power, despite the wishes of politicians and activists who longed for a supposedly golden age of benevolent empire, both major parties, when in power, largely accepted the view that a war had to be fought on the most vulnerable drug users at home. London often supported Washington's drug-war rhetoric and policies — particularly evidenced by prime minister Margaret Thatcher's embrace of US president Ronald Reagan during the 1980s and his war against Central America — but Britain mainly caused damage to its domestic population.

And yet none of this was sustainable. Many police officers, politicians, and conservative media-commentators continued to demonise drugs and the citizens who took them, but as *Mixmag*, Britain's clubbing magazine bible, wrote in 2014, the world was no longer in the grip of a 1960s-style moral panic over drugs. 'When the daughters of police, politicians, and journalists started to take ecstasy', it explained, 'drug users began to be seen in an entirely new light by those in authority; they were not drug fiends, they were just teenagers having fun.'[8]

During the years that Labour was in power, from 1996 until 2010 under prime ministers Tony Blair and Gordon Brown, Britain continued to fight the drug war with a variety of justifications. Arrests soared, and young people were stigmatised regardless of whether they used cannabis or heroin — two drugs with vastly different effects. In 1997, Blair announced that he wanted to 'breathe new life into the battle against drugs. We will hit hard on drugs and the drugs trade.' By 2004, his rhetoric had increased, and he announced a new policy that promised harsher sentences for anybody who dealt drugs near schools. To show how serious he was, Blair took a drug test for cocaine and heroin at a police station in Slough. It was negative.

Blair took a conventional view on drugs — any leniency sent a 'wrong message' to young people who might be considering using them — and ramped up the threats. Yet his government knew it was all for show. A secret report leaked in 2005 found that police needed to seize 60–80 per cent of drugs in the country for there to be any tangible effect on drug flows, and yet they'd never achieved a seizure rate higher than 20 per cent.[9]

Blair understood the power of tabloid scares. In 2004, after consulting with police and experts, his government reclassified marijuana from a Class B to a Class C drug, rendering it akin to anabolic steroids and prescription antibiotics. But then his government threatened to de-reclassify it as a Class B drug, despite the scientific community and the government's own Advisory Council on the Misuse of Drugs (ACMD) warning this was a bad idea that was likely to increase the use of cannabis. Blair's successor, Gordon Brown, ignored the advice and changed the classification in 2008; his home secretary, Jacqui Smith, claimed it was to 'protect the public'. Jail sentences for possessing the drug rose from two to five years.

The most insightful person on this period is David Nutt, a leading British neuro-psychopharmacologist with vast experience in researching drugs and how they affect the mind. After having been appointed in 2008 as chairman of the ACMD, he was fired by Labour the next year for daring to suggest that ecstasy use was just as safe as horse riding, and for advocating a more sensible classification of drugs. 'It turns out that horse riding, particularly if you jump, is more dangerous than taking ecstasy', Nutt told me. 'The government went hysterical because I was challenging one of the prime pillars of the British establishment, that horse riding is a good thing.'

He showed with scientific research that alcohol and tobacco were more dangerous than cannabis, ecstasy, and LSD, and therefore argued that all drugs should be treated legally in order of the harm they did. He said that 'the obscenity of hunting down low-level cannabis users to protect them is beyond absurd', and argued that the reclassification of cannabis to a Class B drug was politically motivated. His honesty was greeted with dismissal.

In a 2011 blog post, Nutt condemned Blair for having classified magic mushrooms as one of the most dangerous drugs in 2005 — before then, the drug was legal — despite not consulting with the ACMD. 'By no metric are mushrooms as harmful as the real

Class A drugs such as crack cocaine and heroin', he wrote.[10] Nutt had become one of Britain's most outspoken and informed critics of the drug war, arguing that harsh laws that targeted users didn't reduce harm and, if anything, 'it may be actually aggravating harm from alcohol'.[11]

During a long conversation I had with Nutt where he now worked as a professor at Imperial College London, he told me that, ever since the 2000s, Blair and Brown had 'decided that they had to get the right-wing press onside, so they started becoming hard on cannabis'. Nutt said that a key reason why Brown reclassified cannabis was a secret deal he'd struck with the conservative *Daily Mail* newspaper. The *Mail* had supported Hitler, Mussolini, and British fascists in the 1930s.

Nutt alleged that the-then editor of the *Mail*, Paul Dacre, told Brown that he would back him if he reduced the top rate of income tax from 50 per cent to 45 per cent and put a cap on immigration. Brown, desperate to win the 2010 election, agreed — but still lost to the Tories, led by David Cameron. Brown regularly hammered cannabis in the public debate, Nutt said. 'Then they started really attacking cannabis users. That's where it all changed. Since then, it's all been politics. Harm reduction is out the window.'

I can't independently verify Nutt's claim — there's little on the public record about this secret meeting, with no notes taken between Dacre and Brown — but he's a respected figure with a history of telling unpopular truths.

'When you go into British politics', Nutt explained, 'the first thing every department does every morning is see what the *Mail* has said about them. It's hugely powerful.' The *Mail* continues to push an anti-drug agenda, despite the harms associated with it. A front-page story in 2019 was headlined, 'Cannabis Surrender: police chief [from the West Midlands] admits his officers won't even warn users'.

Nutt was leading the research on Alcosynth, a synthetic alcohol that didn't produce any of the side effects of traditional alcohol. The drink would still provide a buzz, but without leading to hangovers or contributing to failing health.

The *Daily Mail* isn't the only relevant paper in Britain. Rupert Murdoch's *The Times* editorialised in 2016 that all drugs in Britain should be decriminalised as a first step towards legalisation and regulation.[12] It was a rare position for a major newspaper to take. The last similar media initiative was *The Independent on Sunday* in 1997 pushing for the decriminalisation of cannabis (although ten years later it reversed its position, saying that the strength of skunk marijuana and its connections to mental-health problems justified the change of heart). The self-described liberal *Guardian* was also cautious, only supporting cannabis decriminalisation in 2016.[13] But in 2019, after Mexican drug lord El Chapo was found guilty in a New York court, the newspaper called for a continuation of the war on drugs and for there to be no 'surrender' in fighting it. Because 'cocaine, like alcohol, and unlike heroin or marijuana, has no recognised therapeutic role', the *Guardian* pushed for a kinder, gentler drug war along unspecified lines. 'The war on drugs must be fought', it concluded.[14]

Britain doesn't suffer from American levels of drug-related incarceration, but huge numbers of people still languish in the criminal-justice system. Those in prison for drug offences are overwhelmingly there for having supplied illegal substances. In 2016, 102,000 people were cautioned, sentenced, given a penalty notice, or warned about using cannabis or khat (a plant with stimulating properties). Nine thousand of them were sent to jail. Nonetheless, in some parts of the country and for some groups — though often not minorities — police had unofficially decriminalised cannabis.

In recent times, the highest figure for drug-related offences were recorded in 2008–2009, with over 213,000 offences; in 2017–2018, the

number dropped significantly to just over 109,000.[15] The total population of the country was around 67 million. This showed a steady
change in how the police approached drugs, even though the laws
remained stuck in a different era. Despite these improvements, however, Britain and Wales had the highest incarceration rates in western
Europe, many of which were drug-related.[16]

The Conservatives have maintained high levels of financial support for law enforcement and its war against drugs since taking office
in 2010. Despite the Tories spending £1.6 billion annually on a drug
strategy, an assessment of the government's policies by Transform
Drug Policy Foundation in 2017 found that it was 'squandering'
any chance of success because the level of societal drug use had not
reduced since the war began in 2010 when Theresa May was home
secretary. Transform said that the policy hadn't affected the availability of drugs, and was instead 'harming the young and vulnerable
through criminalising them'.

It concluded: 'And for what? Drug use hasn't fallen for eight years.
More importantly, drug deaths have hit record levels for four years
in a row. This document [a government audit showing that illegal
drugs remain available] proves the ongoing commitment to drug war
enforcement is not about new evidence — it is serving other political
and ideological interests. It's truly scandalous that the poor and vulnerable are dying as a result. The Government are responsible, and
must be called to account.'[17]

One of the Tories' ideas for tackling drug use was the introduction in 2016 of the Psychoactive Substances Act, which was sold as
battling the new generation of dangerous drugs, including the previously legal synthetic cannabinoid, spice. Although such drugs could
cause harm — deaths from spice in British prisons continued to rise
— David Nutt blamed drug laws, because 'these illegal drugs [spice]
were created to get around prohibition of cannabis'. There was also a
real risk that such drugs would be pushed underground.

Nutt said that the Psychoactive Substances Act had been lobbied for by ultra-conservative, puritanical, prohibitionist-style American activists who infiltrated British policy groups — such as the organisation co-founded by the former Conservative leader Iain Duncan Smith, called The Centre for Social Justice. 'They would like to abolish all drugs, including alcohol', Nutt said. 'Obviously, they aren't going to take on alcohol, and their attitude is that drugs are morally reprehensible.'

Duncan Smith's vision for Britain was directly inspired by the darkest aspect of Washington's drug war, and his views were respected in the Conservative government. His group released a report in 2018 that pushed for increased stop-and-search powers for police to tackle London crime. It advocated police stopping people without suspicion in areas that were deemed problematic. Unsurprisingly, this meant suburbs where minorities lived and worked.[18]

This US zero-tolerance style appealed to politicians and media commentators who talked about being 'tough on crime and drugs', but the overwhelming evidence from around the world was that such policies didn't work. For example, a US justice department report on Baltimore in 2016 found that zero tolerance was a failure because it both shattered the relationship between police and the community, and African-Americans were disproportionately targeted to rack up statistics.

Amidst the daily political clamouring to fight a drug war that was guaranteed to fail, a rare voice of reason emerged in 2018. A former lord chancellor, Charles Falconer, who had known Tony Blair for decades and had served in senior roles in his government — including running the justice department between 2003 and 2007 — publicly apologised for his role in the war on drugs. His admitted that it had been a 'tragic disaster' for the poor in Britain and globally, and that the drug laws were 'disproportionately enforced against black people', and urged profound change:

'We need to accept there are alternatives to policies that have failed so many working-class communities. We need to admit that we abandoned whole generations to the scourge of drug addiction. We need to confront our political failures and listen to those police chiefs pushing for saner policies.

'Above all, we need to take back control of drug supply from the most violent gangsters. And it needs to be done sooner rather than later.'

Falconer wanted the Labour Party under 'radical' leader Jeremy Corbyn to 'call for an end to the drug war and commit to the legal regulation of drug production and supply in its next manifesto … For much too long, the Labour Party has failed to engage with these issues and ended up following a stale consensus driven by right-wing Republicans such as Richard Nixon and Ronald Reagan.'[19]

~

Neil Woods worked as an undercover policeman between 1993 and 2007, and estimated that his work had contributed to drug criminals being put in prison for a combined total of 1,000 years. 'Everything I did while undercover was a waste of time,' he told *Vice* in 2014. 'All I did was make the lives of the vulnerable more unbearable.'[20]

When Woods was growing up, he told me, his beliefs about drug and alcohol users were negative. With his views inspired by his parents and tabloid media, he believed that 'people should only have so many chances'.

Now in his late forties, Woods explained that he gradually changed his views about his job, eventually seeing that he was contributing to the drug war getting worse and more futile.

Every morning, he would leave his wife and three young children, put on shabby clothes, and arrive in a new area such as Leicestershire, acting as a drug taker. He'd befriend dealers and gangsters with the sole aim of infiltrating, understanding, and eventually arresting them.

'I justified what I was doing manipulating these people because I saw the end justified the means', he said. 'Their lives are going to be made worse by coming into contact with me. I gradually felt increasingly more guilty of that, but I always justified that position because at the end of the operation six months later I'd be capturing the local nastiest gangster.'

But after many years, Woods recognised one startling fact: 'I was perpetually seeing organised crime getting more violent and it was literally down to the police tactics that were being used', he told me. As he explained to *The Guardian*: 'Every year the police get better at catching drug gangs, and the gangsters' most effective way of fighting back is upping the use of fear and intimidation against potential informants. The most efficient way to stop people grassing them up is to be terrifying. In other words, organised-crime groups were getting nastier and nastier as a direct result of what I was doing.'[21]

This led to phenomena such as county lines being set up across the nation, where children, some as young as 11, were sent to provincial areas by gangs to sell Class A drugs. The National Crime Agency estimated in 2018 that there were more than 1,000 lines across Britain. The profits accruing from them for criminal gangs were estimated at £500 million annually.

What Woods described was the side of the drug war that its most passionate supporters didn't discuss or acknowledge, preferring to trade in platitudes about fighting back against drug-traffickers. Woods shared his insights with his colleagues, especially after he left undercover work, but they were generally unresponsive. 'They just basically fell back on, "Well, what can we do about it? All we can do is keep going. You've just got to keep locking them up." None of them were willing to talk or to even consider any other way of doing things.'

Unsurprisingly, Woods developed PTSD. 'I was haunted by the memories, really intense memories, of people who I had manipulated, and people whose lives had been made distinctly worse as a result of contact with me.'

After writing a memoir in 2016 about his work as an undercover policeman, *Good Cop, Bad Cop*, he was initially shunned by many former colleagues, but said that in recent years more police were accepting his way of thinking about the pointlessness of the drug war. He became deeply involved in an organisation called Law Enforcement Against Prohibition (LEAP), which had been started in the US but was growing internationally, of former and serving police, military, and intelligence officers who opposed the war on drugs because they'd seen the damage it caused.

Like many police with whom I spoke for this book, Woods had clear views about how Britain should regulate drugs. He opposed the 'capitalist free-for-all' taking place across the US as a result of marijuana being legalised (many UK cannabis investors wanted to follow suit, however, and they told me so). He preferred the model in Uruguay, where the key aim was to remove the black market and institute a health-based approach.

Woods wanted his country to follow Switzerland, where heroin was prescribed for problem addiction, but he would encourage authorities to be 'far, far more liberal' than that European nation. 'If someone has a problem with it [heroin], remove them from the exploitation of organised crime and provide them with the heroin in a completely non-judgemental way ... There isn't a drug out there that wouldn't be made safer by regulation.'

Even the *British Medical Journal* agreed, editorialising in 2018 that it now supported 'efforts to legalise, regulate, and tax the sale of drugs for recreational and medicinal use'.[22]

Woods was an optimist, and thought that British drug laws would inevitably liberalise, because a growing number of politicians, police, and the general public were demanding it — ranging from establishing drug-consumption rooms to unofficially decriminalising the possession of small quantities of drugs.

This was the position of campaigning police chief Mike Barton, who headed the Durham police force in north-eastern England. He exploded into national consciousness after the *Observer* newspaper led its front page in 2013 with a story headlined: 'Time to end the war on drugs, says top UK police chief'. Barton said that all Class A drugs should be decriminalised and that the National Health Service (NHS) should allow those with drug dependency to access them.

'In my force area, we have 43 organised-crime groups on our radar', he wrote. 'Most have their primary source of income in illicit drug supply, all of them are involved in some way. These criminals are often local heroes and role models for young people who covet their wealth. Decriminalising their commodity will immediately cut off their income stream and destroy their power.'

The-then Conservative prime minister David Cameron, who before his time as leader had spoken critically about the drug war, condemned its futility, and voted to consider the legalisation and regulation of drugs, came out against Barton's suggestion. 'Drug policy has been failing for decades', Cameron said in 2005 before he became prime minister. Back in the day, Cameron was far more sensible, and would have seen the benefit of Barton's thinking.

Barton said that Cameron's change of heart was because he was a 'coward' and 'scared of the *Daily Mail*'. He admitted that his own views, while increasingly shared by his colleagues, were still rare in the police force.[23] In June 2018, Barton called for the legalisation of cannabis and said his force would not arrest people in his area who grew marijuana plants for their personal use.

During an interview at Durham police headquarters, Barton told me that his philosophy, which he acknowledged was paternalistic, was that 'we target the bad and not the sad'. With over 1,700 registered heroin consumers in the Durham area and around 1,200 police officers, he said that, 'I don't even have as many cops as registered drug addicts in the county. Even if they just man-to-man mapped the registered heroin addicts who are popping up, they couldn't do any other work. It's just futile for people to think that law enforcement can prevent drug addiction.' Barton instructed his force not to prosecute drug users who sold heroin to fellow users.

Barton spoke with the authority of a man who had spent his professional life around law enforcement. He peppered our conversation with humour, but his ideas were deadly serious. 'I've been involved in policing now since 1980, and drugs are cheaper, stronger, more freely available, and more dangerous than they ever have been. And I've been throwing the kitchen sink at this for 38 years. Any sane individual would say, "I wonder if I might have to have a rethink of our approach here."'

I asked Barton if he'd ever taken illicit drugs — I asked Neil Woods the same question, and he had, because it was an unavoidable part of being an undercover policeman when working against the drug-trade — and he said that he had not. 'I'm curious about cocaine', he said, 'but I'll never take it because I'm sort of hardwired to behave.'

There were few public critics of Barton's moves, although Peter Hitchens, a columnist for the *Daily Mail*, was one of them. He didn't mention Durham or Barton by name, but regularly railed against society's growing liberal attitudes towards drugs. In a 2017 column, he wrote that, 'In secondary schools, illegal drug abuse is now more common than cigarette-smoking. Could this have something to do with the fact that the police (busy painting their nails) long ago stopped enforcing the law against drug possession?'[24]

Sometimes the police and authorities tried to pierce the bubble of middle-class drug takers, but in the process overlooked wider realities. The Metropolitan police commissioner, Cressida Dick, condemned cocaine users in 2018 for ignoring the gross abuses required in getting cocaine to them. 'There is this challenge that there are a whole group of middle-class — or whatever you want to call them — people who will sit round ... happily think about global warming and fair trade, and environmental protection and all sorts of things, organic food, but think there is no harm in taking a bit of cocaine', she said. 'Well, there is; there's misery throughout the supply chain.' London mayor Sadiq Khan argued similarly that 'middle-class parties' where cocaine was bought and consumed fuelled violence in the city.

Unfortunately, they both ignored the wider supply chain in South America and Africa — the source and transport routes of the drug — where the trade inflicted its greatest damage. The wrong response came from Conservative home secretary Sajid Javid, who announced in 2018 that his government would crack down on 'middle-class' drug users, thereby once again criminalising sellers and buyers. The problem with these responses from politicians was that it should be possible to argue both that drug users created victims and that legalising and regulating drugs would hugely reduce the number of victims. It was also wrong to suggest that it was only the middle class using cocaine: the rich, poor, and many in-between snorted the drug. Cocaine was now more popular in Britain than anywhere else in Europe, and hospital admissions for cocaine abuse in Britain had never been higher. The Albanian mafia controlled the £5 billion annual cocaine trade, and ran much of Europe's drug industry. One Western diplomat claimed that the country had become a narco-state, the 'Colombia of Europe'.[25]

With 875,000 people between the ages of 16 and 59 taking powdered cocaine in 2017 and 2018, according to Home Office figures, Britons rarely thought about where their drugs came from. It was a damning indictment that it needed activists to remind them. A rare article about the supply chain, in the London *Telegraph*, brutally explained how 'the lives of the farmers [in Colombia] are a near-constant misery, in ways the average cocaine user in Britain couldn't fathom'. The journalist interviewed a London cocaine user, and she had no idea about any of it. 'I had never really put too much thought into how it got here, just how I can get it', she said.[26]

Despite public opinion shifting quickly in favour of drug reform, Mike Barton was still an outlier in his profession for being so public about his views. However, the former Metropolitan police chief Bernard Hogan-Howe, a long-time critic of marijuana, suggested a government review of cannabis prohibition in 2018, and said it was likely that legalisation would come. Nonetheless, Barton wasn't alone. From 2019, the National Police Chiefs' Council allowed individual chief constables to decide whether to arrest a person with cannabis, warn them, or just release them. Increasingly, the aim was to urge treatment, rather than prosecution, for young people. By 2019, police in a number of areas across the country no longer arrested and charged users with personal amounts of controlled substances, but instead directed them towards education and treatment. Vince O'Brien, the head of operations for drugs, firearms, and other commodities for the National Crime Agency, publicly admitted that the availability of illegal drugs would remain high, perhaps even rise, because demand was so strong.

I asked Arfon Jones, the Police and Crime Commissioner for North Wales Police, a man with 30 years' experience as a police officer until 2008, and an increasingly prominent voice on drug reform, why so few heads of police were more outspoken. 'Chief Constables feel uncomfortable about allowing people to break the law', he said. 'To which I say, "You should be feeling uncomfortable about the high numbers of people who are dying because of the state's inaction."' An ITV/YouGov poll in 2018 found that 75 per cent of Welsh respondents believed that the drug war had failed to reduce drug use.

Jones took an evidence-based approach to societal drug use, and knew that more than 90 per cent of people who took illegal drugs were recreational users and caused no harm to others. He wanted the criminal-justice system to target individuals who hurt other people. He supported the cannabis groups that dotted the country, and had visited the Teesside Cannabis Club that fell under the jurisdiction of the Durham police force — and said it was safe, because only marijuana was consumed (though members had to bring their own drugs). He wanted more set up across the nation.

As a result, Jones advocated selling cannabis in licensed premises, akin to alcohol, giving problematic users the ability to access
their drug of choice on prescription, and enabling recreational users
of heroin and cocaine to purchase their drugs from highly regulated
pharmacies. He told me that organised crime wouldn't suddenly dis-
appear if his vision were implemented, but the aim was to reduce the
power and reach of the black market.

~

Crispin Blunt is a conservative politician who was head of prisons and
probations at the Ministry of Justice from 2010 until 2012 in David
Cameron's government. He's one of Britain's most outspoken politicians advocating drug-law reform. He served in the army between
1979 and 1990, and entered parliament in 1997 representing Surrey.

In a remarkable speech given in 2016 to neo-liberal think-tank
the Adam Smith Institute, Blunt admitted that he had been discour-
aged during his time in government from asking critical questions
about the government's drug policy:

> It always had occurred to me that drugs misuse was obviously a
> major driver of demand in the criminal justice system. When I then
> asked the department to tell me just how much did drugs cost the
> criminal justice system, remarkably, answer came there none. In a
> ministerial discussion, I was told that it might be singularly unpolitic
> to pose this question because it might unpick the Government's
> entire drugs strategy and any suggestion that the criminalisation
> in the UK should be challenged would then begin an exercise of
> unpicking drugs law and sending the wrong message.[27]

Blunt expanded on these insights during an interview with me,
and said that he sensed at the time that the Home Office didn't seem

capable of or interested in doing any robust analysis on what the end of prohibition in Britain would look like. As result, the status quo remained. 'One of the saddest things I would see in my time as prisons minister — I visited 70 prisons — would be the queue of emaciated men queuing up to get their methadone', he said. 'With the nurse making sure that they swallowed it in front of them so they couldn't trade it in the prison.'

The Home Office acknowledged in a 2014 report that it knew prohibition was futile, and yet it would do nothing to change the law: 'We did not in our fact-finding [in Portugal] observe any obvious relationship between the toughness of a country's enforcement against drug possession and levels of drug use in that country.'

The former deputy prime minister and leader of the Liberal Democrats Nick Clegg said that there had been an 'endless wrangle' between his party and the Tories about what part of the 2014 report would be made publicly available. He said that the then prime minister Theresa May and her colleagues wouldn't budge.

'I think part of the problem is that for some of them [he named former prime minister David Cameron and chancellor George Osborne] when you say drugs to them, they think of Notting Hill dinner parties', he said. 'They think it is all a slightly naughty recreational secret. They don't think of whole countries, like Colombia, that has been brought to its knees. They don't think of some very unscrupulous criminal gangs who are preying on people who we should be protecting rather than chucking in jail.'[28]

Clegg was articulating the class nature of the drug debate. This was too rarely discussed in Britain, where certain drugs — including ecstasy, cocaine, and LSD (for middle-class people wanting to expand their minds) — were increasingly tolerated, and even accepted, in some circles, while others — such as heroin, crack, and spice — were frowned upon. This was the whispered and unofficial argument: party drugs were fun and medicinal in the 21st century, especially if the user was white, but hard drugs were hurting poor people and turned them into criminals that the state had to control.

Nonetheless, although illegal raves in London were soaring, and clubs and pubs were ill-equipped to deal with rising deaths related to ecstasy and cocaine, the government still did little to address the crisis; for them, closing down 'problematic' venues was the solution. It was a head in-the-sand policy. It took groups such as The Loop, dedicated to harm reduction, to provide pill testing at music festivals and to launch pop-up drug-testing sites in major British cities. Growing numbers of universities were also providing easy access to pill-testing kits. Even the Home Office finally agreed in 2019 to license its first drug-checking service in Somerset, where users could check their illegal substances without fear of arrest.

Blunt had described his party's position on drugs as having 'ceased to be based on the evidence'. He opposed the 2016 Psychoactive Substances Act, claiming it was 'fantastically stupid', and admitted to using alkyl nitrites, also known as poppers. 'I was astonished to find that it's proposed they be banned and, frankly, so were very many gay men', he said.

Blunt used cannabis for the first time in 2018, eating ten milligrams of THC pills and walking around San Francisco's Asian Art Museum with his partner. He didn't enjoy it. 'I didn't like it very much because everything slowed down', he told *The Strangler*. 'For a politician to feel a loss of control is rather alarming', Blunt said. 'So I don't quite get what all the fuss is about.'[29] But this experience had no impact on his belief that drugs should be widely available through a regulatory system.

I asked Blunt how he squared his views with those of the wider Conservative Party, where such public talk was incredibly rare. Blunt argued that his political party used to be more open, and he thought it could be again. 'The party I joined had the flag of freedom, the torch of freedom, as its logo', he said. 'Personal responsibility, personal freedom, and taking responsibility for those decisions is central to what I would see as the politics of the centre-right. I would certainly describe myself as a small "l" liberal conservative. Socially liberal, fiscally liberal, and protecting and enhancing the nation's institutions are central to my outlook, not least as a product of one of those institutions being the army.'

He admitted that the then prime minister, Theresa May, wasn't going to change the drug laws. She was a strong supporter of DrugFAM, set up by one of her constituents, Elizabeth Burton-Phillips, who had lost one of her identical-twin sons to heroin. May shared her views on continuing to fight the drug war, and the party struggled to tackle the issue sensibly. Drugs minister Victoria Atkins, who opposed cannabis, had a husband who managed a company, British Sugar, that grew non-psychoactive cannabis. The hypocrisy of the Conservative Party was laid bare when frontbencher Michael Gove admitted in 2019 that he'd used cocaine in the 1990s and yet his own party backed harsh penalties for that very behaviour.

However, former Tory leader William Hague disagreed, pushing for cannabis legalisation in 2018, and said that trying to stop people smoking marijuana was 'about as up to date and relevant as asking the army to recover the empire'.

Blunt said that the 2017 election, in which May barely scraped back into power, was a 'clusterfuck' because the Tories arrogantly believed that 'the electorate weren't going to be so stupid as to do anything other than give [Labour leader] Jeremy Corbyn an enormous political bath'.

Blunt claimed that his party was looking to better appeal to young people. 'It might be an idea to actually have a policy that protects them rather better from the health implications of their inevitable drug use, as they want to go to music festivals, go clubbing, and use drugs like ecstasy and the rest. If we're killing a regular number of them because they don't know what they're buying and it's criminally supplied, then I think that's an argument we ought to be able to make as to why we're going to make them safer.' Blunt was one of the British parliament's most vocal backers of medical marijuana.

Despite the country's draconian views on cannabis for its own citizens, the UN found in 2018 that Britain was the world's biggest producer of the drug for export for medical and scientific purposes. After a number of high-profile cases in 2018, when parents couldn't get access to medical marijuana for their epileptic children, the Conservative government relented and allowed doctors to prescribe the drug. This change had a profound effect on public opinion towards cannabis. In May 2018, only 43 per cent supported legalisation, according to a Populus poll; by October 2018, two-thirds of Britons backed it.

Blunt looked at the experiences of Portugal, where drug decriminalisation occurred in 2001, and favoured Britain examining going down the same route. 'Even if you get halfway in terms of decriminalisation, you don't even go the whole way in terms of ending prohibition and getting to a proper licence-regulated place', he said. 'Consumption drops, and the public-health consequences get better. This would appear to be a win-win on a rather impressive scale, and you take a half-a-trillion-dollar business out of the hands of organised crime, you put it into the legal environment, and you tax it.' Development group Health Poverty Action released a report in 2018 that advocated legalising cannabis because it would provide extra tax revenue in the billions of pounds annually to the under-funded National Health Service.

Blunt wanted a royal commission to help build an evidence-based approach to examining prohibition globally and in Britain, so that politicians wouldn't simply mouth the usual platitudes that 'drugs are bad and they are banned'. He was relentless in his commitment to the issue. In 2019, after the NHS reported a large increase in under-19s being admitted to hospital in 2018 with severe disorders caused by cannabis, he called for the legalisation of the drug to reduce the influence of criminal gangs and to regulate the potency of marijuana products on the market. King's College London released the biggest study of its kind in 2019, which found that constant pot-smoking and high-potency varieties caused increased mental-health problems, including psychosis in some users.

No politicians I spoke to mentioned the central role that London financial institutions played in laundering drug money. Europe's biggest bank, HSBC, paid a US$1.9 billion fine in 2012 after it was found to have allowed Mexican drug cartels to launder hundreds of millions of dollars. One of the world's experts in the field of drug-trafficking, Italian journalist Roberto Saviano, said that, 'Mexico is its heart, and London is its head.' Little action was ever taken politically because, Saviano argued, much of the laundered money was used for election campaigns in Britain.[30]

Blunt was part of an unofficial grouping in the British parliament that was pushing for changes in the country's drug war. Labour MP Paul Flynn was another long-time outspoken advocate, especially on the subject of cannabis. He told me that he'd never personally taken drugs, but the current laws were an 'astonishingly stupid, wasteful policy which kills people and ruins lives'.

In a 2015 column for *The Mirror* newspaper, advocating the legalisation of cannabis, Flynn wrote that a '50-year experiment in drug prohibition has been a disaster and is crumbling worldwide. In 1971, the UK had fewer than a 1,000 heroin and cocaine users. After 45 years of the harshest drugs policies in Europe we have 320,000.'[31]

Flynn, elected in 1987 to represent Newport West in Wales, urged people to 'break the law', to smoke cannabis in parliament and to see how the government reacted. He was advocating the legalisation of medical marijuana at the time, and admitted to having made a cup of cannabis tea on the House of Commons terrace years before for a woman who was a multiple sclerosis sufferer and died in 2011. Flynn despaired that his own party had 'not got a policy' on drugs that satisfied him. He didn't see much courage within Labour ranks to seriously tackle drug-policy reform, although a colleague, Labour MP David

Lammy, had criticised the failure of British politicians to address drug laws that perpetuated the status quo.[32] Flynn died in 2019.

Fellow Labour MP Thangam Debbonaire entered parliament in 2015 for Bristol West. She urged policy-makers to consider allowing the sale of ecstasy, cannabis, and other drugs over the counter in a regulated manner, and wanted far more labelling on alcoholic beverages because of its potential danger to society.

Debbonaire's thinking about drugs was partly influenced by what she saw in her own constituency. She told me that drug use was destroying the public's ability to enjoy their lives, because heroin was being injected in apartment buildings, used syringes were being left in parks, and drug takers were defecating and having sex in public. One of the main reasons she backed the trialling of drug-consumption rooms was to help people use the drugs in clinically supervised situations and get them 'off my constituents' stairwells'. 'I hate drug dealers, they put misery in my constituency', she said. 'I want to bust their business model.'

Debbonaire took a novel approach to fighting substance abuse by going after liquor companies. After she was diagnosed with breast cancer in 2015, she returned to work healthy, but in 2016 she discovered the dangerous connections between alcohol and cancer of the breast, liver, colon, rectum, oropharynx, larynx, and oesophagus. A survey by Cancer Research UK in 2018 found that only one in ten Britons knew the cancer risks of drinking alcohol, although a majority of respondents supported placing a cancer warning on the labels of alcoholic beverages.[33] Debbonaire stopped drinking after having fallen victim to cancer and wanting to reduce her risk of getting the disease again.

She saw far greater dangers in drinking than drugs, simply due to the sheer number of people who consumed the former compared with the latter (although she stressed to me how dangerous many drugs could be for society). 'The two most dangerous drugs — alcohol and tobacco — are both entirely legal,' she told *The Guardian*. She didn't want to be seen as a nanny-state ideologue, but condemned how normal drinking was in the halls of parliament. 'I'm concerned that alcohol is built into the parliamentary way of working.'[34]

Debbonaire told me that the powerful alcohol lobby, which feared their product becoming as politically toxic as tobacco, with rates of consumption dropping, opposed any moves to have labels on drinks listing calories, ingredients, suggested limits, and cancer risks. She said that they had emailed her and contacted her on social media to send research that, they said, proved alcohol didn't cause cancer. She had refused to meet their representatives.

In June 2018, Debbonaire partnered with fellow Labour MP Jeff Smith to launch the Labour Campaign for Drug Policy Reform, a grouping established to draft forward-looking Labour drug-policy. Smith was a public backer of legalising cannabis. The duo wrote that the time was long overdue to have a 'grown-up debate that focuses on how to tackle the organised-crime networks profiting from the drugs trade, how to ease the strain on our stretched public services, and how to reduce the risk to those who are suffering from addiction'.[35]

I asked Debbonaire if she had asked her Labour Party leader, Jeremy Corbyn, about his views on drug reform, and she said she 'genuinely had no idea' what he thought. She had long criticised Corbyn's leadership. The Labour leadership was overly cautious historically, if not antagonistic, on the subject of drug-law reform; the party had condemned the Liberal Democrats during the 2015 election for being 'soft on crime, drugs and thugs' and advocating that imprisonment wasn't suitable for drug users. In my view, it was a shameful position to take.

Labour under Corbyn remained unfocused on drugs, although there were more people in the party pushing for change than in the Conservatives. Shadow Home Secretary Diane Abbott said in 2018 that the drug war was a failure, but legalising cannabis for recreational use wasn't on the agenda. Instead, she backed more treatment facilities for troubled drug takers — an important step, but hardly a satisfactory one.

~

I spent an afternoon with Wayne, a homeless man outside the King's Cross station in central London. He lived with his dog, Tyson. He was 42 years old with a blond beard, puffy blue jacket, blue jeans and beanie, and black trainers. Wayne told me that most people who passed him every day didn't want to even look at him. A friend in Newcastle, the drug-reform campaigner Fiona Gilbertson, connected us because she said I should meet Wayne to understand how police abused their powers and how it could nearly destroy a man.

Wayne was insightful, and a qualified drain installer. He had been homeless for five years, the result of his marriage collapsing after his ex-wife came out as gay. He admitted assaulting her, but said he was responding to her physical abuse. There was no justification for any assault by either Wayne or his ex-wife.

He discovered an old friend dead in his home after the man had killed his wife and two children and then committed suicide. These traumatic events led him to the streets in London, Brighton, and elsewhere in Britain. 'I'm a polite, trustworthy, and honest person who loves his dog', Wayne said.

He said that today he feared being inside, unsure how he'd cope with living in a house again under a roof. He had two children: an eight-year-old daughter whom he hadn't seen in years because his mother looked after her and they didn't get along, and an 18-year-old boy whom he saw a few times a year and with whom he had a decent relationship.

He had been offered some long-term accommodation during the harsh winter; but, apart from a few days when he was able to stay in a hotel, paid for by the Dogs on the Streets charity, he preferred to sleep in a car he had got the year before we met. He slept in it nightly, parked in King's Cross, even though it was unregistered and covered daily in tickets that he'd never be able to pay. He feared it would be towed away.

The car provided at least a modicum of protection during the cold nights. In the depths of winters, though, Wayne said that the condensation dropped from the roof of the car onto his sleeping bag, often leaving it wet and impossible to dry. When it was cold, a number of local cafés would offer him free tea, and strangers sometimes gave him McDonald's vouchers for food or coffee. Some even bought him a coffee.

He bought two grams of the synthetic cannabinoid spice every day. He found the money from begging. The drug cost around £5 for one gram, and his dealer was in Camden. Wayne smoked to ease his boredom, to pass the time, to feel a buzz, and to cope with his tough life. He was introduced to the drug when it was legal, before the 2016 Psychoactive Substances Act, but he soon realised he couldn't stop.

He said everybody on the streets that he knew was on a substance: spice, marijuana, alcohol, or heroin. It was the only way, he said, that he could cope with life. When I asked why drugs were ubiquitous, he responded: 'Try sitting in a yard from seven in the morning to nine in the evening. If you sat in one spot, not moving, just to go the toilet, and then come back with that question.'

'It's my comfort', he said. 'It's my escape. It takes away any boredom, any shit feeling. Like weed does, or a pint of beer. You get stressed out, you go for a pint and chill out. When I get bored and pissed off being stuck here, I'll have a [spice] joint, and I'm alright.' He rolled and smoked a spice joint during some of our conversation, and remained lucid.

Wayne was battling a drug charge that he said had resulted from a set-up by the police, who were looking to meet their monthly arrest target. There was a real chance that he'd be sent to jail — a futile act for a man who had nothing left to lose. He said that he would smoke spice in prison to tackle the tedium. The Prisons and Probation Ombudsman said that synthetic drugs in prison were 'completely out of control'. He was scared of being jailed, surrounded by four walls every day and night, and predicted that his mental health would deteriorate. Wayne hated the hypocrisy of police and judges abusing alcohol, drinking excessively, or drinking and driving, and yet arresting homeless people for alcohol abuse.

Spice looked like marijuana, but he said it was ten times stronger. (Research suggests that it's up to 100 times stronger.) When he started smoking it a few years before, after using cannabis from the age of 11, he sometimes smoked too much, which risked him overdosing. He rarely drank alcohol. He was asked multiple times daily by passers-by if he had drug-dealer phone numbers. 'They think just because you're homeless, you're on heroin or crack', he said.

He carried his life around with him. His large backpack contained some food, a change of clothes, a sleeping bag, dog food, and a dog bowl. His life mostly involved watching people outside King's Cross station, and he said that he noticed most people walking past looked miserable. He thought he seemed more content with his life, even though he had nothing and everybody else had so much more.

'London, you're miserable bastards', Wayne told me. 'Fucking hell. You work in London, you're earning good money, the majority of jobs, yeah? Fucking cheer up. You're doing better than most. I sit there smiling, looking at the miserable, rich people walking past, who've supposedly got everything that people ever wanted. I've got nothing, and I'm happier than them.'

Wayne appreciated the few people who stopped to talk to him despite the stigma attached to homeless people. In 2017, at least 440 homeless people died across Britain, according to the Bureau of Investigative Journalism. Government figures indicated that more than 4,751 people slept rough every night that year, a number that many charities claimed was a gross underestimate (although even this conservative figure had doubled since 2010). The charity Lifeshare said that 95 per cent of homeless people in Manchester used spice.

'I never chose this life, I never chose to become homeless', Wayne said. 'I know 80 per cent of the others out here didn't choose to become homeless. Don't judge a book by its cover. You've got to read it first to understand. That's what I like about some of the people that stop and actually talk to me and ask me. Because any real true people, they want to know.'

He explained to me the difference between different kinds of people on the streets. Anybody who carried a large backpack with them was likely to be legitimately homeless. Wayne said that the homeless people around King's Cross were predominantly men. The ones who sat around asking for money with just a sleeping bag could be trying to get money for heroin, and they'd go back to a hostel to use it.

Wayne said that very few people survived on the streets beyond the age of 45. The conditions were brutal, particularly in winter, and he told me that he couldn't imagine being outside for another winter. He hoped to get a job driving long distances. If he stopped smoking spice, he said he could get this kind of work.

I spent five hours with Wayne. We talked about life, drugs, relationships, the tabloid media, Britain, and his best friend, his dog, Tyson. Wayne was articulate, but in a dangerous cycle that was worsened by drug taking. Speaking to him also brought a silent acknowledgement from me; I wasn't going to judge him for smoking spice or for how he lived his life. Begging for money to spend on spice made sense if I put myself in his shoes. He wanted an escape from the grim reality of his life, and spice provided that. Spice wasn't a solution, but it gave him comfort.

~

Britain was facing a drug epidemic of epic proportions. Even Rupert Murdoch's *Sun* newspaper, a publication with a history of demonising drug takers, seemed shocked in 2018 when new figures revealed that Britain had 'more drug deaths per head than any other country in Europe'. The number was, on average, four times more than other European nations such as Spain, Italy, France, and Germany. The Office for National Statistics found that legal and illegal drugs killed 3,756 people in England and Wales in 2017 — the highest number since records began in 1993.

The *Sun*'s editorial encouraged 'change' because 'it is clear that our current laws and programmes are not working ... It may even be worth a look at experimenting with decriminalisation.'[36] The paper had already paved the way for this stance in 2014 when it released the result of a reader poll that found seven out of ten respondents believed the drug war would never be won. 'That means we can't just carry on with the status quo', it wrote.[37]

Despite these startling mortality results, the conservative government was uninterested in taking action. It was left to activists, drug-support networks, and former users to help those whom official society wanted to ignore.[38] I met a range of such individuals across Britain, and they all told me how the system was deliberately failing people with drug problems and those caught in a cycle of drugs, poverty, and dependency.

Demonising the vulnerable was an effective silencing tool, said Fiona Gilbertson, co-founder of Recovering Justice, a group dedicated to removing the stigma around drug use, because 'it worked. It crushes poor people. It criminalises them. It puts them in prison. It shames them. It gets them to self-regulate communities, and it's destroying communities.'

Spending time with Gilbertson in Newcastle — she used to take heroin herself, and has become an active and connected member of the movement to change Britain's drug laws — showed me what was possible with few resources and boundless energy. Born in Edinburgh, Gilbertson told me that she 'wanted to be dead before I was 21 ... I had a thing for Sid Vicious.' She was attracted to heroin by the age of 17, and felt it was 'like meeting God'. She saw violence committed by police and gangs. She contracted HIV from a dirty needle when using heroin, but thankfully received treatment. 'I'd been brought up by people who didn't know how to create resilient adults', Gilbertson said.

Now 48 years old and drug-free for many years, she had created an organisation in the deprived north-east of Britain to help former users. Gilbertson likened Westminster's war on the region to the country's colonial heritage: a nation that used to invade and occupy other states, impose rules on them, and silence them had turned inwards. 'When we could no longer export it to the rest of the world, we brought it back here', she explained.

Recovering Justice had built a bridge between the recovery movement and drug-policy reform. Gilbertson worked to divert people from the criminal-justice system to healthy outcomes. 'We thought it was going to be difficult to sell to people in recovery — that we should legalise and regulate all drugs — and it hasn't been', she said. 'When you talk to most people that have had problematic substance use, they know that 90 per cent of people that use drugs won't use problematically, but they get that because they're the 10 per cent that have ended up in the criminal-justice system.'

Gilbertson was particularly active in Glasgow, Scotland, where an HIV outbreak had emerged since 2016, the worst in the United Kingdom since the 1980s. Despite this, the Home Office refused to allow a safe injecting centre. Glasgow Central MP Alison Thewliss condemned it as 'despicable to put party-political dogma ahead of people's lives ... Glasgow already has drug-consumption rooms — they're in back lanes in the city centre, they're in abandoned waste ground, in dangerous, derelict buildings, and in bushes and boardings near to my constituency office.'[39]

Gilbertson said that authorities knew that homelessness was a major driver of drug use, and yet appropriate resources weren't being spent on adequately reducing the problem. 'When we talk about the unintended consequences of the war on drugs, I think we need to stop doing that', she said. 'This is intended. Fundamentally intended. And Theresa May knows it. All of the Tories know it. It's a policy that is killing poor people.'

This grim reality requires on-the-ground assistance. Release is Britain's only charity that provides a free legal and drugs-advice service. Founded in 1967, its head, Niamh Eastwood, told me that the organisation saw around 1,200 clients per year. The majority were male from the age of 30 upwards. The helpline operated for 20 hours per week, took around 5,000 calls per year, and was principally for people who had charges of low-level possession with intent to supply drugs. 'The guys who are higher up the food chain don't need a free legal helpline', she said. Release provided drugs-expert witnesses to help individuals fighting cases in court.

Release was critical of the transformation, which had started under a Labour government 15 years before, to privatise drug-treatment services and harm-reduction options. The result had been devastating for countless Britons who needed adequate support. A 2017 report by the Care Quality Commission, the independent regulator of social care and health in Britain, found that the vast majority of detoxification facilities it had visited failed in at least one aspect of care. This was due to the Conservative government cutting tens of millions of pounds from drug and alcohol assistance in the last years. This meant that whichever provider offered the cheapest option was likely to get the contract.

Release advocated for the decriminalisation of drug-possession offences. Legalisation of all drugs could come later. Eastwood didn't want a legal cannabis market that just 'benefited rich, white men while taking away, albeit an illicit income, from poor communities. That's not an answer.'

Perhaps the most influential drug-reform campaigner in the country is Danny Kushlick, director of Transform, founded in 1996 to push for a global, regulated drug market. He has worked with senior politicians, journalists, and editors for decades to steer the debate away from prohibition. During my research in Britain his name came up again and again, talking about the need to change drug laws.

Like so many other experts in the field, Kushlick feared the crass commercialisation of drugs, and talked about regulation, not legalisation. He wanted the government to be deeply involved in the process, to ensure that corporations didn't make a financial killing from the process. The state had to stop 'the worst tendencies of capital to exploit consumers', he said.

'Legalising drugs is not radical', Kushlick told me. 'Prohibition is incredibly radical.' He believed that the only way for the world to treat drugs seriously and responsibly was to 'switch to the idea that the normative position is that we regulate adult risk-taking behaviours'.

~

One-quarter of London residents who took the Global Drug Survey (GDS) in 2018 — the world's biggest survey of recreational drug takers, with 130,000 people responding to questions across more than 40 countries — said that it was quicker to get cocaine delivered than pizza. Nearly 37 per cent in Glasgow said so; 30 per cent globally answered in the affirmative.

'It compounds the addictive potential of a drug like coke,' said the survey founder and consultant addiction psychiatrist, Dr Adam Winstock, to *Vice*. 'Good-quality drugs delivered to a place of your convenience in record time is a bad combination if you're looking to control drug use.'[40] One of the questions on the 2019 GDS was whether users would pay more for cocaine produced under fair-trade and ethically sourced standards. Over 70 per cent of participants who had recently used cocaine said that they wanted a safe and regulated market to help local producers. Eighty-five per cent said they were willing to pay around 25 per cent more for this type of cocaine. Some drug dealers in Birmingham were already keeping in touch with their buyer's ethical concerns by offering re-usable plastic vials for cocaine.

The Global Drug Survey was started in 2012. From that year, alcohol has remained the number-one consumed drug, the one most likely to send people to hospital, and yet the majority of respondents have no idea of their country's drinking guidelines. By 2018, little had changed in the survey's results on this issue, although many said that labels on alcoholic beverages would make them consider drinking less and inform them of the links between cancer and alcohol.

Winstock said that he started the survey because he wanted to understand 'happy and functional' drug users, the majority of people who took substances. Vast parts of the world were absent from the study — including China, India, much of Africa, and Russia — and Winstock was working to address this.

'No one pays any attention to them until they [drug users] mess up', he told me. Winstock aimed to create a reliable sample of global drug use that could be used to spot trends. For example, if the quality of MDMA/ecstasy tablets was poor, there was a market waiting to try something more effective, often available through online drug stores, all free of government funding or oversight.

Winstock came from a position of accepting that drug use would remain ubiquitous, so how could society and the GDS help make it as safe as possible? One of Winstock's first revelations — something that should be considered if and when Britain legalises cannabis — was that marijuana was a gateway drug to tobacco. The majority of people mixed the two drugs. 'It's the great hidden public-health harm', he said.

Winstock supported the government-led initiatives in Australia and Britain to reduce smoking rates, but worried that the US had regulated cannabis without providing any national guidelines or details about harm reduction, cannabis withdrawal, or dependence. 'I just worry the cannabis industry will become evil like the alcohol industry, and that was the government's fault. They had an opportunity to regulate it differently, and they didn't.' He blamed the cannabis lobby for not honestly addressing related problems, such as the use of cannabis by young people having detrimental effects; instead, the lobby merely praised the health benefits of the drug.

In the 2017 GDS, 10 per cent of British cannabis takers revealed that they smoked a joint within an hour of waking up, and 31 per cent of them said that they wanted to use it less. The vast majority said the government should introduce guidelines for safe consumption, similar to alcohol, though most respondents didn't know what these safe levels were, and most alcoholic beverages currently provided too little useful information for them. Sadly, the British government has given no indication of doing so for marijuana before the drug is legal, but it has a unique opportunity, on the cusp of a legal and regulated market, to implement these sensible ideas.

According to the 2018 GDS, Britons were the highest users of online drug stores in the English-speaking world — 25 per cent of people accessed them via the dark web —purchasing ecstasy, cannabis, LSD, and novel drugs. Forty-eight per cent of English respondents had used ecstasy in the previous 12 months (compared to 28.5 per cent globally), and 43 per cent had used cocaine (compared to 17 per cent globally). Cocaine is now widely available in Britain, with Uber cars being used by street distributors. High-level dealers can even contact a call centre in Belgium, France, the Balkans, and Spain with an encrypted number, and large amounts of cocaine will be quickly dispatched by courier to them.[41]

The country was awash with synthetic cannabinoids, and Winstock said he worked in prisons and saw the rapid uptake of spice because it often didn't show up in urine tests. 'You've got a captive, deprived, vulnerable audience who become dependent on the drug really quickly', he said, worsened by the British government making it illegal in 2016.

Winstock's experiences with a range of unregulated drugs, from LSD to psilocybin mushrooms, convinced him that there was a need for the public and governments to discuss how much to take safely. I asked if he believed in a legal and regulated drug market, and he was cautious. 'For the potential benefits of a legalised drug market, you need to have an adult population and an adult government that is happy to have honest conversations that accept that there are risks', he said. 'The UK does not have honest conversations with its population, and neither do the Australian or US governments.' He wanted governments to have open discussions with their populations about how prohibition had failed and how a pilot program could be introduced to test a regulated market.

Winstock wasn't a utopian believer in a legal drug regime, and I shared his caution. He worried about the effects on the poor, who suffered the most from the drug war, and could in the future. It was a lesson for Britain and any other nation that believed flicking a switch from 'illegal' to 'legal' solved all the problems. 'Unfortunately with transgenerational marginalised, vulnerable populations in Australia, the UK, and America increasing, that functional underclass aren't going be liberated by non-criminalised drugs', Winstock argued. 'They'll still be left unemployed and forgotten. For those people, you need to reduce inequality. You need to invest in early-childhood programs. You need to secure housing. That's the thing that would make the difference.'

~

Reporting across Britain revealed a sad reality about the country's attitudes to drugs. It was a similar feeling I experienced in Australia. Drug use and harm was soaring, but neither country wanted to lead on drug reform. There was inertia, ignorance, and little desire to spend political capital on a problem that seemed too hard and unwieldy to manage. Those most affected by illicit drugs were seen as bringing the problem on themselves. Britain wasn't a leader — it was a follower of Washington — and the result was a deadly carelessness towards the most vulnerable people in society, who were literally dying because the authorities didn't have an effective policy to stop the carnage. Change will come to Britain — legalising or decriminalising cannabis will be the first step — but the voices of those most affected by prohibition must have a central role in whatever comes next.

CHAPTER SIX

Australia

'[Former Federal Health Minister Christopher Pyne said
that] Dr Caldicott is the latest in a long line of health
professionals who pedal the dangerous myth that drugs
policy is about health and not morality and law enforcement.
I put that on a damn T-shirt. On a gravestone. Damn straight
that's where I'm coming from.'

DR DAVID CALDICOTT, EMERGENCY DOCTOR IN CANBERRA[1]

'I grew up in an alcoholic, very dysfunctional, very abusive family',
Kym told me. 'Once I found heroin, I left alcohol alone. I still leave it
alone. I don't like it.'

Kym (not his real name) was a fit man, 62 years old, wearing a
red shirt. He had tattoos on both his arms, though he said there were
many more that I couldn't see. He was highly articulate, passionate,
and political. He took heroin, but didn't fit the stereotype, with no
obvious signs that he used regularly. He didn't look his age.

I met Kym at Sydney's medically supervised injecting centre in
Kings Cross, Australia's first such facility. Having opened in 2001, it
was run by the Uniting Church, and until recently was the only safe
injecting space in the southern hemisphere. It was also the first of
its kind in the English-speaking world. The second one in Australia
opened in Melbourne in 2018 after years of campaigning by activists.

I was granted exclusive access by the church in Sydney to meet and interview users of the centre, the first time a journalist had ever been officially allowed to do so.[2] Both users and the church were rightly wary of journalists who demonised drug takers and the Kings Cross premises.

Kym had grown up in institutions and jail. 'I had nothing but a criminal mentality from the ages of 14 to 23', he said. He was jailed for ten years in 1972 for manslaughter after being involved in a drunken fight. Fighting over a girl, he had killed his best friend with a knife. Both boys were in gangs, and alcohol fuelled their rage. Kym was first sent to a juvenile institution because of his young age. When his parents visited, they didn't believe what he told them about the troubles he was experiencing inside. His father was a Korean War veteran, 'anti-communist, anti-left, anti-anything that isn't right of [Donald] Trump', and the result was a complete severing of his relationship with them. 'I've been on my own since I was 14 years of age', Kym said.

He had never touched heroin before the late 1970s while in prison, and even then only tried it a few times. He told me that the only drug that featured in his life in the 1960s was alcohol, and he had his first alcoholic drink at eight years of age, given to him by his drunk mother. He immediately liked heroin. 'It put me to sleep virtually straightaway at night. That was early use, of course. I just primarily liked the way it made me feel.'

After being released from jail in 1982, Kym worked at a pork tannery, and started using heroin a few years later. His friends were the former convicts that he'd met in prison. He admitted to me that he was a 'criminal' by then, and started dealing heroin to acquaintances in inner Sydney. For him, there was only one drug, then and now: heroin. 'I'm an opiate addict — I don't use anything else', he said. 'I don't like cocaine. I detest this bloody [methamphetamine] ice shit they've got coming around now.'

A few years after being released from prison, Kym was arrested by the police and charged with supplying an illicit substance. He escaped jail time and received a two-year suspended sentence. It had no effect on his drug dealing and using — often multiple times a day — if he could get the drug. He knew nothing about HIV or hepatitis when sharing needles, but eventually contracted a blood disease. He's now cured after taking medication.

When we met, Kym was living with a regular heroin habit, a way of life to which he knew no alternative. 'I don't know any better, for lack of a better phrase', he told me. 'In the beginning, it's quite nice. You can withstand it all the time. The next time, I knew you were just maintaining a habit to stop yourself going into withdrawal. And then it becomes a way of life. Nowadays, I probably only use once or twice a day.'

Kym stopped dealing drugs full-time in the early 1990s, though he continued to occasionally sell drugs to satisfy his own habit, and had worked in various jobs ever since, including landscape gardening and teaching English as a second language. To teach, he had to obtain a university degree — even though he had never gone to high school, and had learned to read and write in jail. It was a remarkable achievement, and Kym said that he never believed it was possible for a person like him.

The safe injecting centre was a lifeline for Kym because it was non-judgemental and safe. He said that he used to shoot up heroin on the streets and alleys in Kings Cross. 'People were dying out there, and since this place has been opened there's been no deaths recorded', he said. It was true that at Kings Cross and all other injecting centres around the world, nobody had died while in them. 'This place is clean, sterile, and you're looked after. If you overdose, you're taken care of straightaway. It cleans up the streets. I personally think all the people [living] around here, while they might not agree with the whole idea of an injecting centre, like the fact that it's here. It's getting people out of their back lanes, backyards, and public toilets.'

When he used heroin, Kym visited the facility more than once daily. 'Just about everyone I know is an opiate addict or a drug addict', he told me, and they all came to Kings Cross to shoot up safely.

Kym's solution to heroin addiction — apart from providing safe spaces for injecting — was prescription heroin, a program tried successfully in Switzerland, Denmark, the Netherlands, and other European nations that both reduced government costs and saved lives.[3] Based on his experiences, Kym believed that a potential patient should prove to a doctor that they'd gone through multiple detox programs, and had used methadone and failed. 'Be a heroin or opiate addict for at least five years [before getting prescription heroin]', Kym said. 'I've got a list of ideas and rules around how it should be.' His ideas are being increasingly adopted by the experts: a prominent research group in Vancouver, Canada, urged the state in 2019 to provide pharmaceutical-grade heroin to users in a regulated way at members-only clubs, and to avoid the dangers of fentanyl abuse on the streets.

While Australia was rarely viewed globally as a leader on drug policy — it was still ruled by a prohibitionist mindset — the lives that the injecting centre had saved was testament to a more complicated narrative. On this issue, Australia was a trailblazer. However, Kym wasn't convinced (while backing the Kings Cross facility). 'We're a conservative nation', he said. 'We're still stuck with the whole stuff that came out of the United States in the 1950s.'

He made it clear that using heroin, with regular breaks during the year when he visited friends in the country to get away from the drug-using scene, was a choice because he 'liked it'. Kym had been using for 30 years, half his life. Although he didn't imagine being an 80-year-old user — 'I think I'm one of the oldest people on the street in Kings Cross' — he said that he'd 'have to make that decision [to fully stop using], and it's a decision I haven't made yet.' He had two adult children living in Melbourne with whom he had irregular contact.

Another client of the facility was Manet (not his real name), who had been sexually abused as a minor by an Anglican youth leader. He had only started regularly using heroin in his thirties (he was 50 years old) with his then-partner. After remarrying several times, becoming a successful businessman, and earning $130,000 every year and gambling, heroin was a relief and release. He said he kept his addiction hidden from his wife — this tactic was not uncommon among high-income users — and he welcomed the opening of the Kings Cross injecting centre. He recalled 'shooting galleries' in the area before it existed, businesses that illegally rented out rooms for shooting up, and it repulsed him. He had to hire female prostitutes to get him a hit.

Manet used irregularly these days, and only visited the safe injecting centre once a week or month. His current partner 'begrudgingly' accepted his heroin use. Manet volunteered at the facility, and helped with its annual art exhibition where users expressed themselves creatively. He painted himself, and showed me some of his sketches. Manet was aiming to change his career and become an artist full-time.

He believed that drug laws should be far more lenient. He opposed the hypocrisy in society's attitude to drugs, whereby smoking cigarettes and eating to excess was legal. Five members of his family had died from smoking, 'I would much prefer to give up smoking than heroin', he said.

Manet wore a white shirt and looked like a middle-aged businessman. Like Kym, there were no obvious signs that he was a user. He was articulate and confident, with a slight handshake. I wanted more people to meet these two men, so they could see that the ugly stereotype of drug users that still polluted media coverage was out of touch: it was possible to be a contributing member of society while taking illicit substances.

~

The injecting centre was situated on a busy road in Kings Cross, the heart of inner Sydney. There were no obvious markings, just a pink sign saying 'Uniting'. Christian philosophy underpinned the centre's approach to its clients, and the Uniting Church was proud of its long-standing support for those affected by drugs and alcohol. (In 2018, the church and other groups lobbied the New South Wales government to decriminalise all drugs for personal use. By 2019, prominent broadcaster Alan Jones and the New South Wales Bar Association had joined the decriminalisation bandwagon.) The centre was near the 'Bada Bing' nightclub on a street with many strip clubs. I'd walked past many times and never noticed it.

It was an open and airy facility with one unarmed security guard. The large open-plan space where clients shot up was brightly lit so staff could see everybody and help them, if required. All tools for heroin use were provided, including needles, spoons, tourniquets, and cotton buds. Clients were told to dispose of their needles in safe yellow boxes in their booth. There were useful signs helping clients to locate the safest spots on their body to inject. Other signs asked clients about their mental health. Tobacco, not heroin, was the biggest killer of visitors, so anti-smoking messages were plastered on the walls.

Every two weeks, clients could see the visiting psychiatrist, and a dental hygienist was also a regular feature. Users were encouraged to wash their hands before shooting up because it reduced bacteria. The only people excluded from entering were people under 18, pregnant women (an employee said the centre disagreed with this condition), anyone intoxicated, and first-time users. The typical client was a 50-year-old who had been using heroin for decades. The majority of visitors were male, homeless, and mentally unwell.

I didn't know what to expect before visiting. I imagined private booths where people shot up, but that was exactly the wrong perception. The centre was a warm and inviting place. It didn't aim to encourage drug taking — one of the persistent myths about the facility — but implicitly accepted that a minority of the population engaged in this activity, and aimed to help them. It was a proven harm-minimisation strategy.

The centre's priority was to provide a safe space to take drugs, though no drugs were provided on the premises; clients had to bring their own. While heroin remained illegal, it was legal inside the facility, and police supported the program and didn't arrest people on the premises. However, sometimes over-enthusiastic young police arrested users possessing heroin outside the centre.

The evidence backing the benefits of having established the injecting centre were strong. It had reduced deaths from overdoses in the area, given treatment and counselling, reduced the incidence of needles being disposed of in public places, and reduced blood-borne diseases such as HIV. It was funded by the New South Wales government from the confiscated proceeds of crime. Most locals and businesses supported the centre because they saw the benefits it brought to their community.

As far back as the late 1990s, when Kings Cross was the national epicentre of people dying from overdoses, loud public voices and a New South Wales government–backed drug summit encouraged the opening of a safe injecting centre. Before it opened, however, Reverend Ray Richmond of the Uniting Church's Wayside Chapel illegally opened a safe injecting room in the area, called the 'Tolerance Room', as a form of civil disobedience in the face of recalcitrant politicians and police. He and some users were arrested for breaking the law, but the point had been made: *Take action to address this deadly problem, or we will.* In 1999 alone, there were 677 ambulance call-outs for heroin overdoses in the area, and 10 per cent of the nation's drug-overdose deaths occurred in Kings Cross.

Although some in the tabloid media, the Vatican, and others opposed an official facility, it received state government backing. It wasn't until 2010 that the 'trial status' of the injecting centre was deemed to be over by government legalisation. The facility was now permanent.

I was taken around the premises by Miranda St Hill, the service operations manager. British-born, she told me that the injecting centre had seen 16,000 registered users since 2001 and 150–200 visits per day (though some people made multiple daily visits). An injecting centre in Vancouver, Canada, received around 800 to 1,200 people every day. She explained that clients didn't need to give their names when they arrived because the focus was on giving them an alternative to injecting on the streets.

The medical director of the facility, Dr Marianne Jauncey, said that in the early days of the centre, media coverage led by Rupert Murdoch's Sydney tabloid, *The Daily Telegraph*, was negative, mostly inaccurate, and aimed to pressure governments to close it down. For example, in 2006 the paper ran a story claiming that 'dozens of syringes' had spilled from a bin in a Kings Cross street, endangering the community. In fact, the syringes had been used on a diabetic cat called Trotsky, and its owner had momentarily left the needles unattended in the street. The needles then magically appeared in a rubbish bin outside the injecting centre, photographed by *The Daily Telegraph*. It was a set-up, revealed on ABC-TV's *Media Watch*, and yet failed to achieve its goals.[4]

Jauncey told me that public opinion had moved significantly since these tabloid scares, and most people now backed safe injecting centres. 'The ongoing argument [of opponents today] is that you're making it too nice for people, you're sending the wrong message', she said. 'Equally, if you don't get everybody drug-free, then there is no success ... Overall, there is a shift to much more supportive community attitudes towards harm-reduction services.' Across Europe over the last four decades, as legal drug-consumption rooms mushroomed across the continent, this approach had been proven to save lives.

She had worked in the drug-and-alcohol field since the late 1990s, and her views on the legalisation debate had evolved. Decades before, she believed that making illicit and dangerous drugs more available would harm the people most vulnerable to them. Today, however, she advocated removing criminal penalties for personal drug use. She didn't back the legalisation of all drugs — fearing it had never been tried anywhere in the world and could increase harm — but opposed the stigmatisation of drug users who suffered while drugs remained illegal.

~

It's easy to conclude that many Australian politicians, tabloid-media commentators, and members of police forces have taken a draconian view of drugs and the people who use them. There are too many examples to prove this point — knee-jerk and unscientific responses to the growing number of Australians who consume illicit substances on a weekly basis, and constant media stories of drugged-out citizens and drug busts.

Two individuals died of drug overdoses and two others were sent to hospital in a critical condition in September 2018 after they had attended a Sydney dance festival, Defqon.1. The premier of New South Wales, Gladys Berejiklian, pledged to close down the festival and never allow it to operate again in her state. In the wake of the tragedy, she established a government panel to advise on drug safety at music festivals; but pill testing, checking the chemical make-up of drugs at festivals for users and medics, was not part of her solution.

The need to test ecstasy tablets in Australia became urgent after a 2015 study — based on a global, ten-year analysis of 25,000 tablets — found that local MDMA pills contained some of the most lethal ingredients.[5] Experts worried that there were more types of pills available on the market than ever before, and that nobody knew what was in them.

'We do not support a culture that says it is okay to take illegal drugs,' Berejiklian said. 'Anyone who advocates pill testing is giving the green light to drugs. There is no such thing as a safe drug, and unfortunately when young people think there is, it has tragic consequences. I want to send a strong message to every young person ... You should not take drugs at these events or anywhere else, and last night's tragic consequences demonstrated this.'

At Defqon.1, 180 police conducted hundreds of searches, found large amounts of illegal drugs, and arrested many people for carrying them. Up to 700 people sought medical help at the festival. Acting assistant commissioner Allan Sicard told the public that, 'Illicit drugs are illicit. Do not take them. They are dangerous substances.' When asked about introducing pill testing, he said it would be a 'bad look for the government' and police because drugs remained illegal. Berejiklian's 'solution' to the issue was to warn drug dealers that they would face 25 years in jail if they supplied drugs that caused overdoses.

After another man died at a Sydney music festival from a drug overdose in December 2018 (with more dying at summer events in 2019), Berejiklian told young people that 'you can die if you take an illegal substance'. She again dismissed pill testing with the argument that, 'If we thought it was going to make a difference we would go down that path. We don't think it will.'

This was evidence-free politicking, and also flew in the face of public opinion, according to a 2019 Essential poll that found a majority of Australians favoured pill testing. In 2019, in an attempt to stimulate public debate and support pill testing, New South Wales Greens politician Cate Faehrmann became the first Australian politician to admit taking ecstasy. She wouldn't be the last to acknowledge consuming illicit substances. A fellow state Greens politician, David Shoebridge, publicly pushed for the legalisation of ecstasy in 2019, arguing it should be available over the counter at pharmacies to individuals over 18 years old. His party also committed to expunge the criminal convictions of individuals charged with marijuana possession. Over 40,000 people had been convicted of cannabis possession in New South Wales in the 2008–2018 decade.

At the Groovin the Moo music festival in Canberra in April 2018, pill testing was conducted legally for the first time in Australian history, with the collaboration of local police. One hundred and twenty-eight people visited the pill-testing tent, and 85 drug samples were tested. Fifty per cent turned out to be pure MDMA (ecstasy), and 50 per cent were 'other' (paint, sweetener, or lactose), of which two were deadly. Harm was reduced, some bad drugs weren't consumed, and many festival-goers praised the initiative, pushing for a country-wide roll-out after the deadly Defqon.1 debacle. The Melbourne *Age* editorialised with this very suggestion, and Britain's only pill-testing organisation, The Loop, which had rolled out similar services in the UK at 12 music festivals in 2018, said it was inevitable that Australia would eventually embrace a policy that saved lives. The Australian Medical Association came out in support of pill-testing trials, and New Zealand pledged to introduce pill testing at all music festivals by the end of 2019. Groovin the Moo conducted a second successful pill-testing pilot in 2019, and once again discovered dangerous substances in pills that were then discarded by users.

International examples prove that pill testing reduces harm. Britain's first academic study of pill testing, based on a music festival in Cambridgeshire in 2016, found that pill testing alerted users to many dangerous substances in drugs, and saved lives, compared to previous events where pill testing didn't take place.[6]

At the biennial Boom music festival in Portugal in 2018, an NGO called Kosmicare Association provided devices for the first time that allowed party-goers to test drugs for impurities, strength, and quantity. Close to 700 samples were tested, and many pills were found to contain exceptionally high levels of MDMA. As a result, alerts were posted that suggested users start with half a pill or less.[7] It was a responsible policy, which showed that organisers had acknowledged that drug taking would occur.

Australia's history with drugs mirrored the racial agenda of the US and its attempts to control minorities with drug laws. Australian authorities routinely looked for ways to discriminate against non-whites by using laws that reeked of racism. The country's first drug law was enacted in 1857 — white settlement had begun in 1788 — when an import duty was imposed on opium. Opium was demonised and taxed extensively in the years to come, but the aim was not to eradicate the drug itself; rather, it was to try to stop Chinese people arriving.

Despite these concerns by authorities, opiates became massively popular for Australians in the 19th century, and they became some of the world's biggest consumers of this class of drugs. Medicines often contained morphine or alcohol. Laudanum was a popular choice given to calm children, despite it containing opium and alcohol. Tellingly, laws against opium were only directed against it in its smoking form, to attack the Chinese, and therefore didn't affect the European, white consumers of the drug.[8]

Desmond Manderson, a professor of law at the Australian National University, writes that Australia's drug laws have never been about addiction or health. Instead, 'They have been an expression of bigotry, class and deep-rooted social fears, a function of Australia's international subservience to other powers, and a field in which politicians and bureaucrats have sought power.'[9]

By the early 20th century, racial anxiety was arguably the key driver of drug laws in Australia, the US, and many other equivalent Western nations. Opium was framed as the devil's drug, and white officials were determined to target the poorly assimilated Chinese population. Like US authorities at the time, who attacked Hispanics and blacks because they smoked marijuana, the fear of white women in Australia being seduced by Chinese men was the stated driver of anti-opium laws. The *Bulletin* magazine published this in 1886:

> One of the girls now kept in a den on the Rocks, says … 'I went to … place when I was only about 16 because he used to give me presents. He then wanted me to smoke, but I never would, because the pipes looked so dirty. But one day he put a new pipe before me, and made it ready, and after the first whiff from it, he or any other man … I was completely at their mercy, but so help me God I was a good girl before that.'[10]

Manderson compares officialdom's view of smoking opium, as a drug that took control of white women and forced them to act against their will, as akin to the attitude to witchcraft in an earlier era. In both cases, 'possession' was central to the fear that unacceptable social behaviour was the fault of the drug, or the devil, and that invisible demons were to blame. In the modern version of this twisted theory, harmony would be restored if the drug were removed from society.

This is still the position of many in the prohibitionist movement. Drug laws in Australia and globally, both at the beginning of the 20th century and today, have been at least partly about providing a scapegoat to relieve societal anxiety about the sexuality and morality of minority groups.[11] It was once explicitly stated that drugs laws were designed to suppress or control ethnic minorities, and that the Chinese in Australia were the first targets.[12] Now it's futile for governments, police, and many in the media to warn of the harsh consequences of importing, using, or dealing drugs, given how little effect this has on the ever-widening consumption of drugs in a population of over 25 million people.

'The function of illegality is not to stamp drugs out, but to make it more public, more dramatic, more theatrical', Manderson explains. 'Zero tolerance is a faith and not a policy, a faith at the heart of which lies the importance of social rules, obedience, and respect for the distinctions between right and wrong ... Behind that faith lies fear: fear of the consequences of a loss of certainty, fear of a weakened legal capacity, and fear of a "permissive" world in which such bright lines can no longer be drawn.'[13]

The 20th century saw a radically shrinking space in Australia for what were once widely available substances, when social hysteria around drugs was whipped up across the globe. Cannabis had been sent to Australia on the First Fleet, which arrived in 1788, in the hope that hemp would be grown commercially in the new colony, and it was smoked casually in cigarettes until the 1920s.

However, its use was banned in various states from the late 1920s as Australia followed international (US-led) campaigns to demonise the drug. The now defunct *Smith's Weekly* newspaper, viewed as patriotic in its day from 1919 to 1950, ran *Reefer Madness*–style stories in the late 1930s to expose the 'evil sex drug that causes its victims to behave like raving sex maniacs'.

Heroin was finally banned in Australia in 1953 after global pressure, despite it being widely used as a painkiller and in cough mixtures. Until its prohibition, Australia was the world's biggest per capita user of the drug, as it was legally available on prescription.

Meanwhile, alcohol, prohibited in the US from 1918 to 1933, never faced the same antiquated attitudes in Australia, and many advocates defended it as a necessary part of prolonging the white race. British settlers brought opium, tobacco, and alcohol in vast quantities, and substance abuse remains a major problem to this day amongst the majority white and small indigenous populations. The political power of the alcohol lobby in the 21st century has successfully headed off legislated impediments to its ability to market its products, despite it being far more dangerous than all illicit drugs combined.

After World War II, Australia moved into the US orbit and was less influenced by Britain. While Canberra never followed Washington's obsessive pursuit of the drug-trade, anti-drug paranoia was coupled in the public imagination with the fight against communism. This message emanated from the US; fighting drugs was vital to avoid 'communist heroin traffickers' and infiltration from the Red menace.[14] Ironically, mainstream drug use in Australia didn't occur until the 1960s, but fear of this happening had been successfully inculcated from the 1950s.

The 1960s was a transformative age for drug use and prohibition, and Australia is still living in its shadow. In the face of the Vietnam War and profound social change, more people started smoking marijuana and taking LSD and heroin, but authorities reacted with horror and brutality, not compassion. The modern 'war on drugs' in Australia was born at this moment. This included high-profile police raids on youth smoking cannabis, and breaking up hippie parties where illicit substances were being consumed. There was an increasingly synchronised message from successive governments and the media that drug users were morally deficient and had to be punished.

'We do believe in penal populism [in Australia]', CEO of the Noffs Foundation, Matt Noffs, told me. His organisation is the country's largest youth drug-and-alcohol treatment service. 'Australia loves punishing people. Perhaps that stems from being convicts and being a convict culture. And, at the same time, we also love the antihero, the [outlawed bushranger] Ned Kellys, because we come from a criminal past.'

Noffs cited the conservative Liberal Party's obsession in 2018 with drug-testing welfare recipients — despite there being no evidence that this would motivate people to find work, and in the face of opposition from experts in the field — as a modern example of vilifying somebody for the ills of society. The plan was likely to worsen drug addiction and push people into criminality to support their drug habits. If this happened, it would allow supporters of the 'war on drugs' to justify harsh punishment. The unhealthy cycle of blame was never-ending.

While Australia never developed the mass-incarceration culture experienced by the US — except for indigenous Australians who are imprisoned in some states at rates akin to those in apartheid South Africa — criminal convictions for minor drug offences became ubiquitous, negatively affecting a person's job prospects and life. Whereas once Australia aimed to regulate and control drugs that were used principally for medicinal purposes, harsh penalties for their use, possession, and supply were introduced in the modern era.

The failure of the federal government in Canberra to reform its drug laws forced the states to act independently. South Australia decriminalised the personal use of marijuana in 1987, and users received a small fine for possessing less than 25 grams. However, in 2018, a newly elected conservative government pledged to fight a renewed 'war on drugs', and to hugely increase financial penalties, introduce jail time for cannabis possession, and send sniffer dogs into public schools to search for drugs. Under pressure, the government relented on prison terms but increased fines. Many other states still viewed the use and possession of marijuana as a criminal offence, but convictions for possessing small amounts for personal use rarely resulted in time behind bars. Instead, the response was mandatory treatment and diversion programs.

A national drug strategy was introduced by states and the federal government in 1985 to incorporate harm-minimisation tactics (although border control and policing receive the majority of funds to this day). 'It was a serendipitous moment of public policy-making',

John Ryan, head of the non-profit Penington Institute, told me. The prime minister at the time, Bob Hawke, had a daughter who was addicted to heroin, and his health minister, Dr Neil Blewett, feared that HIV transmissions in the gay population would spread to the heterosexual community. It was a common concern of the day.

Nevertheless, the political speeches in parliament from that period showed a contempt for drug users, according to Ryan, who was also head of Harm Reduction International. There was a 'moral repugnance around injecting drug use and the higher goal of protecting the broader community'.

'I think we haven't actually progressed [politically] since about the mid-1980s', he lamented. 'We have not yet come to understand that people who use drugs are normal and that they should be treated like normal people. We still generally criminalise them, and marginalise them, and then we all suffer the consequences, but they suffer most acutely.'

One of the most successful ideas was a needle-and-syringe program from 1988 that helped reduce the spread of HIV and hepatitis C among drug users. Between 2000 and 2009, according to government figures, clean needles prevented 32,050 HIV infections and 96,667 hepatitis C infections. Accidental drug overdoses continued to surge, however, which led to a 1997 royal commission and Justice Wood's recommendation to create an injecting centre. The Kings Cross facility opened its doors in 2001.

One of the key advocates for the needle program and injecting centre was Dr Alex Wodak, a former director of the Alcohol and Drug Service at St Vincent's Hospital in Sydney and president of the Australian Drug Law Reform Foundation. He recounted the thinking behind Australia's approach in trying to save lives by contrasting it with 'identifying and quarantining' people, which had been undertaken by other nations (Cuba excluded its entire HIV population in the late 1980 and early 1990s in specialised sanatoriums). Instead, the Labor federal government worked with the affected communities to devise a strategy. 'The inclusive approach would work, and the exclusive approach would be a disaster, though politically attractive', Wodak told me.

The Australian Capital Territory (ACT) bravely attempted a heroin-prescription program in 1997. It was modelled on the successful Swiss model, which had been introduced in 1994 and resulted in marked reductions in overdoses. But it was scuttled before it began by a furious conservative prime minister John Howard, helped by media mogul Rupert Murdoch and his Sydney tabloid, *The Daily Telegraph*, which campaigned vociferously against it. 'Drug pushers in suits' was one headline targeting the ministers who backed the program. Even the US ambassador pressured the ACT to drop the idea.[15]

One of the key backers of the trial, former ACT politician and president of the World Federation of Public Health Associations, Michael Moore, never gave up his campaign, and today advocates for a safe injecting centre in Canberra. The ACT continued to push, or at least argue, for serious drug reform more seriously than any other territory or state in Australia. In October 2018, at an annual memorial to remember more than 250 victims of drug misuse, the attorney-general, Gordon Ramsay, said that 'an exclusively prohibitionist policy does not work and will not work'. Instead, 'the evidence is overwhelming that treating addiction as an issue of right and wrong not only is ineffective; it simply does not stack up to what we know about the biology and psychology of drug use.'[16]

One of Australia's leading advocates for drug reform, Dr David Caldicott, moved to the country from Britain in 1999. He told me that at the time he was struck by the 'Nancy Reagan "Just say no" and very primitive American-style policy' that was being pursued by the Howard government. He despaired at the infantile level of public debate, damning the federal Liberal health minister, Christopher Pyne, in 2007 when he claimed that his government was winning the drug war by strongly opposing pill testing and safe injecting rooms. Caldicott blamed 'wowsers playing to fringe electoral groups for cheap votes'.[17]

Despite, or perhaps because of, the various scare campaigns against all illicit drugs, teenagers were increasingly using less alcohol, tobacco, and other drugs.[18] Results from the 2017 Australian Institute of Health and Welfare's National Drug Strategy Household Survey found that young people were trying drugs at a later age, but that Australians aged between 35 and 55 were consuming more drugs than ever before.[19] Australians bought narcotics using the dark web and online marketplaces, at a rate that was only second per capita to the Netherlands.[20] Increasingly, this was how Australians were purchasing their illicit drugs, without having to worry about a drug dealer in a dark alley or nightclub. It made purchasing illegal drugs a seemingly clean endeavour, although law-enforcement officials didn't agree. In 2019, police arrested and charged three individuals for engaging in what they claimed was the biggest dark-web business in Australia, selling more than $17 million of ecstasy and LSD.

The use of ice (a crystal form of methamphetamine) had increased, posing a challenge for hospitals, ambulances, and mental-health workers due to its devastating effects. Australia had some of the highest per capita users of ice in the world. The highly addictive opioids fentanyl and oxycodone were being taken at record rates, especially in rural areas. That was why there were growing calls to make the drug naloxone more widely available, like in the US, as it was the drug that saved people in the grip of an overdose.

Shockingly, unintentional overdoses — caused by a combination of painkillers, alcohol, heroin, and other illicit substances — were killing 142 people every month, according to a report by the Penington Institute in 2018. It was an indictment on one of the richest nations on earth that such deaths were surging in frequency and didn't cause public outrage. I feared it was because the media and politicians had spent decades demonising drug users, so that public sympathy was lacking.

The Global Drug Survey, released in 2018 with 130,000 anonymous respondents from over 40 countries participating, found that Australia had the highest per capita number of emergency-department visits for LSD, and the second-highest for methamphetamine and MDMA/ecstasy. The Australian Drug Trends Report found in 2018 that people were taking more cocaine than ever recorded, and purer forms of ecstasy. Drug use was common, widely accepted, and uncontroversial for vast swathes of the population. The political class hadn't yet caught up, and still subscribed to the narratives from the 1950s. The huge Australian interest in cocaine led to an explosion of cocaine smuggling routes through vulnerable Pacific nations. Cocaine and meth were being trafficked from Latin America.

The Reserve Bank of Australia released a report in late 2018 that found Australians spent US$9.7 billion on illegal drugs in the year through August 2017. Methamphetamine and cannabis were the biggest sellers. The bank suggested that nearly 2 per cent of its banknotes were used for drug deals; the $50 bill was the most popular note.[21]

In 2019, the Australian Criminal Intelligence Commission released a report into wastewater treatment plants, and found that Australians consumed $9.3 billion of illegal drugs in 2018. Cocaine was twice as popular in Sydney than Melbourne, while 80 per cent of drugs consumed were methamphetamines. The scale of drug use was massive. The Melbourne *Age* began a story about the findings in a stark way: 'Australians are spending almost as much on illicit drugs every year as they do on brunch and coffee at cafes.'[22]

Australia has rarely been a global leader in drug policy, although needle exchanges from the 1980s was a notable case of sense trumping fear. It was far ahead of the US, where a federal ban on providing federal funds for clean syringes was introduced in 1988 and continued through into the Obama administration. Politicians only infrequently led the call for sensible drug laws, so it was left to the public to demand it.

According to surveys, a majority of Australians supported the decriminalisation of marijuana. Medical marijuana became legal in 2016, and the Greens released a policy in 2018 that backed the full legalisation and regulation of cannabis. The Australian Medical Association opposed the idea, because it believed that the drug negatively affected people's mental and physical health.

One in ten Australians had used cannabis in the previous 12 months, according to a report issued in 2018 by the Australian Institute of Health and Welfare. In announcing his party's policy, Greens leader Richard Di Natale argued that, 'Nearly seven million Australians choose to use cannabis. That choice can land them with a criminal conviction, which can impact their opportunity to get a job. They're sourcing products of unknown quality and purity, and of course all they're doing is feeding the mega profits of criminal syndicates and criminal gangs.' The Melbourne *Age* applauded this 'toughest and most enlightened policy on drugs and crime because it would obliterate a black market, reduce harm and fund prevention education.'[23]

The federal health minister, Greg Hunt, from the conservative Liberal Party, said that the Greens' plan was 'risking the health of Australians', and he believed that cannabis was a gateway drug to other drugs such as methamphetamines. Legalisation would not happen under his watch. Prime Minister Scott Morrison has also opposed legalising cannabis for personal use, as has the opposition Labor Party, though some of its own politicians have bucked the trend and pushed for legalisation.[24] The former federal Labor leader, Bill Shorten, condemned the Greens' policy on the basis of no evidence, and falsely alleged that the Greens wanted to legalise ecstasy. (In fact, the party aimed to decriminalise most drugs.) Any cheap insult would do against those pushing for a more sensible drug policy.

It seemed inevitable that cannabis would become legal in Australia, but the country wasn't interested in leading global moves to arrive at that position. It was a familiar stance, taken by Australian political elites for decades: pick and choose the most effective tools of control from the US 'war on drugs' without adopting its most egregious methods of mass incarceration and police violence. Nonetheless, Australia was slowly edging towards a US-style system, whereby people wait in prisons for over 12 months until being sentenced for drug crimes and other offences, while receiving no drug-treatment during this period. Crimes rates were falling, and yet prison populations soared.[25]

Australia lagged behind many equivalent Western nations on drug policy, and there was little organised public pressure for change. Unlike same-sex marriage, which attracted massive support in 2017, legalising cannabis was not an issue that generated large public passion. Change was coming, albeit slowly. A coroner in New South Wales said in November 2018 that prohibition was akin to state-sanctioned racism. Deputy State Coroner Harriet Grahame argued that 'in a hundred years from now people will look back' and would be 'incredulous' about how governments treated drug users. 'It will be like the way we look back at when we didn't allow black people to vote', she said.[26] In 2019, Grahame went a step further and called on the government to hold a drug summit to examine the viability of drug decriminalisation for personal use.

'Australia will end up being shamed into modernising its drugs policy because everybody else will', emergency doctor David Caldicott said.

~

Restrictive drug laws don't stop activists, doctors, and users from pushing the limits of what the state will tolerate. Australian war veteran Mick Harding is the founder of Weeded Warrior, a group dedicated to helping former soldiers deal with PTSD. After being involved in an incident in Afghanistan in 2010 when a colleague was shot and killed, Harding began suffering from a major depressive disorder. He was medically discharged from the army in 2012, and was subsequently prescribed anti-depressants Lexapro and Avanza, and the anti-psychotic Seroquel. It made him worse, pushing him to the brink of homicidal and suicidal acts. His weight ballooned.[27]

The Department of Veterans' Affairs dismissed any interest in cannabis as a treatment for PTSD. Despite at least 84 veterans committing suicide in 2017, the government told Harding that marijuana was an unproven and illegal remedy. Even though medical marijuana became legal in Australia in 2016, the government severely restricted its availability to doctors and users.

Harding told me that he had smoked hash during downtime in Afghanistan, given to him by the Afghan army, but never regularly. On his return to Australia, he regularly abused alcohol by mixing spirits and three different psychotropic medications. 'I got to a point I couldn't afford the alcohol habit', he told me, 'so I actually started brewing my own spirits.'

Harding started smoking cannabis more regularly from 2012, and found that the drug soothed his condition. After reading about war veterans in the US who used marijuana to treat their PTSD, despite its use being illegal in many states, he visited the US to see how these former soldiers treated their symptoms. He returned to Australia and founded Weeded Warrior. Harding knew that alcohol made his condition worse, and that although weed 'didn't take things away, it took the edge off so that you could interact with people again. You'd start having some form of quality of life back again.'

Weeded Warrior arranges monthly meet-ups for veterans in Brisbane and down the east coast of Australia to discuss their experiences and how to manage them. It's not just about finding ways to smoke cannabis; Harding is a supporter of yoga, meditation, healthy food, and flotation therapy. He doesn't fear arrest or imprisonment for using and suggesting marijuana — an unlikely outcome for a white Australian male — but resents authorities telling him how to manage his pain.

'We put our lives on the line for the country so that not only the people of the country but their bloody ungrateful politicians that get to sit down in Canberra enjoy their high life and get to do what they do', Harding said. 'I think the least bit of decency that we can get is to be able to treat and manage our conditions from that service in the most effective way that we deem possible.'

He was overwhelmed with the number of messages he received weekly from veterans, their partners, and their families thanking him for offering alternatives to traditional medication. Harding is moved by the sentiments. One told him: 'Thank you so much for what you've done. You saved my partner's life. He was about to overdose. The amount of meds that he's on, his organs were shutting down, and now he's reduced that by half and he's back to functioning. He's lost ten kilos and he's a dad again.'

'To me, how is that criminal?', Harding asked. 'The real criminals are the people making us criminals for doing that.'

The lack of easily accessible cannabis means that many veterans are forced to source it on the black market. Although Weeded Warrior isn't focused on other drugs to help veterans, Harding said that he was personally interested in the ayahuasca brew and the naturally occurring psychoactive substance ibogaine, both said by supporters to help with mental-health problems. There was a growing underground movement in Australia to use psychedelic psychotherapy — based on MDMA, LSD, and psilocybin (magic mushrooms) — to help patients with such problems.

Harding's vision was a legal and regulated cannabis industry in Australia. He wanted the drug to be viewed like fruits and vegetables and taxed accordingly, so that veterans could 'cultivate cannabis, giving them purpose back and allowing them to support their mates, other veterans, as well as the broader community'.

Extending the use of drugs for medical purposes is also what motivates Dr Minh Le Cong. He works with the Royal Flying Doctor Service in Queensland, and has spent much of his professional career researching and using the anaesthetic agent ketamine to treat people with extreme depression. Although the drug is illegal for recreational use — it's used as 'Special K' by some ravers at parties for its psychological effects, and there are dangers with abuse — Cong believes that it has 'revolutionised' aeromedical retrieval. He works with desperate people in remote areas or country towns where there are no psychiatric facilities or psychiatrists, and some times has to fly a patient to bigger cities or towns that are up to two hours away.

Before the use of ketamine, Cong would use sedatives for patients, but they would often rapidly deteriorate and be rendered comatose during the transfer because of their extreme condition. He questioned these measures, and soon pioneered the administering of ketamine instead. Even light doses had a calming effect. The drug is now used widely across Australia by many aeromedical services.

Cong was a leader because there were virtually no global examples to mimic. The distances are so vast in Australia, and most psychiatric facilities are situated on the coasts; only Canada uses ketamine while transporting patients. The drug was discovered in 1962, and was first used as a battlefield anaesthetic during the Vietnam war.

I asked Cong about the ethics of using ketamine medically — one known side effect is hallucinations, although they're short-lived and can potentially be influenced by medical practitioners — and if he had received any backlash for doing so. He told me that although it had been a novel and experimental treatment more than a decade before when he started using it, he had spoken to senior psychiatrists, who had backed the practice. They understood that if administering the drug avoided a person having to be placed into a medically induced coma, after which it would take days for them to wake up and be treated in a hospital, ketamine was ethically justifiable — the psychiatrist could get to work soon after the plane and patient arrived. It was also justified because keeping the aircraft safe for operation was a priority, and wildly out-of-control patients threatened the flight.

Cong believed in changing public perceptions about a drug that was mostly associated with parties. 'Ketamine does have a notorious street drug reputation', he said. 'It does have a reputation as a drug of abuse, and a lot of doctors are still very concerned about this.'

This wasn't helped by a scandal that rocked the industry in 2015 when a medical clinic in Sydney, Aura Medical Corporation, was giving depressed patients vials of ketamine to take home and inject. Although many patients told *ABC News* that ketamine had stopped them from committing suicide and had improved their mental health, the company behind the plan was condemned by many doctors for both commercialising the practice and for using a drug without proper long-term testing. The clinics were closed down.[28] A ketamine nasal-spray trial was ended in Australia in 2018 after some of the most severely depressed participants suffered a temporary loss of motor skills and psychotic-like effects.

Although there is a growing body of scientific studies to show the benefits of using ketamine with depressed people — Israeli researchers at Tel Aviv Medical Centre released a report in 2018 that indicated taking ketamine orally could reduce depression within hours — Cong recognised the downside of Aura shutting its doors. 'Some of those clients did actually get significant benefit from the therapy, which is sad', he said. 'Because once it was cut off, they really had no other avenue, and this is the current problem of using ketamine as a depression therapy — there are only a few practitioners willing to take on that reputational risk to prescribe it.'[29]

~

'I grew up in a time when there weren't that many drugs around or available', Australia's former Federal Police commissioner Mick Palmer told me. 'We all got on the booze, I guess, more than we should have.'

Palmer served as Australia's top policeman between 1994 and 2001, and acknowledged that his views on drugs changed radically during his decades in the force. He recalled arresting a few men in the Northern Territory in the late 1960s for 'having a pot party', and the case ended up in the state's Supreme Court. One of the accused had cut his hair and had a shave by the time he arrived in court. When Palmer gave his evidence, he explained that, 'I spoke with the accused, John Brown, who at the time was dressed in a caftan, had long hair, and a beard.'

At the first break in the court proceedings, the judge called Palmer to his chambers and said, 'I know you intended well, but what the man looked like at the time you apprehended him has got nothing to do with the charge he's facing. I think you were trying too hard to paint a picture to me of somebody who was an obvious drug user, and it didn't do you guys any favours.'

This experience, along with some he had as a lawyer representing young people who were facing serious charges for the simple possession of cannabis, changed Palmer's thinking, because he saw that harsh drug laws were destroying people's lives.

Palmer served as police commissioner during the first years of the Howard government until his retirement in 2001, and he praised the former prime minister for his priorities to do with drugs. Although Howard talked tough and spent huge amounts of money targeting drug-traffickers, Palmer said that he also focused on areas that received far less media coverage. The Howard government gave federal money to the states and territories to support their needle-exchange programs, devised diversionary programs for some drug users to avoid the criminal-justice system and be placed in drug-treatment, and aimed to reduce the spread of HIV across Asia.[30]

Palmer said that he didn't believe all drugs would ever be legalised and that there was a need to 'get tough and have a criminal attitude toward criminal drug-trafficking'. And yet he knew that it was all futile. 'We didn't make any damned difference', he said. 'No matter how effective police became, intelligence sharing and technology has allowed them to make strikes and identify movement of drugs in a way that they weren't able to do before. We've made no difference, or almost none, to the level of supply. The best intentions of government have failed. No one's suggesting it wasn't a well-intentioned policy, but it just hasn't delivered.'

The political challenge of changing drug laws was what scared politicians, Palmer said, because they feared the media and public backlash, despite public attitudes in Australia having changed radically in the last decades. He had had many conversations with politicians over the years, and told me that their private views on drugs were often more liberal than their publicly stated positions. 'Because of the nature of politics, the more that parties like the Greens support something, the more likely that it is that a conservative coalition may not wish to do so', he said.

What Palmer knew, he said, was that, 'The current law-enforcement, prohibition approach to drug policy has been an abject failure. We haven't reduced supply. We haven't done any-thing about reducing price. We haven't reduced demand. There's no evidence anywhere around the world that there's much difference between user levels in countries that have very tough drug policies and countries that have very lenient ones. The reality is the vast majority of the people who use drugs do so socially at a low level, hold down decent jobs, and don't commit crimes. It doesn't impact on their lives.'

Palmer admitted that the police, the government, and some in the press loved stories about big drug busts. 'The media gives a lot of coverage to big seizures and the violence that surrounds drug use.

That frightens the hell out of mums and dads and the public.' I asked Palmer how to change this media narrative, to not make such stories so appealing to news editors and reporters looking for an easy take-down. He wasn't optimistic. 'The media's hungry for that sort of information because it's good news. I've been part of media coverage where we've burned cocaine in a commercial incinerator and thrown heaps of cocaine into the furnace.' Palmer said that he wanted journalists and the public to care about big drug busts, because that level of criminality needed to be stopped.

I've lost count of the number of news reports I've seen, in the commercial media and the ABC, that have been little more than regurgitated police press releases about the 'biggest drug bust of the year'. It is lazy journalism from spoon-fed reporters who don't care or dare to ask questions about the supposed benefits of the police action, and it reinforces the false notion that law enforcement can win the drug war. In each case, drug supply is rarely affected, and nothing changes. Another almost identical story appears the following month. One scare campaign, circulating in 2019, revolved around 'monkey dust', a synthetic drug: it can indeed cause harm, but doctors said that the hysterical media coverage was completely out of proportion to the relatively minor risk.

Such hysteria makes drug reform much more difficult, Palmer said, which was why he supported a more concerted campaign to reach the public and explain why the current drug laws weren't protecting their children. 'We haven't been very successful in personalising much of this', he argued.

Palmer's vision for the police was for them to stop arresting young people at music festivals for small amounts of drugs, and go after the criminal syndicates instead.[31] He said that most police supported a change in their mission, and wanted to be viewed as a support network and not the enemy. He worried about young people quickly swallowing huge amounts of drugs that they were carrying when they

spotted a police officer or a sniffer dog at a dance party or rock con-
cert. It was dangerous, and served no purpose.

Although the legalisation and regulation of all drugs was Palmer's
ultimate ambition, he acknowledged that this was unlikely to ever
happen. He backed pill testing at music festivals, supported the
Greens policy of legalising marijuana, opposed drug-testing welfare
recipients, wanted more safe injecting centres, and supported more
money for harm minimisation programs.

One of the more innovative suggestions that received very little
attention in Australia, put forward in 2016 by Palmer and Australia
21, the independent think tank with which he's involved, advocated
'moving psychoactive drugs from the black market to the "white"
market'. This would involve taxing and regulating the supply of currently illegal drugs that cause the least harm, with the regulation of
supply being introduced over a period of time. Advertising of any
regulated drugs would be banned.

~

The Kings Cross injecting centre was a failure, argued Sydney's *Daily
Telegraph* columnist Miranda Devine in 2010. After the New South
Wales government ended the long trial of the facility and made it
permanent, this writer was livid. It had 'done nothing demonstrable
to reduce heroin use, or cause drug addicts to abstain from the substance that is ruining their lives', she wrote.[32]

Back in 2003, two years after the centre opened, Devine longed
for the Kings Cross of the 1990s, when she lived in the area, because
'it still had charms'. Sure, she admitted, 'there might have been the
odd gangster beaten to death in the middle of the night and mys-
terious screams outside. But, in those days, drug dealers weren't
obvious unless you were looking.'[33]

The pastor of the Wayside Chapel in the area at the time, Reverend

Ray Richmond, told a vastly different story because he was on the frontlines of the drug crisis, and Devine was not. 'In Kings Cross [in the 1990s], the police and ambulance services were stretched beyond limits', he wrote. 'Council workers disabled all public-park taps. Restaurants shut toilets to patrons, and users were entering private property for water to mix drugs for needle injecting. Trade in restaurants, coffee shops, and nightclubs decreased. Kings Cross was too dangerous.'[34]

This background is important because Devine has been one of Australia's most vociferous opponents of drug reform for decades. There's arguably no public commentator who has been more vocal and at times influential in delaying or stopping drug reforms due to her closeness to the Liberal Party and ability to dominate the news cycle. In an interview via email, Devine explained that she advocated tough 'war on drugs' rhetoric and practice to dissuade people from using illicit drugs.

'They claim we have lost the so-called war on drugs but no one ever claimed it was a war that could be won', she wrote in 2014. 'What we have done before and can do again is make drugs harder to procure. That starts with zero tolerance, not a nudge nudge, wink wink.'[35] Devine would be unhappy with New South Wales magistrates deciding from 2018 that jail time for minor drug dealers was pointless, and instead sentencing them to intensive correction orders.

Devine opposed 'drug liberalising', which she accepted had become 'received wisdom' among health and criminology academics. Locally, she blamed Dr Alex Wodak, 'probably the most influential in Australia', and the Greens; and, globally, the billionaire philanthropist George Soros, and the founder of the US-based Drug Policy Alliance, Ethan Nadelmann.

She accused the 'harm minimisation doctrine' of teaching Generation Y that 'alcohol is worse, or at least as bad, as illicit drugs and if you must "use", here's how to do it safely.' This was a strange argument, because alcohol use has fallen amongst young Australians in recent years, but Devine blamed the 'successful demonisation' of alcohol for the increasing use of drugs.

Alcohol causes more damage to society than illegal drugs do, by a wide margin. A 2010 study by Britain's Independent Scientific Committee on Drugs investigated the harm caused by tobacco, heroin, cannabis, crack cocaine, and alcohol: it found that alcohol, with all its associated health and societal harms, was the most destructive drug.

When the Australian government released its National Drug Strategy in 2017, ice was deemed the most serious problem, despite less than 1.5 per cent of Australians ever consuming it. The Australian Medical Association condemned the report as indulging socially acceptable drug taking, such as drinking, despite the government noting that 'alcohol is associated with 5,000 deaths and more than 150,000 hospitalisations each year — yet the strategy puts it as a lower priority than ice'.[36]

Devine admired the Howard government's Tough on Drugs campaign that started in 1997, because 'for the first time in three decades, fewer young people experimented with drugs and those who did were older'. Devine celebrated the huge numbers of drug seizures and arrests of drug mules, and the strong emphasis on law enforcement. The heroin drought at the end of 2000 was thanks to Howard, she told me, quoting the Australian Federal Police's international network manager, Mike Phelan. 'We believe law-enforcement efforts have contributed to the heroin drought', he said.

Myanmar was the primary source of heroin coming into Australia, and there was more than an 80 per cent drop in production from 1998 until 2006. Australia was lucky that less heroin was arriving on its shores at the time, but this trend didn't continue; Myanmar once more became a global leader in poppy production.

Devine didn't mention Myanmar, but claimed that, 'The tough on drugs strategy led directly to a heroin drought and falling crime rates — a real world rebuke to criminologists and drug-liberalisers who claim law enforcement attempts to control supply are doomed to fail.'

What Devine ignored was that Howard's drugs strategy wasn't just about law enforcement, but a range of other practices to reduce drug taking. The former prime minister responded to an ABC-TV program in 2002 that had challenged his 'zero tolerance' approach to drugs. Howard claimed that roughly 60 per cent of his Tough on Drugs funding was 'provided to prevention, education, rehabilitation, and diversion of illicit drug users'. He praised what he called the 'unprecedented increase' of seized illicit drugs since his policy had been launched in 1997.

Nonetheless, Australians weren't just changing their drug intake because of police actions alone, as Devine suggested, but for a range of other reasons (including inconvenient ones pursued by her political hero). Like Devine, however, Howard opposed the Kings Cross injecting centre because it sent 'exactly the wrong message to the community'.

Australia spends around $1.7 billion annually on fighting illicit drugs, with nearly 65 per cent going to law enforcement, 2.2 per cent on harm reduction, 9.5 per cent on prevention, and 22 per cent on treatment. Devine clearly believed that police should receive an even bigger piece of the annual spending pie.

Although Devine didn't state that she believed in US-style mass incarceration of drug users and dealers, she blamed the local courts for being too lenient. In her view, too few people were going to prison for supplying cannabis, ecstasy, and even amphetamines. 'For drug users, it's a slap on the wrist … drugs are ubiquitous and the ambivalence of authorities has rendered them powerless to protect young people from the perils of drug taking. There is next to no penalty for use or dealing. It's a waste of police time to take it to court. This is de-facto decriminalisation.'

Implied in Devine's answers to my queries was deep frustration that more people weren't sent to prison, despite the US being a prime example of how catastrophic this policy had been (all without reducing drug taking amongst the population).

I asked Devine what she wanted the 'war on drugs' to look like. Many of her columns, and her paper, *The Daily Telegraph*, used war rhetoric when describing the battle against illicit substances. She knew that 'drug use will never be eradicated, but no one said it would. That's the straw man created by [Alex] Wodak and [Ethan] Nadelmann and pals. But diligent police and customs work to target dealers, penalise possession, stop drug shipments, and educate young people about the dangers has been proven to work.' She argued that legalising marijuana was a mistake, and would lead to greater use and mental-health problems.

Devine and I agreed — and it was the only time — when she claimed that, 'Drug use isn't a victimless crime. We've been bombarded with campaigns about blood diamonds, sweatshop sneakers, fair-trade coffee and cruel fur. But the case against recreational coke snorting is more compelling. It fuels the drug-trade, causing misery and corruption in places such as South America and West Africa.'

Devine is right about this, and it's an issue that rarely gets mentioned in the drug debate. This book reports on the misery, poverty, corruption, and violence in Central America and West Africa caused by the cocaine trade, leading to many people's lives being undeniably ruined or at least negatively affected by the use and abuse of cocaine in the West. Despite this, I've rarely seen a sustained public campaign in Australia or globally to connect the dots and explain what this demand leads to in the poorest nations on earth. How about encouraging a belief in ethical drug taking? In fair-trade cocaine? Devine's reason for arguing this is different from mine — I support a healthy, safe, and legal recreational drug market, while she does not — and yet she inadvertently highlights what snorting cocaine in Sydney,

London, or New York means for a poor farmer in Guinea-Bissau.

One of Devine's more controversial columns was published in 2016. Headlined, 'Ice them: time to sterilise drug-addicted parents', she called for a 'truly radical program [that] would be to offer addicts a sterilisation bonus, like the baby bonus, so they can wreck their own lives but no babies are harmed in the process. If that's too draconian, how about an incentive to take long-term contraception?'[37] Devine wrote this after her newspaper was outraged about the government providing a 'taxpayer-funded nanny' to an ice user who had had her eight children removed by the state.

Devine's desire to treat drug addiction as a crime, and to punish users in the process, was an example of tough love that has never worked and has pushed victims onto the streets. She wanted people who took ice to be judged harshly and rejected by society. Devine condemned what she claimed was a welfare industry that 'turbo-charges the underclass. It incentivises hopeless drug addicts to keep having children they can't take care of, because it provides them with more money for each child and priority social housing.'

Devine told me that her call for sterilisation came from a place of worrying about future generations of drug users, and that many commenters on *The Daily Telegraph* website approved of the suggestion. TV host David Campbell strongly opposed it, however, saying that sterilisation 'worked really well in Nazi Germany, but this is Australia so that's not really an argument'.

Devine positively cited the US group Project Prevention that pays drug addicts US$300 to volunteer for birth control, including sterilisation. Its founder, Barbara Harris, has been criticised for saying that, 'We don't allow dogs to breed. We spay them. We neuter them. We try to keep them from having unwanted puppies, and yet these women are literally having litters of children', and 'We campaign to neuter dogs and yet we allow women to have 10 or 12 kids that they can't take care of.'

Devine was a puritanical Catholic who loathed the changes in modern society, from the prevalence of single-parent families to the acceptance of same-sex marriage. (She partly blamed the 2011 London riots on 'the manifestation of a fatherless society'.) Her opposition to drug use fitted this worldview, whereby individuals who took illegal substances had to be punished. Liberalism had to be rejected as a virtue. I never saw her question why the government deemed certain drugs illegal, and whether it made practical and moral sense to do so. Devine had more influence years ago, as did her paper, *The Daily Telegraph*. Since then, growing numbers of Australians have either taken drugs or know somebody who has, and they have realised that in the majority of cases it was a harmless and fun activity.[38]

~

Australia's health minister, Greg Hunt, said in early 2018 that, 'We would like to be, potentially, the world's number one medicinal cannabis supplier.' After the government approved therapeutic marijuana products for export in January 2018, stock prices shot up for Australian cannabis producers by up to 50 per cent. Companies expressed excitement at the prospect of making huge profits from the drug, as well as helping people lead less painful lives.

Leading pharmaceutical company AusCann produces cannabinoid medicines, and its managing director, Elaine Darby, was optimistic that the opportunities were wide open with a potential market of three million Australians who suffered regular pain. Globally, around 7 to 8 per cent of people experienced neuropathic pain, and Darby said Australia should exploit the fact that major markets such as Germany were getting their cannabis supplies from the Netherlands and Canada only.[39] She told *The Sydney Morning Herald* that her firm went out and educated doctors about the benefits of medical cannabis, hoping they would prescribe it to their patients.

By 2018, despite Australia having legalised medical marijuana in 2016, around only 350 Australians had obtained legal cannabis for their health conditions, not helped by the hundreds of pages of supporting documentation and evidence that authorities required to begin the never-ending process of getting the drug. Ignorant and fearful doctors, limited supply, expensive cannabis, and unending bureaucracy made the situation complex and frustrating for those who needed it most. Brisbane-based Lindsay Carter and his mother, Lanai, became the public face of this situation because Lindsay suffered from extreme seizures due to a brain tumour and epilepsy. He often couldn't access the drug in Australia, forcing him and his mother to travel overseas to purchase it, but this was time-consuming and enraging.[40]

The Australian government had clearly not planned the rollout of medical marijuana well, prioritising the wishes of big cannabis firms over patients. Bastian Seidel, the then-president of the Royal College of General Practitioners, explained in July 2018 that in a country with 38,000 GPs, only one of them was an authorised prescriber of medical marijuana. He said the drug was 'pretty much inaccessible' for those most in need. 'The hurdles are still in place. It is frustrating for us because medicinal cannabis might be an option of last resort for patients where we've tried absolutely everything in the book.' This meant, according to Iain McGregor, a psychopharmacologist at Sydney University, that about 100,000 Australians might be accessing illegal cannabis for medical purposes.[41]

The hype around medical cannabis is strong. One of the world's leading experts is Dr Michael Dor, the senior medical advisor for the Israeli government's Medical Cannabis Unit. He said that it was inevitable that cannabis would soon be used by doctors as a first-line treatment, not as an alternative when other drugs failed. During a visit to Australia in 2018 at the invitation of Australia's only private cannabis company, MediFarm, during which they wanted the Israeli doctor to educate local doctors about the drug's benefits and history, Dor acknowledged that research on the benefits of marijuana remained incomplete. In 2019, Israel allowed the export of medical marijuana, and as a result the country's cannabis industry is growing rapidly.

Although the evidence pointed to clear benefits for children with autism and epilepsy, and pain relief for cancer sufferers, much was still unknown about its wider applications. Israel has one of the biggest proportions of patients treated with the drug: more than 37,000 people out of a population of nine million (excluding the occupied Palestinian territories) have been treated with medical marijuana.[42]

Dor was right about marijuana's growing acceptance, with public attitudes shifting, and governments around the world rushing to encourage corporations to grow, produce, sell, and market the drug to consumers. This has advantages if patients are helped, but not if it principally leads to profits for the companies. Australian firms were rushing to make locally made products widely available at pharmacies across the country, and the drug's take-up in cannabis oils and tinctures (alcohol-based cannabis extracts) was assured.[43]

The pathway to legalising recreational marijuana would likely follow in the years to come after other nations tried it first. Many local and international companies are investing in the Australian cannabis industry because they believe it will soon take off. Venture capitalist Ross Smith, who made millions of dollars from investing in the industry for years while threatening opponents, said that, 'There's no question in my mind that medical cannabis is the Trojan horse for recreational cannabis.'[44]

~

'I think that communities have moved a long way [on attitudes towards drugs], but there's a fear of you having a puff on a joint and ending up in the gutter using heroin', Fiona Patten, leader of the

Reason Party, who sits in the Victorian Legislative Council, told me. 'The myth is still out there.'

The founder of the Sex Party in 2009, dedicated to fighting censorship and advocating for drug reform and same-sex marriage, Patten changed the party's name to the Reason Party in 2017. Today she's one of the more outspoken advocates for a radical shift in Australia's drug policy. Her ideal vision was the legalisation of all drugs, but she acknowledged that the community didn't share this view. Instead, the decriminalisation of use and possession was her first step — the Portugal model.

She pushed for a ground-breaking (in Australia, at least) Victorian parliamentary inquiry that investigated the state's drug laws and whether they should be changed. Released in 2018, the report called for establishing a new government advisory council to determine whether adults should be allowed to use marijuana. Patten said she was proud of the way the report was gathered. It stated that Victoria could 'no longer arrest its way out of the drug crisis'. The report was correct; in 2016–2017, Australian police made a record 154,650 national drug arrests.

Its recommendations were relatively cautious. Patten told me that she wished they were stronger, but they included telling police not to charge people with small amounts of drugs and instead sending them to rehabilitation; reviewing the use of police sniffer dogs at music festivals due to the risks of young people ingesting large amounts of drugs; trialling pill testing; and examining new pharmaceutical options for heroin treatment.

Patten said that the parliamentary inquiry took a policeman overseas for the first time ever during its investigations — to Portugal, where all drugs are decriminalised, and Vancouver, Canada, where supervised injecting centres are saving lives — and he influenced the thinking of other participants. 'He came back seeing first-hand what was possible', Patten said.

The reluctance of the Australian political class to embrace drug liberalisation was because 'they don't know how to message it. They don't have the language to talk to the community about this. We haven't got people out there in the community saying that 99.9 per cent of drug users are recreational users. That they may age out of using drugs when they get mortgages and children. Or they may continue to use drugs on a recreational basis and be very successful people. Like I have said many times, [I enjoy] a joint with a glass of wine at the end of the day, because it relaxes me. I don't think there's anything wrong with that.'

Patten's vision included legalising cannabis and having cafés where consumers could openly smoke it. She was critical of how Amsterdam had managed its decriminalised weed industry — the drug remained illegal, but its personal use was accepted — because she argued that the Dutch didn't change their laws to fully acknowledge the realities of cannabis-selling coffee shops.

The Netherlands employ *gedoogbeleid* (a tolerance policy) whereby prosecutors turn a blind eye to certain laws being broken, including businesses selling weed. Understandably, Patten told me that she didn't want to exactly follow the Amsterdam model. Pro-cannabis activists that I met in Washington, DC, also expressed concerns about adopting the model, not wanting to turn cities into drug havens.

Tourism has soared in Amsterdam over the last decades, due to the easy availability of sex and marijuana, but the result is that many locals now resent the 'urban jungle' it has created. This includes criminal activity, human trafficking, Moroccan gangs running the ecstasy market, and dirty streets.[45] Dutch police warned in 2018 that the nation risked turning into a 'narco-state' due to the size of a parallel criminal economy.

The growing belief that the legalisation of marijuana was inevitable in Australia was a relatively new phenomenon; the debate had shifted in some circles to how to manage this legal market, rather than wondering if it would ever happen. Patten disagreed with the Greens' blueprint for a legal cannabis market in Australia, with the government as grower and dispenser — akin to the model in Uruguay, the first country in the world to legalise marijuana in 2013. Patten said she believed that this would give the government too much power over the drug. She preferred private firms to be the producers, with minimal government interference. She wanted the state to regulate but not have control over the drug's growth and distribution.

'I certainly don't think that the sale of cannabis or the growing of cannabis should be government-owned', Patten said. 'The government doesn't even own the cultivation of opium poppies in Australia. Why would we restrict this plant to government? I think it sends the wrong message about it. I think it's presenting the plant as dangerous, sold by uniformed people in locked government offices. That's not how I feel about cannabis. I don't think it's what the community feels about it, either.'

Patten concurred with Uruguay in the need to legalise cannabis to remove the huge influence of criminal elements; organised crime was benefitting from a multi-billion-dollar industry. The best estimates, in Victoria alone, was that the retail market was worth over $8 billion annually, and that the wholesale market was worth $1.5 billion.[46] On these figures, it was one of the state's biggest businesses, and yet its illegality meant that crime gangs from Vietnam and Albania often controlled the industry.

~

Australia is never going to be a leader on drug reform — a sad indictment on the many politicians who don't have the courage to express their real views publicly. They're scared of a tabloid backlash in a nation where Rupert Murdoch's newspapers, traditionally hostile to drug reform, have more influence than any other media company. As with same-sex marriage, abortion, and euthanasia being practised in legal, quasi-legal, or illegal form, Australia will have to look overseas for inspiration, take the best ideas and models, and adapt them to local conditions.

In the context of the Asia-Pacific region, Australia is an ocean of calm compared to the drug-war hysteria in the Philippines and increasingly in Sri Lanka, Indonesia, and Bangladesh. Many nations execute traffickers. However, this is not to insulate Australia from necessary criticism of its policies, including its overseas impacts. Canberra still refuses to stop sharing information with its foreign law-enforcement partners in relation to drug crimes even when there is no assurance that capital punishment won't be carried out. The Australian Federal Police still defends its role in helping Indonesia capture the so-called Bali Nine in 2005, many of whom were subsequently executed for drug-trafficking.

If a nation such as the US can be so obsessed with punishment and still move towards legalising marijuana, there's hope for a nation such as Australia to move out of its subservience to Washington and follow its lead.

CHAPTER SEVEN

Solutions

'I start from the presumption that nature is all that there is
and gravitate towards scientific explanations of phenomena
… Was it possible that a single psychedelic experience —
something that turned on nothing more than the ingestion
of a pill or square of blotter paper — could put a big dent in
such a worldview? Shift how one thought about mortality?
Actually change one's mind in enduring ways?'
MICHAEL POLLAN, *HOW TO CHANGE YOUR MIND*, 2018[1]

The longevity of the drug war has surprised many of its most fervent
opponents. Even though it's been a catastrophic failure in reducing
drug supply and usage, its benefit to political and law-enforcement
elites should never be under-estimated. For these reasons, alternatives to the war on drugs have never been more relevant. How to
access illicit substances in the face of prohibition, the beneficial uses
of psychedelic drugs, and what a legalised and regulated market could
look like are three areas that deserve examination.

As long as the drug war continues to ravage communities in the
West and drug-producing nations in South America, Asia, and Africa,
resistance to its twisted logic is necessary. This isn't a signal to consume
more drugs, but rather an acknowledgement that a regulated and legalised system is the best way to improve health and reduce crime.

~

The explosion of the dark net — online, mostly anonymous, crypto-markets — has provided a new frontier in selling and procuring drugs. It has allowed consumers to browse countless stores to find what they're looking for, usually without exposing themselves to law-enforcement threats or gang violence. I've checked out some of these websites, many based in Australia and Europe, and seen every drug imaginable on sale, from heroin to fentanyl. I could order the drug, and it would arrive at my home or office within a matter of days or weeks. The vast bulk of the product reaches the intended customer, with police only intercepting a small fraction of it.

Research released by criminologists in 2017 found that Australia had more online drug vendors per capita than any other country, apart from the Netherlands. Vendors sold opioids and ecstasy,[2] and more than one-quarter of the dark net's methamphetamine market was facilitated by Australian online dealers. Prices for drugs varied greatly, but Australian vendors often charged more for products than their overseas counterparts, meaning much of their market was domestic.

One of the researchers behind the study was Dr James Martin, associate professor in criminology at Swinburne University in Australia, who argued that there were positive signs revealed by the study. He wrote that dark net consumers usually purchased higher-quality drugs than those sourced from traditional places, and had greater knowledge of the drugs' composition.

There was one huge caveat, however. 'Unfortunately, crypto-markets are unable to resolve the worst, intractable systemic drug violence in source countries such as Mexico', Martin wrote. 'In the absence of a legal market for these drugs, this violence will continue unabated, much as it has since the beginning of the war on drugs.'[3] The dark net did little to stop the brutality around the production of drugs in Africa, South America, or elsewhere.

The dark net entered the public consciousness with the Silk Road marketplace, run from 2011 until 2013 by Dread Pirate Roberts, later exposed as American citizen Ross Ulbricht. He was found guilty in 2015 of narcotics trafficking, money laundering, running a criminal enterprise, and computer hacking, and was sentenced to life in prison without the prospect of parole. Before his sentencing, Ulbricht told the court that Silk Road was 'supposed to be about giving people the freedom to make their own choices' as an expression of his libertarian values.

But it had all gone horribly wrong, as prosecutors alleged that he had paid money to have six people killed (although the murders were never carried out). Dozens of drug sellers on Silk Road were prosecuted globally after Ulbricht was imprisoned. The US government and those involved with Silk Road who evaded detection eventually tried to sell some of the hundreds of millions of dollars of bitcoin that they recovered or kept after the site was shut down.

The US government argued that closing down Silk Road was a necessary step in tackling illegal drugs. After the verdict was announced, the Manhattan US attorney, Preet Bharara, said that, 'Ulbricht was a drug dealer and criminal profiteer who exploited people's addictions and contributed to the deaths of at least six young people. Ulbricht went from hiding his cybercrime identity to becoming the face of cybercrime and as today's sentence proves, no one is above the law.'

James Martin, some of whose work was used by the Ulbricht defence team, unbeknownst to him, told me that Silk Road was pioneering, and for that reason the US government had to crush it because it was an 'overtly politically, subversive act' to sell illegal drugs on such a large scale. 'I think it really highlighted the limitations of state power', he said, because it took years of high-cost investigations by the FBI, DEA, and Europol to get Ulbricht. 'Terrorists and paedophiles get a lighter touch [prison sentence] than Ulbricht, and his biggest crime was making a fool of the whole system of drug prohibition.'

Ending Silk Road was only a momentary victory for US officials, because many similar sites blossomed soon after. Martin welcomed this as a positive development. 'The dark net does offer this kind of unexpected third way where at least some of the harms associated with the drug-trade can be ameliorated', he said. 'Street dealing is typically the riskiest part of a drug-supply chain. The reason for that is because drug dealers need to have some minimal level of public exposure to get customers.'

Martin's research offered unique insights into the drug-trade, whereas its traditional trafficking methods made it close to impossible to track. Via encrypted chats, many online sellers shared details about their motivations with Martin and his colleagues, detailing their financial returns as well as their deliberate subversion of what they viewed as absurd drug laws.

While nations from Australia to the US maintained a tough prohibitionist strategy against drugs, the dark net was a buyer's market rather than a seller's market. Interested parties had thousands of options to browse through, even able to check online reviews of products on their very own trip advisor. As in the legit world, selling bad drugs would generate poor reviews. There was still no guarantee of quality, unless the drugs were tested on arrival — toxic fentanyl was being sold to consumers with sometimes deadly results — but reviews gave users a sense of what the seller was offering. Drug samples were also sometimes given to 'drug critics' as a way to boost a seller's reputation and sales. Some suggestions were emerging that dark-net dealers might develop an effective and safe method of testing drugs themselves to reduce the risks of consumption for users. Increasing numbers of people were also buying legal prescription drugs on the dark net because they couldn't get the drugs they believed they needed to treat their medical conditions.

Some dark-web operators stopped selling fentanyl in 2018, fearing that its potency and toxicity might attract the attention of law enforcement. A 2019 study by the Australian National University found that fentanyl was being sold on the dark net, but that 99.7 per cent of the listings on various dark-net sites were not of the deadly drug.

In a study released in *Addiction* journal in 2017, Martin challenged his own belief that the dark net would necessarily reduce violence associated with the drug-trade. Although there was evidence that proved such reductions would be 'modest' — because ecstasy and cannabis were the biggest sellers online, and the drugs that were least associated with violence — 'the demographic characteristics of cryptomarket users may also exclude those market participants who are typically most vulnerable to systemic violence (eg sex workers, rough sleepers).'[4]

Some of the more entrepreneurial dark-net sellers used the language of ethical drug taking in their advertising. It was impossible to verify the accuracy of their claims, and it was unlikely that drug sellers had the ability to completely avoid the destructive supply chain that was inevitable in the production of drugs such as cocaine, but some clearly believed it was an effective tool to attract business. One advertisement read:

> We are a team of libertarian cocaine dealers. We never buy coke from cartels! We never buy coke from police! We help farmers from Peru, Bolivia and some chemistry students in Brazil, Paraguay and Argentina. We do fair trade!

Another one read:

> This is the best opium you will try, by purchasing this you are supporting local farmers in the hills of Guatemala and you are not financing violent drug cartels.[5]

Martin acknowledged that the dark net was open to abuse — such as doxing, fraud, hacking and sellers stealing funds — but 'to date, not a single instance of physical, intra-market violence between cryptomarket drug-traders has been recorded. This fact is likely to be of no small comfort to those who increasingly choose to buy and sell illicit drugs online, and the absence of violence associated with online drug-trading may be a significant factor driving its growth in years to come.'

The attitude of law enforcement towards the dark net was still evolving, he said. Officials knew it was impossible to shut down all websites selling illicit drugs, just like they could never arrest their way into a drug-free society, but cryptomarkets presented an existential challenge to the normal ways of policing drugs with busts and surveillance. Online drug markets were undeniably less harmful than the traditional drug-trade, so the public interest would be best served by allowing these sites to remain open (a view not shared by all police). One of the biggest dark-net sites, Dream Market, closed in 2019 amid rumours that the DEA or FBI had caused its failure.

Martin said that the dark net also presented an ideological challenge to the drug war, because the rhetoric for decades about illicit substances emphasised the violence that inevitably occurred. But with Silk Road and others, Martin explained, they were 'just a bunch of nerds. You've got these guys who are sitting behind a computer. You've got no violence. You've got no scary people hanging around corners or hanging around schoolyards or any of the other sort of symbols of drug-war propaganda. It's pretty difficult to scare people with that.'

~

Beckley Park is a beautiful old property situated 30 minutes from the centre of Oxford in England. Down muddy tracks, past lush, green fields and old farmhouses, I visited on a glorious, crisp sunny day. Founded by Amanda Feilding in 1998, Beckley Foundation pushes for global drug reform and the scientific study of psychoactive substances.

I spent the day with Feilding, in her mid-70s, and discussed her life-long quest to normalise the use of psychedelic drugs and cannabis to help people in mental need. She was passionate and knowledgeable, clearly frustrated by the slow pace of drug reform. She believed that LSD, mushrooms, and cannabis should be a central part of treating depression and mental-health problems.

Evidence was building to support her thesis. Two 2016 studies — one at John Hopkins University and the other at New York University — showed that a single dose of psilocybin (magic mushrooms) could have immediate, lasting, and profound effects on cancer patients dealing with depression and anxiety. An earlier study found that cancer sufferers who faced imminent death felt more comfortable with this outcome after taking psychedelics. Another study at John Hopkins University from 2014 found that taking magic mushrooms helped 80 per cent of participants end their nicotine addiction.

Beckley's grand house, parts of which dated back hundreds of years, surrounded by a moat and perfectly manicured hedges near fighting swans in the lake, made for a curious setting to the serious and revolutionary message she was pushing. She told me that although she had befriended many rich people — including some in the tech world — who talked positively about using psychedelics and how it helped their creativity, very few were willing to put up money to support scientific research into the drugs' perceived health benefits.

Feilding told me that, after decades of psychedelic drugs being demonised and dismissed, science could restore its rightful place in society and show with evidence that mind-altering drugs would help the world. 'Science is the kind of new religion', she said, as other religions had become less respected in the West.

Due to the drugs' illegality and the widespread belief that working with them would harm careers, only a few brave souls engaged in this issue, though it was becoming far less controversial to research these drugs. Feilding had to play the long game, pushing for change over decades. Only in the last years had it become more socially acceptable to advocate for these drugs, but her frustration with the slow progress of change was palpable. Feilding wasn't a trained scientist, but understood much of the science around psychedelic drugs and its properties.

She had launched a for-profit cannabis business, Beckley Canopy Therapeutics, to capitalise on the booming legal marijuana business and to develop cannabis-based medicines. She hoped to put some of the profit generated by this business into more scientific research on psychedelics.

Feilding had had an interest in mystical experiences from a young age. Her godfather had become a Buddhist monk, which gave her a taste for global adventures. She left school at 16 because she didn't 'like the constrictions and not being allowed to learn what I wanted to learn, but I always self-educated pretty compulsively. I got the best tutor in the world in religions and Arab studies.'

She started smoking cannabis at Oxford University in 1960, and tried LSD for the first time in 1965. 'I found my mission in life', she said. 'I had kind of a visionary spirit. My mother was Catholic, my father was agnostic, so I had a bit of both. I dreamed of doing great things for the world. One of my dreams was watering the desert. And then I came across this knowledge [about the benefits of psychedelic drugs].' To this day, Feilding wanted people to have access to these drugs and to the science that supported its use. 'I'm not against recreational use at all. I'm against recreational misuse.'

The Beckley Foundation was born from an idea that Western societies, including Britain, had copied US drug policies for the wrong reasons. We were a 'lapdog', she said. 'I started the Beckley

Foundation to build a scientific evidence base, to share why the policies of criminalisation and prohibition were causing much more harm than they were solving. You need to deal with the drugs individually, and psychedelics and cannabis cause very few harms. The harm is mainly caused by prohibition.'

Feilding's vision was a future where psychedelic drugs weren't viewed as a novelty but as part of a vital way of life. 'In an ideal society, there would be retreat centres', she told me. 'Places in the country where people can go and have people around who are experienced guides [with drugs] to help the traumatised in bad situations — experiencing altered states with the intention of self-improvement.' Psychedelics or cannabis could help people with Parkinson's disease and PTSD.

LSD was discovered by Swiss scientist Albert Hofmann in 1938 — he was the first man to take an acid trip in 1943 — but the drug only entered popular consciousness in the 1960s. He spent his life opposing the drug's prohibition. He took it himself because he saw it as a 'sacred drug' and argued that, 'I see the true importance of LSD in the possibility of providing material aid to meditation aimed at the mystical experience of a deeper, comprehensive reality.' Hofmann was aware of the drug's danger if not used in a well-controlled, professional psychiatric setting, but remained a committed advocate for its therapeutic benefits.

For decades, Feilding's advocacy was restricted to a small audience, but in the last decade public attitudes and scientific research had evolved; psychedelic drugs were no longer viewed as an evil that had to be restricted. 'I'd like my legacy to be to integrate the possibility of altered states into society, because I think they are valuable to the human's survival', she said. 'What we find noble in humans, including bravery — these compounds can help bring that out.'

The Beckley Foundation regularly featured in the British conversation about drug reform. In 2011, the organisation co-ordinated a public letter in *The Guardian* and *The Times* that declared the 'war on drugs' a failure and pushed for an end to prohibition. It was signed by current and former leaders of Colombia, Guatemala, and Mexico, countless Nobel Prize winners, and many others.

Feilding had worked with one of Britain's leading scientists in the psychedelic field, Dr Robin Carhart-Harris, who was head of Imperial Psychedelic Research Group at Imperial University. (Imperial opened the world's first psychedelic research centre in 2019.) Carhart-Harris often partnered with Dr David Nutt, the famous British neuropsychopharmacologist. At his home in Oxford, Carhart-Harris told me that he had long believed that there was a need for rigorous scientific studies on psychedelic drugs to give them credibility in the wider community. He was shocked to learn that there had never been a brain-image study with LSD until he released one in 2016. It was possible to prove with evidence that LSD was fundamentally changing how humans viewed the world.

Carhart-Harris said at the time:

> We observed brain changes under LSD that suggested our volunteers were 'seeing with their eyes shut' — albeit they were seeing things from their imagination rather than from the outside world. We saw that many more areas of the brain than normal were contributing to visual processing under LSD — even though the volunteers' eyes were closed. Furthermore, the size of this effect correlated with volunteers' ratings of complex, dreamlike visions.
>
> Our brains become more constrained and compartmentalised as we develop from infancy into adulthood, and we may become more focused and rigid in our thinking as we mature. In many ways, the brain in the LSD state resembles the state our brains were in when we were infants: free and unconstrained. This also makes sense when we consider the hyper-emotional and imaginative nature of an infant's mind.[6]

Carhart-Harris explained that there was still much that humans didn't understand about the brain, but psychedelic drugs ranging from ayahuasca [an Amazonian hallucinogenic brew] to LSD had the possibility of reshaping consciousness. He imagined a world in the not-too-distant future where a patient visited their local doctor, explained they had depression, obsessive-compulsive disorder, addiction, an eating disorder, phobia, a speech impediment, or chronic pain, and, instead of prescribing an anti-depressant, the doctor would say that there was a viable alternative. Carhart-Harris imagined a doctor saying to the patient: "There is this other treatment model, but it requires something of you. It's not just about passively giving you medicine. You have to go into this treatment willing to engage. If you're interested, I can refer you to this clinic that's called the Psychedelic Treatment Clinic."

It would take a week or longer at a psychedelic spa to be given certain psychedelic drugs, under professional supervision, along with access to healthy food, teaching, and yoga, and at the end of the process the person would, hopefully, be vastly improved, if not cured. Carhart-Harris was critical of many psychoanalysts working today whom he viewed as not being open to using psychedelic drugs with their clients. 'They're almost in this religion rather than in scientifically directed method and practice', he said.

Carhart-Harris admitted that psychedelic retreats would be difficult to support in a public health-care system without a major shift in government thinking, although the Food and Drug Administration in the US was changing its views. In 2016, it allowed final trials on ecstasy for PTSD patients before possible legalised prescription use of the drug from 2021. Such treatment would be principally available to those who had private health care; it would likely be inaccessible to most people in the non-Western world, who barely had access to decent health care, let alone a psychedelic spa. Take Honduras, the Philippines, or Guinea-Bissau. Carhart-Harris acknowledged that this was a major problem and there should be a concerted effort to not keep these medical advances just for Western patients. There was a risk of creating an 'elitist division', he said, when only the wealthy, connected, or highly educated could access the drugs.

The New Yorker magazine ran feature stories on the use of aya-huasca in Brooklyn and Silicon Valley.[7] 'The drug of choice for the age of kale' was the headline on its 2016 story. Novelist Ayelet Waldman gained publicity in 2017 after admitting to micro-dosing LSD, using small amounts of the drug to manage her depression (although it can also help to improve creativity). The Beckley Foundation and Imperial College London started the world's first scientific study into micro-dosing in 2018. The practice exploded in Silicon Valley from 2010, with the use of small amounts of LSD or magic mushrooms allowing for hours of intense concentration, and it soon crossed over into more popular use.

These kinds of stories didn't mean that the drugs weren't helping people, but the benefits needed to be more widely shared than just with elites on the American coasts. Public attitudes were shifting rapidly. A YouGov poll in 2017 found that nearly two-thirds of Americans were keen to try psychedelic drugs if they were proven to help with their condition. The level of education determined a person's belief in the drugs. Fifty-three per cent of respondents supported medical research into psychedelic drugs, but this increased to 69 per cent for people with graduate degrees.

During the years I spent researching this book, I started seeing more articles in the mainstream press from PTSD sufferers who swore that ecstasy had saved their lives. The illegality of the drug undoubt-edly affected its use and popularity for medical purposes (but this has had little impact on its widespread recreational use).[8] Although I've never been an evangelist for psychedelic drugs, I've become convinced that the West's obsession with anti-depressants is a funda-mentally unhealthy way to manage life. If psychedelic drugs can even partially ameliorate the pain that's convinced so many people to pop anti-depressants, it's surely a path worth exploring.

The growing acceptance of psychedelics, and the possibility of them becoming more widely available, also raised issues about the privatisation of knowledge and production — similar to the concerns being expressed about the legal cannabis industry. Activists worried that companies would steal the wonders of the drugs for their financial benefit; I saw little debate around the for-profit corporate medicalisation of psychedelics, but it seemed like a necessary conversation.[9]

Looking much further into the future, with artificial intelligence likely to dominate the 21st century, I asked Carhart-Harris about the possibility of giving psychedelic drugs to robots if they were depressed. The character Marvin, the paranoid android, in Douglas Adams' book *The Hitchhiker's Guide to the Galaxy* was prone to depression and boredom; I thought he was a prime candidate for psychedelics. Carhart-Harris found the idea intriguing, and said that, 'If we create them [robots] in our image, then they'll suffer like we do.'

Zachary Mainen, from the Champalimaud Centre for the Unknown in Lisbon, told a conference in New York in 2018 that intelligent robots, like humans, might need anti-depressants because 'an autonomous AI will need to have its own interests and its own goals, and if those are thwarted it will be angry or sad in the sense of the same type of reactions that animals and people have.'[10]

Despite the scientific successes, and a growing body of evidence that proved the health benefits of some psychedelic drugs, Carhart-Harris was cautious. 'I should be more conscious of the runaway enthusiasm that's happening now [around psychedelic drugs], and just keep that in check a bit', he said. He worried that some of the therapy that used these drugs wasn't grounded in well-researched science. 'What is the therapy, because it's not something that looks that familiar to me. It's not cognitive behavioural therapy, as I understand it. It's not even psychoanalysis, as I understand it. It's its own thing. What is that? That's a completely legitimate question, because it needs to be better documented and manualised so that others can understand the model and then replicate it and test it. You can't just assume that the model that you're using, which is left over from the 1960s, is the right one.'

Many of the teachings and mentorships that influenced this movement, from the 1960s until today, came from people with a mystical bent. 'As a secular scientist, I need to think carefully about that', Carhart-Harris said.

Many of the people I spoke to about psychedelic drugs stressed that they wanted to avoid what they viewed as the mistakes made by the 1960s generation. The message back then, personified by psychedelic drug preacher Timothy Leary, was to 'drop out of high school, drop out of college, drop out of graduate school.' The effect was a successful government campaign to demonise the drugs, and decades of wasted years when valuable scientific studies could have occurred. Today, the target audiences for advocates aren't hippies but the political and medical elites, to show them how valuable the drugs are. As the libertarian *Reason* magazine put it in 2017, the message is clear: 'Stay in school. Apply for research grants. Design clinical trials. Show your work. Evangelize, yes, but with a new audience in mind — not the counterculture, but the Man himself.'[11]

The US Drug Enforcement Administration (DEA) had placed MDMA on its Schedule One list in 1985, making it illegal to manufacture, sell, buy, or prescribe it. A Democrat from Texas, Lloyd Bentsen, had pushed the DEA to act after a spate of medical emergencies related to the drug. Nonetheless, one year later, a DEA administrative judge, Francis Young, concluded that the DEA had been mistaken and that MDMA should be a Schedule Three drug, allowing it to be prescribed by doctors. 'The overwhelming weight of medical opinion evidence received in this proceeding concurred that sufficient information on MDMA existed to support a judgment by reputable physicians that

MDMA was safe to use under medical supervision,' Young argued. 'No evidence was produced of any instances where MDMA was used in therapy with less than wholly acceptable safety.' His view was ignored.[12]

The practical application of psychedelics is a live issue today. Dr Ingmar Gorman is a New York-based psychologist who has researched the use of supervised ecstasy in the treatment of PTSD. He has also focused on using such drugs to treat substance abuse (a 2017 study published in the *Journal of Psychopharmacology* found that LSD and psilocybin helped people reduce their dependence on opioids). He was committed to the concept of MDMA becoming a recognised and accepted form of medicine.

Many decades ago, including in the US, doctors and psychiatrists used to take the same drugs as their patients, including psychedelics, to give them an insight into their effects. In the course of his research, Gorman interviewed these older doctors, and they agreed that it gave them a unique understanding into the use and applicability of psychedelic drugs under a carefully controlled scientific setting.

William A. Richards, a psychologist at the Johns Hopkins School of Medicine in Maryland, said that it was a 'perfectly rational thing for a professor to give LSD or psilocybin to a graduate student' in the 1960s, such was the normality of dishing it out to doctors and psychologists.[13]

Many doctors who advocated psychedelic drugs for treatment, personal growth, and insight spoke of the possibility of one drug-taking session having the potential of changing an individual's life. Some patients talked about taking these drugs as 'rebooting the brain.'[14]

Richards told *New Statesman* that, 'People may only receive the drug once and experience its effect for four to six hours but the benefit comes from the memory of that experience and how it changes your view of yourself, other people and the world.'[15]

Gorman's primary focus was on helping people with severe PTSD who were treatment-resistant, meaning that psychopharmacology and other psychotherapy didn't work: soldiers and people who had experienced war, torture, or sexual abuse. Jessi Appleton had been violently sexually assaulted when she was young, and had participated in the MDMA trial for PTSD set by up one of the US's leading groups advocating for psychedelic drugs, the Multidisciplinary Association for Psychedelic Studies (MAPS). She wrote in 2017 that, 'My MDMA sessions allowed me to process my past traumas and learn to live a life with compassion and self-love.'[16] Nonetheless, there were growing stories of sexual assaults occurring in the psychedelic community, which too often received little public attention. A #MeToo reckoning was required.

Although Gorman wanted MDMA to be more widely available as a medically provided treatment for trauma than it currently was, he worried about its overuse because not enough was known about its long-term effects. 'People can be very vulnerable when they're on these drugs', he said. 'My fear is that there could be some kind of negative consequence to willy-nilly prescription of psilocybin [mushrooms] or MDMA.' Instead, he wanted these drugs to be better integrated into normal medical treatment.

What motivated Gorman to continue his work was seeing the tangible results of patients using psychedelic drugs. 'Therapy with MDMA is kind of like driving a Ferrari', he explained. 'People refer to psychedelic therapy as accelerated therapy. I could use psychiatric terms to describe it, but it's like night and day. It's a transformation. From somebody who cannot smile, who doesn't have the joy in their life, to somebody who then has that, and it's incredibly motivating. It's moving. To be able to release that control, it's something that in therapy, without these drugs, can take decades. You see it over the period of three months [with ecstasy].'

It wasn't just ecstasy that provided potentially huge benefits to patients. Ketamine was also being tested to treat alcohol addiction (and it was proven to help some people with depression and anxiety). Elias Dakwar, a professor of clinical psychiatry at Columbia University in New York, led ketamine tests on patients with substance-abuse problems. 'The thinking on ketamine's effect on depression is that it reverses depression-related adaptation through neuroplasticity', he told *Vice Motherboard* in 2016. What he meant was that the brain became more open to creating new connections, and could stop old and unhealthy patterns of behaviour. Therapy with the drug held open the possibility of improving lives.[17]

Growing numbers of doctors wanted the option of using ketamine, because they had so few other medical ways to stop highly disturbed and distressed patients intent on suicide. Ketamine can be that powerful. Although the US FDA approved a ketamine-like nasal spray for release on the market in 2019 — to be made by pharmaceutical giant Johnson & Johnson — many doctors expressed reservations over the haste with which the product was approved, considering its still unknown long-term effects. Nonetheless, it's surely worth using judiciously on the 25 per cent of patients with depression who don't respond to current drugs.

Dakwar conducted a study on the use of ketamine to treat crack cocaine addiction. Early, unfinished results showed that the craving for cocaine was reduced with the use of small amounts of ketamine. If successful, ketamine could be used to rewire the brain to be less attracted to drugs such as cocaine and others like it that caused personal and societal damage if abused.[18]

Dakwar told me that despite the benefits of some psychedelic drugs, he did not support the full legalisation of them, because they required a 'medical context for administration. The risks associated with irresponsible use, which unfortunately we might predispose to if they're so freely available, are just so grave. There's potential psychosis that persists beyond the experience.'

These concerns led to the opening in New York in 2017 of the first US therapeutic facility for users of psychedelic drugs. Andrew Tatarsky, founder and director of the Centre for Optimal Living, said that the growth in experimentation with these drugs convinced him to open a space in which reliable information could be obtained about the opportunities and risks associated with them.

The Psychedelic Education and Continuing Care Program was another US-based initiative that aimed to both educate the wider public about the use of such drugs and reduce any harm. This movement was moving into the mainstream, with growing numbers of university students researching psychedelic science and better understanding the properties and possible benefits of the drugs. There was also a focus on getting more women and minorities involved in the movement.

~

What a legal and regulated drug market would look like is one of the great questions of our age, because no country has ever tried it. Throughout this book, I've included ideas, suggestions, and insights from drug takers, experts, academics, and politicians around the world about how it could be done, and why they think it's the most sensible way to tackle widespread drug use and misuse.

And yet it's only relatively recently that the public conversation in the US has momentously shifted, from why the drug war has been disastrous and should end to how this could be done. Growing anger over mass incarceration and increased support for legal cannabis have generated enough heat to lead the new conversation.

'Depending on how the issue is framed', an American writer on the drug war, Dan Baum, argued in 2016, 'legalisation of all drugs can appeal to conservatives, who are instinctively suspicious of bloated budgets, excess government authority, and intrusions on individual liberty, as well as to liberals, who are horrified at police overreach, the brutalisation of Latin America, and the criminalisation of entire generations of black men. It will take some courage to move the conversation beyond marijuana to ending all drug prohibition, but it will take less, I suspect, than most politicians believe.'[19]

I would quibble with Baum's characterisation of conservatives and liberals — many conservatives and liberals, especially since 11 September 2001, accepted vast government and corporate surveillance over their lives with little protest, and takers of cocaine rarely thought about the harm it caused to South American nations — but his overall point was correct. It's unimaginable that every nation in the world would suddenly legalise all drugs one day and that the drug war would simply end. Some countries would take incremental steps, such as starting with the legalisation of cannabis, and then potentially become open to further ideas leading to full legalisation. Others could follow the Portugal model, and decriminalise.

Let's imagine, with hard facts, what a different world could look like. We must consider the best ways to minimise harm in a legalised drug environment. Abuses and crime will occur; mental-health problems may ebb and flow, depending on access to proper treatment and medication; and it's possible that problematic drug use could worsen. A utopian legal and regulated drug market — a world where billions of citizens use substances responsibly — won't happen. Advocates of a different system must think through what could go wrong, to try to lessen any harmful consequences from the first day when strong and weak drugs are prescribed legally by a doctor and bought online, over a store counter, or at a pharmacy.

The evidence from Portugal is encouraging: troubled drug use has declined since 2001, and the state has spent huge amounts of money on treatment for any problems that have occurred since decriminalisation. Nonetheless, the outcome of legalisation in a larger country such as the US, Britain, or Australia is unclear. Demand for drugs remains sky-high across the globe, so for many experts the question is therefore clear: how can harm be mitigated?

Mark Kleiman, a professor of public policy at New York University, opposed the drug war for decades, and told *Harper's Magazine* that he believed the evidence pointed to a likely increase in problematic cocaine use after legalisation, roughly equivalent to the number of alcoholics in the US (around 17.6 million people). He feared that the government wouldn't spend enough on treatment to help. The result, he argued, could be higher numbers of troubled cocaine and alcohol users. 'A limit to alcoholism is you fall asleep', he said. 'Cocaine fixes that. And a limit to cocaine addiction is you can't sleep. Alcohol fixes that.'[20]

Even if Kleiman was correct — and there was no way to know with certainty until a country legalised all drugs — this didn't mean that a responsible state shouldn't move to end the far-worse system of prohibition, and aim to minimise harm in a regulated environment. Decades of hard evidence have proved the damage done by trying to police personal habits, with the enrichment of organised crime and the prevalence of associated ills an unavoidable by-product of the drug war.

A minority of people abuse alcohol chronically, but making it illegal is unthinkable. Instead, a rational society finds ways to warn people of the risks of excessive drinking, and offers treatment for those who fall between the cracks (although few nations achieve this successfully). Likewise, in a legalised drug market there would need to be tight controls over access, distribution, taxes, advertising (ideally, none at all), and care for anybody who didn't manage their drug habit properly. It's wildly irrational to imagine that every young person would start shooting up heroin at school if the drug suddenly became legal (and data from Portugal showed that overdoses and HIV infections dropped hugely after decriminalisation was instituted).

No legal market should encourage people to take drugs — in fact, the dangers associated with them should be made plain — and yet the widespread recreational use of such substances can't be discounted. Many of the problems that do occur in the recreational drug market are due to drugs that are mixed with deadly chemicals, or to the street violence that comes with drug dealing. A legal drug market would control the chemical composition of the drugs. The dark net or shady dealers could still sell unsafe drugs, but the prevalence of this activity would decline.

Anybody who wanted to take ecstasy at a party, for example, would know where to find clean, tested pills. Young people would be taught not to take them excessively — in lessons that should start in high school — and a legal market would allow scientists to far better understand the long-term effects of drug use. This research is currently highly restricted because the substances are illegal.

Steve Rolles is a senior policy analyst of drug policy with the Transform Drug Policy Foundation in Britain, and he's one of the most informed thinkers on the subject. In 2019, he released the world's first book on how to regulate cocaine and other stimulants. He explored the viability of consumer cocaine products such as energy drinks, lozenges, and gum, and whether the general public would use them if they were regulated and produced safely.

His 2017 book, *Legalising Drugs: the key to ending the war*, laid out a clear path towards a sustainable and sensible drug policy. 'Working towards reducing harm would shift the focus of policy from reducing use per se to reducing problematic use (in other words, use that creates significant negative impacts for the user or those around them)', Rolles wrote.[21]

US writer Dan Baum argued that there had to be a state monopoly over drug distribution; otherwise, the profit motive would corrupt the process. 'That the government should profit from a product it wants to discourage could be seen as hypocritical but that's the way things stand with tobacco, alcohol, and gambling', he wrote.[22] He advocated that state funds, as in Portugal, be directed to helping troubled drug takers, producing education campaigns aimed at dissuading the use of drugs, and establishing a range of services (from public infrastructure to health care) from tax income.

Baum could foresee that criminal networks that today make huge amounts of money from the drug-trade would diversify their interests into other nefarious areas, such as illicit goods or kidnapping, to recover the lost revenue from the legalisation of drugs. But law enforcement should target these groups, and, using the proceeds of legalisation, would have greater funds to do so. Harvard economist and director of economic studies at the libertarian think tank the Cato Institute, Jeffrey Miron, estimated in 2019 that local, state, and federal US governments could reap a US$106.7 billion annual windfall from the legalisation of all prohibited drugs. This huge sum would be derived both from tax revenue and law-enforcement savings.

Although public opinion has shifted radically in many Western nations towards supporting cannabis legalisation, it remains a minority view that all drugs should be legalised and regulated. Despite the Global Commission on Drugs finding in 2016 that the banning of drugs has had 'little or no impact' on drug use globally, there was still a long way to go to convince a sceptical public to back an end to prohibition. I heard this scepticism across the globe. After all, as this book shows, it wasn't the rich who suffered in the drug war. It was the poor and minorities, so it was these groups (and those with the most limited voices in our political and media systems) who would disproportionately benefit from an end to prohibition. On this issue, I can't claim to be an objective journalist, weighing up the pros and cons of legalisation, when I've witnessed the debilitating effects of prohibition. I'm happy to be called an advocate for new and safer ways to address drug use and abuse.

Rolles envisaged various ways to regulate drug supply. The most serious drugs, such as injectable heroin, would be prescribed by a medical practitioner and could only be taken in a supervised facility.

Pharmacies could offer drugs such as ecstasy to interested users and sell it to them in non-branded packaging. Licensed outlets could sell drugs carrying a lower level of risk, such as magic mushrooms and cannabis, with buyers allowed to consume them on the property. International, national, and local laws would need to change and adapt to the new drug regime to work.

The advantages of this system were clear, Rolles explained:

> Legalised and regulated drugs will be of known quantity and potency, will come with dosage and safety information from the vendor and on the packaging. They are also more likely to be consumed in safer, supervised environments that encourage more responsible using behaviours. We have to move beyond the historical preoccupation with reducing the prevalence of use and have a pragmatic focus on reducing risky use and overall harm.[23]

No country would adopt these measures overnight; it would be a gradual process of removing the litany of prohibitionist legalisation, policing, and attitudes. Yet, from what I've heard and seen, I believe that it's the most sensible way to end decades of wasted resources and ruined lives on a war that will never be won. Continuing with prohibition does nothing to address the ballooning profits of criminal groups, or the many deaths from dirty drugs. Legalisation and regulation could transform the way in which we view drugs — from being a danger having to be controlled to providing an opportunity to establish a safer society.

Conclusion

'After writing about drugs for the last 20 years, my
conclusion is that the only way worldwide drug use will be
eliminated is if Earth gets whacked by a colossal meteor.
In the meantime, it's time to do away with the myths and
hyperbole so often used when talking about drugs. Drugs can
be fun. They can also be dangerous. What is for sure is that
they are not going away.'
MAX DALY, *VICE*, 2018[1]

In a world awash with drugs, it's worth looking at Iceland. With a
population of just under 340,000 people, it's a country that could
teach the rest of us a few things about taming excessive drug use.

In 1992, teenagers in Iceland filled out a survey about their
experiences with alcohol and drugs. Over 40 per cent had been
recently drunk, and 25 per cent smoked daily. Today, however, those
figures have radically changed, and the nation's teens are the most
drug- and alcohol-free on the European continent. The percentage of
15- and 16-year-olds who had drunk alcohol fell from 42 per cent in
1998 to 5 per cent in 2016. Cannabis use dived from 17 per cent to 7
per cent, and cigarette smokers also fell from 23 per cent to 3 per cent.

American psychologist Harvey Milkman was recruited to help
Iceland in 1991. An American psychology professor, Milkman knew
that children started using drugs and alcohol to fill an emotional

void, so he posited that they could be stimulated by alternatives such as music, dance, hip-hop, art, and martial arts. He had opened a centre in Denver where he had seen dramatic results. Iceland also introduced a plan called Youth in Iceland, which restricted access to tobacco and alcohol, imposed night curfews on young teenagers, and encouraged greater interaction between parents and their children. The state even gave families a leisure card to spend on activities.[2]

The results were dramatic. Between 1997 and 2012, children played much more organised sport and doubled the time they spent with their parents. Cannabis use, drinking, and nicotine use all dropped. Although Iceland took major steps that many other nations would not (including a large role for the state and a form of social engineering), it's hard to argue with the outcome. Iceland isn't the answer to the world's drug problems — it's a tiny nation whose experiences can't be simply copied in other cultures and places with bigger populations — but it's worth investigating how it works.

This is a more positive side of the drug story that too rarely makes the news. This book is full of horror stories from across the globe, about how the darkest fantasies of prohibitionists have turned the world into a charnel house. Stopping the carnage will take a monumental effort on the part of politicians and the public. Although there are some positive signs that a few leaders are now listening — legalising and regulating cannabis is a strong first step — the vast bulk of the drug war involves other, harder drugs. These substances remain illegal and are consumed by millions; the result is a drug supply-chain that enriches a minority at the expense of a majority who toil for little reward.

The most pessimistic view of the coming decades is expressed in apocalyptic terms. Think of ever-worsening crime wars waged by drug cartels, terrorists, gangs, and mafias with overwhelming military-grade firepower. Narco-cities are already increasingly common in Mexico and Brazil, operating parallel governments that solely exist to grow a drug economy. This toxic cocktail causes huge refugee movements, insecurity, and violence in the Middle East, Central Asia, sub-Saharan North Africa, and Central and South America.[3] With a fragmenting global order, and no central authority or power willing or able to resolve conflicts, these trends are set to continue. Maintaining strict prohibitionist policies, while demand for drugs continues, only exacerbates the problems.

Famed US historian Alfred McCoy, one of the world's experts on the drug war, predicts that China will overtake the US by 2030 to become the globe's leading hegemon with the most powerful economy.[4] What this means for drug policy is unclear, although it's hard to be overly optimistic. Although Washington may no longer have the interest or ability to police and dictate prohibitionist policies that have been the mainstay of drug-war architecture for more than half a century, Beijing is hardly a liberal reformer. China executes more people than any other nation on the planet, often for drug dealing, and punishment can be a harsh drug-rehabilitation facility. If these policies are forced on other countries, like the US has done for decades, legalising and regulating drugs will be even more difficult to achieve.

Travelling across the world for the last four years and seeing the devastating effects of the drug war has been a powerful reminder to me that business as usual must end. The stories I heard in Honduras, the Philippines, Guinea-Bissau, the UK, the US, and Australia were often from individuals caught up in a war that they didn't understand and had no ability to change. Small-time dealers, farmers, fishermen, and users weren't interested in fighting a war against drugs. For them, it was just an economic lifeline.

Let's end the negative judgements around drug use and abuse. It achieves nothing other than making necessary policy change more difficult. But perhaps even more importantly, attitudes need to change towards those who take drugs. As a journalist, I know the damage that my profession has contributed to these false stereotypes. Enough.

In terms of dangers to society, alcohol is undeniably more harmful — the World Health Organisation found in 2018 that alcohol was responsible for more than 5 per cent of global deaths every year, or around three million people — and yet it receives far less media, political, and public concern. This doesn't have to be a permanent state of affairs — both alcohol and drugs should be better regulated in a healthy society — and yet it is cannabis, heroin, ecstasy, and all the others that are often demonised as moral abominations.

The Global Commission on Drugs, composed of former leaders from Africa, South America, and Europe, released a report in 2018 that keeps up the pressure on prohibitionist bodies to reverse course. 'The legal regulation of drugs is rapidly moving from the theoretical to the practical domain', it began. 'This report addresses the reality that over 250 million people around the world are taking risks by consuming currently prohibited drugs. Accepting this reality and putting in place an effective regulatory strategy to manage it is neither admitting defeat nor condoning drug use. It is part of a responsible, evidence-based approach that deals with the world as it is in contrast with ideologically driven and ultimately counterproductive attempts to create a 'drug-free world.'"[5]

This was a direct challenge to the US-led approach to drugs. President Donald Trump had ramped up his rhetoric on the drug war, especially in Washington's sphere of influence, and supported a militarised response that has devastated vast parts of Latin and South America in the past. Nonetheless, hard-line supporters of the drug war would have been disappointed by figures released by Harm Reduction International in 2019 that showed a massive drop in known state executions globally for drug offences (91 known deaths in 2018, compared to 755 in 2015). According to the group, at least 7,000 people remain on death row worldwide for drug offences.

As this book has shown, logic rarely enters drug policy when criminalisation is a far easier solution. And yet facts have an uncomfortable tendency to get in the way. The International Drug Policy Consortium, a global network of 175 NGOs, released a groundbreaking study in 2018 that analysed the previous ten years of the drug war. Its conclusions were shocking yet unsurprising. With nearly half a million deaths every year, an explosion in opium and coca production, a 31 per cent increase in drug use, and increasingly dangerous drugs being consumed without any safeguards, the war on drugs had caused unprecedented upheaval. And yet when was the last time you read these statistics in the media? It's a war that impacts millions of people, and yet they're not important enough to warrant sustained attention.[6] This book is, hopefully, a corrective to this wilful blindness.

I remain haunted by the stories I saw and heard across the globe, and it's hard not to conclude that the drug war continues because some lives matter more than others. A white opioid user in the US warrants sympathy, but a black drug dealer deserves prison. A poor man in Manila is killed in cold blood, and yet many of his fellow citizens support it. Families weep in Honduras as loved ones are murdered, while the Trump administration backs its corrupt government. Drug abuse in Britain has never been worse, but most of the media ignore it. Australians could be saved by pill testing at music festivals, but many politicians refuse to even consider it. Cocaine use soars in the West, while low-level traffickers toil for little reward but big risk.

This is what the war on drugs looks like on the ground in every corner of the globe, and it will never end until African, South American, and Asian lives matter as much as white lives in the Western heartland. There are viable alternatives to this reality if we want to see them.

Over the past century, the drug war has been a convenient justification to ostracise, demonise, imprison, ignore, or kill the most marginalised. And yet drugs have never been more widely available, so those ideas have failed. What replaces them is yet to be seen, although I hope this book shows a way forward, in listening to those most affected by the war and imagining a world where a person using heroin or snorting cocaine isn't deemed unimportant or expendable. I hope readers listen to them, and encourage policy-makers to stop blaming the victim and wishing for a world where illicit substances have disappeared. That's the kind of fantasy thinking that created the war on drugs in the first place.

There is nothing inevitable about the drug war ending. As this book has shown, it serves and enriches many people and institutions around the world. Look at the rise of nationalism, hard borders, and the repression of refugees — policies pushed by Trump and many European leaders. The idea held by many progressives that the world would increasingly embrace the outsider has been mugged by reality, and sounds like a naïve wish today. Likewise with the war on drugs: it will take years more of campaigning and fighting back against the wrong-headed though politically powerful messages that have sustained it for so long. The drug war is both real and fake, sustained by fear, effective propaganda, and extreme violence. One can't operate without the other.

As journalist Max Daly wrote for *Vice*, the public conversation around drugs has remained myopic. 'In reality most people use drugs because they are fun, or an escape, not because they are morally corrupt', he explained. 'Drug addiction and street drug selling is a symptom of inequality and lack of hope, not of people simply being lazy or evil. If those who use drugs continue to be treated as criminals before they are seen as people, the need for open, honest reporting on this subject is paramount. It's time to bury the caricatures of pushers selling drugs to kids outside the school gates, zombie junkies, and instantaneous addiction. Now is the time for reality to be represented.'[7]

After working on this book for years, I've come to realise that the required action to stop or avert the drug war isn't going to come in radical waves, as much as I wish it would. The world won't suddenly legalise and regulate drugs. It'll be a messy collection of nations and states experimenting with various forms of legalisation and decriminalisation. Public acceptance of cannabis is a positive step, but will it lead to all drugs being similarly taxed and available? After witnessing the damage that prohibition causes, from Honduras to Australia, I support the complete legalisation and regulation of all drugs, so long as that is accompanied by appropriate safeguards. I hope that at least one of the Latin American nations that has gained nothing but trouble from criminalisation manages to legalise cocaine and show the world how it could be done. That's the ultimate good example, and the best way to reject Washington's disastrous lead.[8]

As with climate change, small incremental shifts won't ultimately suffice to address the drug war. There is a need, as Canadian writer Naomi Klein explains, to fundamentally reorient our societies away from capitalist growth. Similarly, if you consume drugs, it's not enough to become more ethical in drug taking — by all means, consider the source of your drugs, and avoid worsening the lives of the supply chain's most vulnerable victims — in the hope that this will provide a clear path to ending the war on drugs. It may make you feel good, but will do little to help the millions of dealers, drug takers, farmers, and couriers who are caught in this self-defeating war.

For those who believe that the war on drugs has failed, and will always fail, it is time to imagine and work towards a different future.

Acknowledgements

Writing a book is always a collaborative affair. After travelling the world to multiple countries over the last four years to investigate the drug war, I appreciate the invaluable advice, assistance, and friendships I've experienced with hundreds of people. This book wouldn't exist without it. There's justified scepticism about the media and journalists in many nations, so individuals helping me in my quest to reveal and expose the drug war is remarkable. I cherish these interactions, and I remain in touch with many of the sources, fixers, and contacts in this book.

There are many people whose names can't be listed due to safety concerns, but I thank them for their essential work.

In Honduras, Raul Valdivia was a fixer with extraordinary insights, and I thank him for helping me navigate a very challenging nation. He read the Honduras chapter and offered useful suggestions.

In Guinea-Bissau, Allen Yero Embalo guided me skilfully through a country that very few other journalists ever visit.

In the Philippines, Bernardino Testa knew the streets of Manila so well, and helped explain the brutality of the drug war.

In Britain and the US, Johann Hari kindly connected me with many people who knew what the war on drugs meant on the ground. His generosity is an inspiration.

The following friends, family, contacts, and acquaintances provided everything from thought-provoking conversation to useful links, a bed to rest at the end of the day, connections, and guidance:

Yasmine Ahmed, Maryam Alavi, Anthony Arnove, Conor Ashleigh, Wendy Bacon, Reuben Brand, Dan Davies, Paul Farrell, Luke Fletcher, Benjamin Gilmour, Emily Howie, Mark Jeanes, Matt Kennard, Danny Kushlick, Mary and Ross Martin, Anita Martins, Lizzie O'Shea, Mike and Jess Otterman, Selena Papps, Mustafa Qadri, Justin Randle, Jeff Sparrow, Helga Svendsen, and Kaspia Warner.

Thanks to Scribe and Henry Rosenbloom for their guidance, editing prowess, and vital support.

My literary agents, Benython Oldfield, Sharon Galant, and Thomasin Chinnery from Zeitgeist Media Group, who span the globe, read my manuscript, offered great suggestions, and helped push this book into global hands.

Jeffrey Loewenstein is a father with endless supplies of love, energy, and enthusiasm. I thank him for sharing my passion and supporting it. I lost my mother, Violet, during the writing of this book, and I miss her dearly. I like to think she's looking down and smiling at this book because it advocates for a kinder, gentler world.

Alison Martin has been my partner in crime for many years, and she provides never-ending support, love, adventures, laughs, insights, and honesty. I can't imagine travelling through life without her. Our first child, Raphael, was born during the research of this book, and he has brought unimaginable joy (and tiredness) to our lives. Becoming a parent with Ali has reinvigorated my commitment to serious journalism, because at its heart it aims to highlight injustice and imagine a better future for our children. I hope he enjoys this book when he can read big words.

Notes

Introduction

1 Dan Baum, 'Legalise It All: how to win the war on drugs", *Harper's*, April 2016.

2 Michelle Alexander, *The New Jim Crow: mass incarceration in the Age of Colorblindness*, The New Press, New York, 2010.

3 Norman Ohler, *Blitzed: drugs in Nazi Germany*, Penguin Books, London, 2017, p. 24.

4 Matt Kennard, 'Is there a drugs war in Latin America?', *Alborada*, 20 December 2017.

5 Then DEA head Michele M. Leonhart stepped down from her post in 2015 after failing to adequately manage the scandal that saw DEA agents using prostitutes paid for by drug cartels in Colombia. She was a staunch opponent of cannabis legalisation, and stated publicly that 'all illegal drugs are bad".

6 Ginger Thompson, 'Who holds the DEA accountable when its missions cost lives?', *ProPublica*, 19 June 2017.

7 Kate Linthicum, 'Meth and murder: A new kind of drug war has made Tijuana one of the deadliest places on Earth', *The Los Angeles Times*, 30 January 2019.

8 'Trial of El Chapo highlights failure of US war on drugs, but will US ever be held to account?', *Democracy Now!*, 5 February 2019.

9 Deborah Bonello, 'In El Chapo's Mexico, fentanyl is the new boom drug', *Vice*, 18 February 2019.

10 Jessica Loudis, 'In Mexico, the cartels do not exist': a Q&A with Oswaldo Zavala, *The Nation*, 22 April 2019.

11 'El Chapo is behind bars but drugs still flow from Mexico', *The New York Times*, 13 February 2019.

12 Ginger Thompson, '"There's no real fight against drugs"', *The Atlantic*, 20 July 2015; Washington's plan in Mexico was based around the kingpin strategy, decapitating cartel leaders, and yet this led to the fragmentation of the drug business and internal power vacuums. Drug production and trafficking was not affected. See Deborah Bonello, 'El Chapo is on trial. So business for his cartel is booming', *Ozy*, 12 November 2018.

13 Nick Miroff, 'The staggering cost of Colombia's war with FARC rebels, explained

in numbers', *The Washington Post*, 24 August 2016.

14 Natalio Cosoy, 'Has Plan Colombia really worked?', *BBC News*, 4 February 2016.

15 Jana Winter, 'Trump says border wall will stop drugs. Here's what a DEA intel report says', *Foreign Policy*, 29 August 2017.

16 Seth Freed Wessler, 'The Coast Guard's "floating Guantanamos"', *The New York Times,* 20 November 2017.

17 Alfred McCoy, *The Politics of Heroin: CIA complicity in the global drug-trade*, Lawrence Hill Books, 2003, p. 461.

18 Ibid, pp. 16–17.

19 Fernando Henrique Cardoso, the former president of Brazil and chair of the Global Commission on Drug Policy, Cesar Gaviria, the former president of Colombia and Ernesto Zedillo, the former president of Mexico, wrote in 2016 that the war on drugs was an "unmitigated disaster" and the criminalisation of drugs must end. See Fernando Henrique Cardoso, Cesar Gaviria and Ernesto Zedillo, 'Three leaders from Latin America call for decriminalising drug use', *The Los Angeles Times*, 11 March 2016.

20 Maia Szalavitz, 'Why we should say someone is a "person with an addiction", not an addict', NPR, 11 June 2017.

21 Joel Wolfram, 'Don't call people "addicts", Penn researchers say', WHYY, 13 August 2018.

22 Steven Cohen, 'What "Narcos" gets wrong about the war on drugs', *The New Republic*, 30 October 2015.

23 Jon Lee Anderson, 'The afterlife of Pablo Escobar', *The New Yorker*, 5 March 2018.

Chapter One: Honduras

1 Alongside Berta on the night of her death, activist Gustavo Castro Soto was present and shot, sustaining injuries. He survived and returned to his native Mexico, pursuing justice for his murdered friend.

2 Copinh reacted to Mejia's arrest by accusing the Honduran government of dragging its feet over the investigation (a common complaint I heard during my time in Honduras). 'The arrest is thanks to the work and pressure by national and international organisations', it wrote. 'No thanks is due to the attorney general's office, who have tried everything possible to cover up the truth in this case.'

3 Nina Lakhani, 'Berta Caceres murder: ex-Honduran military intelligence officer arrested', *The Guardian*, 2 March 2018.

4 According to the Mexico Citizens' Council for Public Security annual survey in 2017 of the 50 most violent cities globally, 42 were in Latin America and two in Honduras. See Christopher Woody, 'These were the most violent cities in the world in 2017', *Business Insider*, 6 March 2018.

5 'Events of 2017, Honduras', Human Rights Watch World Report, 2018. Copinh and

the Caceres family launched legal proceedings against FMO in the Netherlands in May 2018 for disregarding human-rights concerns over the dam before Berta's murder. One hope of the action was to pressure European banks and companies not to ignore human rights in the future when funding projects.

6 In 2015, a Honduran journalist exposed that millions of dollars of public funds for the health care system were transferred to the National Party for the re-election of President Hernandez, but nobody senior was fired or investigated. See Alexander Main, 'An anti-corruption charade in Honduras', *The New York Times*, 15 February 2016.

7 US Attorney General Jeff Sessions announced in June 2018 that asylum seekers would no longer gain entry into the US by claiming fears of gang violence or domestic abuse. It was a decision that would affect many people fleeing Central America.

8 Before the election of Donald Trump in 2016, Buzzfeed reported that many of the clothes sold under his name were sewn in Honduras by workers who received a pittance. See Karla Zabludovsky and Daniel Wagner, 'Meet the workers who sewed Donald Trump clothing for a few dollars a day', *Buzzfeed News*, 22 July 2016.

9 Official figures of gang members vary widely, from the US government claiming 36,000, to the UN saying 12,000 and the Honduran police alleging 25,000. See Elyssa Pachico, 'The problem with counting gang members in Honduras', *Insight Crime*, 17 February 2016.

10 In Tegucigalpa, I visited one of its most dangerous neighbourhoods, Flor Del Campo (Flower of the Field), and met an outspoken citizen, Juan Hernandez, to understand what a 'war tax' and government-sponsored violence meant. He told me that, 'We always live in a state of terror. It's like your life is hanging by a thread.' A few days before we spoke, in a house where women explained how they were often unable to walk the streets due to extreme violence, a massacre had occurred outside a nearby school and innocent people were killed. Hernandez said that he didn't know anybody who wasn't considering leaving the country. 'In this area, 70 per cent of businesses closed down because of it [war tax]. I had a business plan but it stayed just a plan because of the war tax … People flee their homes and never come back, fearing for their lives.'

11 Sibylla Brodzinsky, 'Inside San Pedro Sula: the most violent city in the world', *The Guardian*, 16 May 2013. Honduran police said that the murder rate in 2017 declined by more than 25 per cent to 42.8 killings per 100,000 people but countless activists I spoke to questioned the accuracy of these statistics. A relation of Berta Caceres, freelance film producer Silvio Carrillo, wrote in *The New York Times* that US ambassador James Nealon admitted in a meeting that Honduran officials manipulated crime figures. See Silvio Carrillo, 'An idealist's martyrdom fails to move Honduras', *The New York Times*, 2 March 2017. Many

women's rights groups said that authorities were focused on narco-trafficking and organised crime while ignoring the wave of killings engulfing civilians, especially women. Sara Tome, programme director at the Centre for Women's Studies Tegucigalpa told the BBC News in July 2017 that, 'we are angry about the constant indifference in the justice system'.

12   Eating foreign junk food for the middle class in Honduras was a sign of success that they could buy their child an American hamburger. I saw similar trends in China of economic advancement intimately tied to consuming the most garish signs of American capitalism. Later in the Honduran trip I visited a petrol station to buy water, but could only find Coke, Pepsi, and any number of sugary drinks. It felt as if Honduras imported the worst aspects of US culture, such as its fatty and unhealthy fast food, and locals were given few culinary choices that inevitably worsened their health.

13   'Where did banana republics get their name?', *The Economist*, 21 November 2013.

14   John Ewing, a US minister in Tegucigalpa, sent a letter in 1914 to the US State Department and explained the power of the United Fruit Company: 'In order to obtain these concessions and privileges and to secure their undisturbed enjoyment, it [the United Fruit Company] has seen fit to enter actively into the internal policies of these countries, and it has pursued this course so systematically and regularly until it now has its ramifications in every department of the government and is a most important factor in all political movements and actions.' See Dawn Paley, *Drug War Capitalism*, AK Press, 2014, p. 195.

15   Jane Hunter, 'Israel funded, armed and trained the Contras in co-ordination with Washington', *Washington Report On Middle East Affairs*, January 1987, pp. 4–5. https://www.wrmea.org/1987-january/israeli-arms-sales-to-central-america-an-overview.html.

16   Battalion 316 was a death squad that disappeared, tortured, and murdered Honduran opponents of regime head General Gustavo Alvarez Martinez. Its existence was denied for years by both Honduran and US officials (even though the CIA had given the Contras an 'assassination manual' to further its goals). At least 184 people were killed by Battalion 316, with many others murdered by other forces in the 1980s and 1990s, and yet its victims still search for justice. See 'Honduras seeks to revive cases from the 1980s dirty war', Reuters, 8 January 2008.

17   A former Honduran politician, Efrain Diaz Arrivillaga, told *The Baltimore Sun* in 1995 that, 'their [the US government] attitude was one of tolerance and silence. They needed Honduras to loan its territory more than they were concerned about innocent people being killed.' See Gary Cohn and Ginger Thompson, 'A carefully crafted deception', *The Baltimore Sun*, 18 June 1995.

18   The former president of the Committee for the Defense of Human Rights in Honduras (CODEH), Ramon Custodio Lopez, wrote that drugs in Honduras

slowly strangled his country in ways that had never been undone: '… Before it [Honduras] was simply a stop-over [for drugs], next came the stage of consumption as part of the new habits of the nouveau riche of high society, but later it became dollar payments for services rendered [and then] payments in kind because there was already an internal market for coca[ine] and we have advanced in the area of money laundering and narco politics.' See Thelma Mejia, 'Unfinished business: the military and drugs in Honduras', TNI, 1 December 1997.

19   Andrew Marshall, 'CIA turned a deliberate blind eye to Contras' drug-smuggling', *The Independent*, 7 November 1998.

20   Robert Parry, 'CIA's drug confession', *Consortium News*, 11 October 1998.

21   One drug-delivery effort from Honduras to Miami in 1981 was called an 'initial trial run' because the Contras claimed that they had to become drug-traffickers 'in order to feed and clothe their cadres'. The CIA did nothing to stop these activities and even encouraged them, sometimes hiring Contras whom they knew were dealing drugs. There were literally hundreds of allegations against Contra officials and nearly 1,000 CIA cables sent back to Washington that outlined the Contras' illegalities. At times, according to the 1998 CIA report, the agency instructed the DEA to avoid inquiring into Contra authorities. See Walter Pincus, 'CIA ignored tips alleging Contra drug links, report says', *The Washington Post*, 3 November 1998.

22   Gary Webb found that a CIA-sponsored Contra group called the FDN had ties with San Francisco drug-traffickers, and after cocaine was sold to a dealer in South Central Los Angeles, the millions of dollars from those transactions were funnelled to the US-backed war against the Sandinistas. Webb showed that poor African-Americans, the community most negatively affected by crack cocaine, were collateral damage in Washington's pursuit of geo-political goals in Central America. Webb wrote that President Reagan feared 'another Cuba taking root in their backyard, another clique of Communists who would spread their noxious seeds of dissent and discord throughout the region.' For these revelations, Webb was smeared by many in the mainstream media; he lost his job, and eventually committed suicide in 2004. See Gary Webb, *Dark Alliance: the CIA, the Contras and the crack cocaine explosion*, Seven Stories Press, 2014. p. 69.

23   A succession of the Honduran elite had been charged and jailed for drug-trafficking in Honduras and the US; it's common for Honduran election campaigns to be paid for with drug money and their leaders beholden to traffickers. See Brendan Pierson, 'Son of ex-Honduran president gets 24 years for US drug charge', Reuters, 6 September 2017.

24   'Open and Shut: The case of the Honduran coup', Wikileaks State Department cable, 24 July 2009. After finishing his term as ambassador in 2008, Charles Ford became diplomatic attaché for the US Southern Command in Miami, the body

tasked to fight the drug war in Latin America.

25 '11 Latin American dictators', School of the Americas Watch, http://www.soaw.
   org/index.php?option=com_content&view=article&id=840.

26 Jake Johnson, 'How Pentagon officials may have encouraged a 2009 coup in
   Honduras', *The Intercept*, 30 August 2017.

27 Stephen Zunes, 'The US role in the Honduras coup and subsequent violence',
   National Catholic Reporter, 14 March 2016.

28 Mark Weisbrot, 'Hard Choices: Hillary Clinton admits role in Honduran coup
   aftermath', Al Jazeera America, 29 September 2014. Clinton emails released in
   2015 shone more light on her actions after the 2009 coup. Despite the Obama
   White House claiming that aid had been suspended after the coup, Clinton
   ensured that more than $1 million continued to the new regime. She turned to
   a lobbyist friend of her family, Lanny Davis, to establish contact with the coup
   leader, Roberto Micheletti, and he publicly blamed overthrown president Manuel
   Zelaya for his downfall. See Bill Conroy, 'Emails show Clinton disobeyed Obama
   policy and continued funding for Honduras coup regime', *The Narcosphere*, 5
   July 2015. Zelaya told *Democracy Now!* in 2015 that he blamed Clinton for being
   'very weak in the face of pressures from groups that hold power in the United
   States, the most extremist right-wing sectors of the U.S. government, known as
   the hawks of Washington.' See 'Clinton and the coup: amid protests in Honduras,
   ex-President on Hillary's role in his 2009 ouster', *Democracy Now!*, 28 July 2015.
   During the 2016 presidential election campaign, Clinton was asked by the New
   York *Daily News* about her role in the coup. She claimed that the regime 'followed
   the law' by ousting Zelaya, and that 'I think in retrospect we managed a very
   difficult situation without bloodshed'. She argued that cutting US aid to Honduras
   would have 'punished the Honduran people' and that was why she believed it was
   unwise to call the events in 2009 a coup.

29 Nikolas Kozloff and Bill Weinberg, 'Honduras and the political uses of the drug
   war', North American Congress on Latin America (NACLA), 20 April 2010.

30 Alan Yuhas, 'Former Latin American leaders urge world to end war on drugs
   "disaster"', *The Guardian*, 12 March 2016.

31 *The Nation* revealed in 2016 that secretary of state Hillary Clinton had spent
   tens of millions of dollars in 2012 on a little-known propaganda program called
   'Honduras Convive' that was aimed at winning the 'hearts and minds' of the
   Honduran people. It involved working with private contractors, including one
   owned by Australian David Kilcullen — a self-described counter-insurgency
   expert who contributed to the failed US wars in Iraq and Afghanistan and now
   runs a for-profit contracting business — to build closer ties between police and
   the community. The unstated goal of the program was to back a regime friendly
   to US business and strategic interests. See Tim Shorrock, 'How Hillary Clinton

militarised US policy in Honduras', *The Nation*, 5 April 2016.

32   In December 2009, the country's top anti-drug official, Julian Aristides Gonzalez Irias, was murdered with the collusion of high-level police commanders and drug-traffickers. It was reportedly because this official had stopped cartel plans to work with police and steal 143 kilograms of cocaine from a rival. A cover-up ensued, and nobody senior was ever held to account for the killing. See Elizabeth Malkin and Alberto Arce, 'Files suggest Honduran police leaders ordered killing of antidrug officials', *The New York Times*, 15 April 2016.

33   Thom Shanker, 'Lessons of Iraq help US fight a drug war in Honduras', *The New York Times*, 5 May 2012.

34   Janine Jackson, 'NYT claims US opposed Honduran coup it actually supported', Fairness and Accuracy in Reporting, 18 August 2017; and Adam Johnson, 'Omitting the US role in Honduran activist's death', Fairness and Accuracy in Reporting, April 2016.

35   Damien Cave and Charlie Savage, 'US rethinks a drug war after deaths in Honduras', *The New York Times*, 12 October 2012.

36   'Honduras profile', *Insight Crime*, 10 November 2017.

37   Mo Hume, 'Why the murder rate in Honduras is twice as high as anywhere else', *The Conversation*, 26 November 2014. One former congressman and police commissioner in charge of drug investigations, Alfredo Landaverde, claimed that one out of every ten members of Congress was a drug-trafficker. He was murdered in 2011.

38   Danielle Mackay, 'Drugs, dams and power: the murder of Honduran activist Berta Caceres', *The Intercept*, 12 March 2016.

39   Joel Brinkley, 'Violence in Honduras has US fingerprints on it', *The Kansas City Star*, 28 June 2013.

40   The Hernandez regime bought sophisticated cyber tools to monitor computers and mobile phones from a notorious arms dealer, Ori Zeller, in 2014. Zeller, a former member of the Israeli special forces, had a long history of working with extremist groups and right-wing paramilitary forces in Colombia. See Lee Fang, 'Former AK-47 dealer goes cyber, supplied surveillance tools to Honduras government', *The Intercept*, 27 July 2015. The UK sold surveillance equipment to the Honduras regime just before the disputed 2017 election. See Nina Lakhani, 'UK sold spyware to Honduras just before crackdown on election protestors', *The Guardian*, 8 February 2018.

41   The Honduran regime paid the leading US PR firm Ketchum US$421,333 in 2015 to burnish its image. See Sarah Lazare, 'Meet the corporate PR firm hired to sell a murderous foreign regime to the American public', *Alternet*, 15 April 2016. In 2016, the Honduras ambassador in the US hired Washington, DC, based–PR firm Curley Company for US$40,000 and two months of work.

42 Israel has a long history of supporting, arming and training right-wing dictatorships in South America, Central America and Africa: see http://dailysketcher.blogspot.com/2009/09/honduras-israeli-connection.html and https://www.wrmea.org/1987-january/israeli-arms-sales-to-central-america-an-overview.html.

43 When nearly 50,000 unaccompanied children crossed into the US from Central America in 2014, Obama pushed Mexico to stop the flow, paying them $86 million for the job. See Nicholas Kristof, 'Obama's death sentence for young refugees', *The New York Times*, 25 June 2016.

44 Congressman Hank Johnson was joined by a number of other Congressmen and women in demanding accountability for US aid, justice for Berta Caceres, and an investigation into whether the US-trained Honduran security forces, Fusina, were involved in her murder. See John James Conyers Junior, Keith Ellison, Hank Johnson, Marcy Kaptur, Jan Schakowsky and Jose E. Serrano, 'America's funding of Honduran security forces puts blood on our hands', *The Guardian*, 8 July 2016.

45 Tracy Wilkinson, 'Congress and the State Department at odds over $55 million in aid to Honduras', the *Los Angeles Times*, 25 October 2016. After the conclusion of the Berta Caceres trial in late 2018, Congresswoman Ilhan Omar pledged to pursue justice to the 'highest strata of the Honduran elite.'

46 Trump started sending back tens of thousands of Hondurans who had been living legally for years in the US in 2018 despite US diplomats claiming the move would further destabilise Central America. See Nick Miroff, Seung Min Kim and Joshua Partlow, 'US embassy cables warned against expelling 300,000 immigrants. Trump officials did it anyway', *The Washington Post*, 8 May 2018. During a visit to Washington, DC, in October 2018, President Hernandez expressed reservations with Trump's separation of children from their parents after they entered the US. 'I cannot go back to Honduras without an answer', he said.

47 Silvio Carrillo, 'America's blind eye to Honduras's tyrant', *The New York Times*, 19 December 2017.

48 President Hernandez had been invited to Israel to attend the country's independence celebrations in 2018, but he cancelled after human-rights groups complained. President Trump threatened to cut off aid to Honduras in an April 2018 tweet after he accused Honduras and other Central American nations of allowing a caravan of Honduran migrants to move through Mexico towards the US. Trump continued this public pressure on Honduras when another caravan made its way towards the US in late 2018. The vast bulk of the refugees in the caravan were from Honduras.

49 Garance Burke, Martha Mendoza, and Christopher Sherman, 'Amid corruption concerns, Gen. Kelly made allies in Honduras', Associated Press, 12 April 2018.

50 Nina Lakhani, 'Berta Caceres's name was on Honduran military hitlist, says

former soldier', *The Guardian*, 21 June 2016.

51   A leading activist in Honduras explained to me how the hit list worked on those being targeted: 'The list just starts circulating on social media, and I doubt anyone knows the origin of it. It was all over Facebook. The US embassy has been asking for the list, but no one shares it with them (or even journalists really) because people know that it won't be taken seriously. The list is very real to people for various reasons ... Most of the people on the list have received death threats or denounced previous incidents of violence against them; and a lot of death threats in Honduras are delivered in an indirect manner, like through neighbours or distant friends telling people to be careful.'

52   There is no trust between peasant farmers and the government. Vitalino Alvarez told me that the head of the Xatruch Taskforce, a military unit designed to help the police in the area resolve land conflicts and battle crime, was an impediment to peace. Army Colonel German Alfaro Escalante 'won't accept that land grabbing is the heart of the problem', Alvarez told me. 'He blames drugs as the key issue, but he accuses campesinos of drug-trafficking, which is false.' Escalante had a history of denigrating peasant leaders, including Alvarez, as far back as 2013, accusing them of 'damaging the image of the Honduran state' by unfairly targeting the Xatruch Taskforce.

53   Nina Lakhani, 'Honduras and the dirty war fuelled by the west's drive for clean energy', *The Guardian*, 7 January 2014. In 2017, peasants sued the World Bank for financing Dinant and accused the private sector lending arm of 'knowingly profiting from the financing of murder'.

54   Dana Frank, 'Wikileaks Honduras: US linked to brutal businessman', *The Nation*, 21 October 2011.

55   Sara Blaskey and Norman Stockwell, 'Miguel Facusse is dead: what does that mean for the people of Honduras?', *The Tico Times*, 25 June 2015.

56   Tracy Wilkinson, 'In Honduras, a controversial businessman responds to critics', the *Los Angeles Times*, 21 December 2012.

57   Frank, 'Wikileaks Honduras'.

58   Historian Dana Frank from the University of California in Santa Cruz revealed that four months before the 2009 coup, a right-wing newspaper in Honduras reported that 1,400 kilos of cocaine had been found in the Aguan on a landing strip owned by Facusse. Dana Frank, 'Wikileaks Honduras: US linked to brutal businessman', *The Nation*, 21 October 2011.

59   Joseph Goldstein and Benjamin Weiser, 'After 78 killings, a Honduran drug lord partners with the US', *The New York Times*, 7 October 2017. In 2017, prominent Honduran businessman Yani Rosenthal was sentenced in the US to three years in prison for money laundering after colluding with the Los Cachiros drug cartel.

60 Over the coming days, Guillermo would explain the Garifuna to me, showing that they were highly educated and successful in many professions. The first Honduran to successfully complete medicine at Harvard was a Garifuna man, and he returned after his degree to open a clinic in his home country.

61 Mattathias Schwartz, 'DEA says Hondurans opened fire during a drug raid. A video suggests otherwise', *The New York Times*, 23 October 2017.

62 The official review into the 2012 massacre, issued in 2017 by the inspectors-general of the Departments of State and Justice dismissed DEA claims that the Honduran police were properly vetted or trained. See Annie Bird and Alexander Main, 'The deadly results of a DEA-backed raid in Honduras', *The New York Times*, 2 July 2017.

63 Roatan was a tourist mecca for foreigners and rich Hondurans to holiday on beautiful white, sandy beaches. One end of the island, West Bay, was where many of the hotels and resorts were located, almost a world away from Honduras, with signs only in English and few local faces except for those working in the hotels. At the other end of Roatan, at French Harbour, where many locals resided, the roads were uneven, homes were decaying, and poverty was highly visible. Drunk men lay on the side of the road. Clara Woods lived in this part of town, where wooden homes were all covered in fading paint.

64 Karen Spring, 'Killing in the name of the war on drugs', *Scoop*, 3 February 2015.

65 On principle, I didn't pay people for interviews, but occasionally I felt it was appropriate to give some financial support and help those in need. I helped Clara Woods buy food for her children and family for three weeks.

66 'Made in the US: the real history of the MS-13 gang Trump talked about in State of the Union', *Democracy Now!*, 31 January 2018. US President Donald Trump routinely attacks the MS-13 gang, calling them 'animals'. They're an undoubtedly violent gang that commits horrible abuses, but their history is largely ignored. Founded in Los Angeles in the 1980s by refugees fleeing the US-backed dirty war in El Salvador, lack of opportunities in the US pushed many to join gangs. In the decades since, successive US presidents have deported many of them to Central America. Now, with violence again consuming Guatemala, El Salvador, and Honduras — often caused by US foreign policy — many are fleeing to the US, where President Trump demonises them as murderers and a threat to security. During the Obama years, countless refugees from Central America were sent back to their deaths. *The Guardian* found that many undocumented migrants fleeing gang violence from Guatemala, El Salvador, and Honduras were deported and killed soon after their arrival home. See Sibylla Brodzinsky and Ed Pilkington, 'US government deporting Central American migrants to their deaths', *The Guardian*, 12 October 2015.

67 Michael Lohmuller, 'Police theft of $1.3 million is mark of Honduran corruption',

Insight Crime, 17 February 2015. I was shown a list by a Washington, DC–based think tank, The Washington Office on Latin America, of the many abuses committed by the Honduran military and Tigres since 2014. The crimes involved kidnapping, robbery, violence, and murder.

68 Lee Fang and Danielle Mackay, 'The President of Honduras is deploying US-trained forces against election protestors', *The Intercept*, 3 December 2017.

69 *The Wall Street Journal* was given access to the Tigres in 2016, but the result was an overly rosy picture of their capabilities. The Tigres were framed as playing an essential role in reducing 'illegal' immigration from Honduras to the US. See Michael M. Phillips, 'US Special Forces take on street violence that drives illegal immigration', *The Wall Street Journal*, 22 February 2016.

70 The effectiveness of US-sponsored propaganda trips in Honduras was clear after Pulitzer Prize-winning author Sonia Nazario wrote a glowing report in *The New York Times* about the US programs for civilians in San Pedro Sula and urged Washington to send even more money. There was no mention of the 2009 coup, but copious amounts of praise for how the US was supposedly reducing crime and violence. See Sonia Nazario, 'How the most dangerous place on earth got safer', *The New York Times*, 11 August 2016.

71 I asked the US ambassador, James Nealon, and Eric Turner about the allegation that US-backed security forces had both been complicit in the killing of Berta Caceres and carried a hit list with her name and others on it. They said they hadn't seen the hit list and that I should give them the list if I saw it, so they could check its veracity. I did not do so.

72 Jake Johnson, 'Informants claim drug-traffickers sought assistance of US-backed Honduran security minister', *The Intercept*, 26 November 2017.

73 The US embassy in Honduras proudly announced in May 2018 that, 'Honduran national Sergio Neftali Mejia-Duarte was sentenced today to life in prison for his involvement in a large-scale international narcotics transportation organization.' Honduran politician Fredy Najera Montoya pleaded guilty in a US court in December 2018 to running a drug-trafficking operation. He used landing strips on his property to land planes from Colombia laden with cocaine and then moved the drugs to the Guatemalan border.

74 Former Honduran army captain Santos Rodriguez Orellana publicly accused the DEA of alleging his involvement in a 2016 plot financed by Tony Hernandez to assassinate the US ambassador, James Nealon. He denied it. See Gerardo Reyes and Juan Cooper, 'From hero to villain: the saga of a Honduran army captain caught in a drug war', Univision News, 22 November 2017.

75 Nina Lakhani, 'Honduras and the dirty war fuelled by the West's drive for clean energy', *The Guardian*, 7 January 2014.

Chapter Two: Guinea-Bissau

1   For centuries, many Muslim locals practised the Sunni strain of Sufism. The CIA World Factbook in 2018 stated there were about 40 per cent Muslims, 22 per cent Christians, 15 per cent Animists, and 18 per cent unspecified. See Anna Pujol Mazzini, 'Sufi West Africa braces amid rise of fundamentalism', *Ozy*, 3 July 2018. US intelligence reports released in 2018 said that terror groups such as Al-Qaeda and Boko Haram were using Guinea-Bissau as a safe refuge. See Anna Pujol Mazzini, 'Islamist terrorist groups are turning their attention to West Africa', *The Washington Post*, 3 July 2018.

2   Grant Ferrett and Ed Vulliamy, 'How a tiny West African country became the world's first narco state', *The Guardian*, 9 March 2008.

3   Alexander Smoltczyk, 'Guinea-Bissau a "drug-trafficker's dream"', *Spiegel Online*, 8 March 2013.

4   Raggie Johansen, 'Guinea-Bissau: new hub for cocaine trafficking', United Nations Office on Drugs and Crime, Issue 5, May 2008.

5   Ibid.

6   Geoffrey York, 'Coup in Guinea-Bissau shines a light on powerful West African drug-trade', *The Globe and Mail*, 13 April 2012.

7   Adam Nossiter, 'Leader ousted, nation is now a drug haven', *The New York Times*, 1 November 2012.

8   Adam Nossiter, 'Six years after murder, Guinea-Bissau autocrat makes a posthumous comeback', *The New York Times*, 12 August 2015.

9   'Guinea-Bissau's President and "biggest drug dealer"', *The National*, 7 March 2009.

10 Toby Green, 'Introduction', in Patrick Chabal and Toby Green (eds), *Guinea-Bissau: micro-state to 'narco-state'*, Hurst and Company London, 2016, p. 5.

11 Ferrett and Vulliamy, 'West African country became the world's first narco state'.

12 David Lewis, 'Special report: West Africa's alarming growth industry — meth', Reuters, 24 July 2015.

13 Charlotte Alfred, 'Recovering addicts battle Kenya's exploding heroin problem', *Huffington Post*, 12 December 2015. Most Europe-bound heroin still took the so-called Balkan-route via Iran and south-east Europe, but East Africa was increasingly targeted by drug-smugglers. The UN estimated in 2016 that up to 70,000 kilograms of Afghan heroin was being smuggled annually via Africa to Europe. See Alexandra Fisher, 'Africa's heroin highway to the West', *The Daily Beast*, 5 November 2016.

14 The head of UNODC, Yury Fedotov, told the UN Security Council in May 2018 that since the establishment of the Transnational Crime Unit (TCU) in 2009, it had investigated '70 cases of drug-trafficking, with 113 persons prosecuted and 71 kg of cocaine and 1,353 kg of marihuana seized'. He lamented that UNODC's funding in Guinea-Bissau was 'drastically reduced' in 2017.

15　In September 2018, the West African Commission on Drugs released a report that called for the decriminalisation of all drugs for personal use to allow law enforcement to focus on organised crime, high-level corruption. and the most serious drug offences.

16　Ferrett and Vulliamy, 'West African country became the world's first narco state'.

17　Joanne Csete and Constanza Sanchez, 'Telling the story of drugs in West Africa: The newest front in a losing war?', Global Drug Policy Observatory, November 2013.

18　Alonso Soto, 'Cocaine smugglers may cash in on Guinea-Bissau politics feud', Bloomberg, 9 December 2018.

19　Anna Pujol Mazzini, 'He's on a mission from God to tackle drugs in Africa's first narco state', *Ozy*, 12 July 2018.

20　Hassoum Ceesay, 'Guinea-Bissau: the narco-state and the impact on institutions in Guinea-Bissau', in Chabal and Green (eds), *Guinea-Bissau*, p. 220.

21　Green, 'Introduction', p. 5.

22　Mark Shaw wrote in the *Journal of Modern African Studies* that the term 'narco-state' was inappropriate for Guinea-Bissau and instead called the key political and military figures behind drug-trafficking part of an 'elite protection network'. He went on: 'In Guinea-Bissau, that network did not act on its own, but relied on a series of "entrepreneurs" who operated as an interface between traffickers and the elite. While the military as an institution is often said to be in charge of trafficking, exclusive control by high-ranking military personnel within the elite network only occurred relatively late. Senior soldiers' attempts to provide more than just protection, and to enter the drug market themselves, led to the network's undoing.' See Mark Shaw, 'Drug-trafficking in Guinea-Bissau, 1998–2014: the evolution of an elite protection network', *The Journal of Modern African Studies*, 10 August 2015.

23　In 2016, Inspector Edgar Ribeiro of the Portuguese judicial police told a gathering in Bissau that Guinea-Bissau was not a 'narco-state' 'although West Africa serves as a circulation platform for drugs from Latin America to Europe'. The Guinea-Bissau economy 'does not live from the production and sale of drugs', he said.

24　In the 2016 Global Index for Peace, Guinea-Bissau was rated as the most violent nation in the Portuguese-speaking world. The index considered around 20 indicators, including public safety, police violence, homicide rates, social justice, and terrorism.

25　Smoltczyk, 'Guinea-Bissau a "drug-trafficker's dream"'.

26　African-American political activists who had worked with black liberation movements, some accused of murder in the 1970s, hid in Guinea-Bissau for years.

27　David Lewis and Richard Valdmanis, 'Special report: how US drug sting targeted West African military chiefs', Reuters, 24 July 2013.

28   Emma Farage and Fernando Pereira, 'Guinea-Bissau sidelines top brass in bid to end coups', Reuters, 19 May 2015.

29   Lewis and Valdmanis, 'Special report'.

30   Ibid.

31   '"Narco-terrorist" deported from US "freely living in Portugal"', *Portugal Resident*, 14 December 2015.

32   Dan Browning, 'Narco terrorist convict deported from Minnesota but where is he?', *Star Tribune*, 10 December 2015.

33   Yudhijit Bhattacharjee, 'Godfather for hire', *The New Yorker*, 30 July 2018.

34   Glenn Greenwald, 'Why does the FBI have to manufacture its own plots if terrorism and ISIS are such grave threats?', *The Intercept*, 26 February 2015.

35   In 2010, the US Treasury Department declared both Na Tchuto and the air force chief of staff, Ibraima Papa Camara, as drug kingpins.

36   Yudhijit Bhattacharjee, 'The sting: an American drugs bust in West Africa', *The Guardian*, 17 March 2015.

37   'Catch me if you can: Exxon complicit in corrupt Liberian oil sector', *Global Witness*, 29 March 2018.

38   Nick Turse, 'The US military's drug of choice', *TomDispatch*, 8 February 2018.

39   Charlie Savage and Thom Shanker, 'US drug war expands to Africa, a newer hub for cartels', *The New York Times*, 21 July 2012.

40   Ginger Thompson, 'Trafficking in terror', *The New Yorker*, 14 December 2015.

41   Ibid.

42   Benedict Carey, 'The chains of mental illness in West Africa', *The New York Times*, 11 October 2015.

43   Sofia Christiansen, 'West Africa's addiction to hard drugs is on the rise', VOA, 19 July 2018.

Chapter Three: The Philippines

1   'Aquino says PDEA killed only three drug suspects in his first 100 days', GMA News Online, 9 January 2018.

2   The Duterte-backed Davao death squads were accused of killing at least 1,700 criminals during his time as mayor, although during the 2016 election campaign Duterte said the number killed was 700. US state department cables released by Wikileaks confirmed that Washington had long viewed Duterte as complicit in the Davao horrors. A Human Rights Watch report in 2009, 'You Can Die at Any Time', found that police gave vigilante groups lists of people to be targeted. In December 2016, Duterte said that when he was mayor of Davao he would ride around on his motorcycle 'looking for trouble', and would kill suspected criminals. He later admitted that he'd killed 'about three' people. Despite knowing about the abuses during Duterte's rule in Davao, IBM partnered with the city

in 2012 to provide surveillance technology to law enforcement. George Joseph, 'Inside the video surveillance program IBM built for Philippine strongman Rodrigo Duterte', *The Intercept*, 20 March 2019.

3   A 2016 Reuters report found that the Duterte government had done little to address the massive influx of drugs coming from China, and had not gone after the drug lords running the trafficking. John Chalmers, 'Meth gangs of China play star role in Philippines drug crisis', Reuters, 16 December 2016.

4   During the Duterte era, jails had experienced huge overcrowding. I visited the facility in Quezon City. It had a 700-person capacity, but when I went there, there were 3,299 inmates; 72 per cent of them were inside for drug offences, mostly serving one to five years, while 50 per cent were shabu users before they arrived. The warden, Ermilito Moral, told me that there was a comprehensive rehabilitation program for inmates that included singing the national anthem, behavioural attitude changes, singing, dancing, massage therapy lessons, learning to cut hair, cosmetics, sewing, handicrafts, making perfume, barista training, and religious lessons. A guard walked me into the prison, and there were bodies everywhere, slammed up against each other on various floors: talking, sitting, standing, lying, and sleeping.

5   During the 2016 election campaign, Duterte joked that he 'should have been first' in the 1989 rape of an Australian missionary in Davao, and accused his daughter of being a 'drama queen' after she said that she had been raped. After Duterte won office, he threatened his son Paolo with death if allegations of drug-trafficking against him were true. Paolo was cleared of trafficking after a government investigation concluded in 2018. Duterte's daughter, Sara, has served as mayor of Davao City.

6   Few political opponents of Duterte spoke out strongly against his rule; they were scared. I met two of them. Representative Gary Alejano told me that he supported Duterte in his ambition to 'stamp out illegal drugs' in the Philippines, but opposed how it was implemented 'through elimination and killing suspects'. Senator Antonio Trillanes was a former navy officer who staged a failed coup in 2003. He said that he backed the idea of a war on drugs, but thought that the Duterte form of 'summary executions' aimed to instil fear in the population. Duterte aimed to arrest Trillanes in late 2018 for his role in the failed 2003 coup. One of Duterte's fiercest critics, Senator Leila De Lima, was thrown in jail by the president in February 2017 over allegations that she had facilitated drug-trafficking while justice secretary. She denied the allegations.

7   Davey Alba, 'Connecting hate: how Duterte used Facebook to fuel the Philippine drug war', *Buzzfeed News*, 4 September 2018.

8   Nicole Curato, *We need to talk about Rod. A Duterte reader: critical essays on Rodrigo Duterte's early presidency* (edited by Nicole Curato), Bughaw, 2017, p. 5.

9   Duterte occasionally mentioned the so-called rich man's drug, cocaine, and claimed that Mexican and South American cartels were bringing in the drug, but his government seemed to care little about stopping the influx.

10   The legacy of the American presence in the Philippines continues to this day. In April 2018, the Trump administration agreed to return a set of church bells that had been captured during a bloody encounter between American forces and locals in 1901. The Philippines and Duterte had pushed for the bell's return for years. See Richard C. Paddock, 'US set to return Philippine bells that once tolled to mark a massacre', *The New York Times*, 13 April 2018.

11   Jason Ditz, 'The Philippines: remembering a forgotten occupation', *Huffington Post*, 18 June 2013.

12   Pankaj Mishra, 'How colonial violence came home: the ugly truth of the first world war', *The Guardian*, 10 November 2017.

13   Adele Webb, 'Hide the looking glass', in Curato (ed.), *A Duterte reader*, p. 134.

14   Stanley Karnow, 'Reagan and the Philippines: setting Marcos adrift', *The New York Times*, 19 March 1989.

15   Brennan Weiss, 'Duterte's death squads were born in America's cold war', *Foreign Policy*, 10 July 2017.

16   Webb, 'Hide the looking glass'.

17   Israel and the Philippines improved their relationship, despite Duterte comparing himself to Hitler, and the former sold military equipment and weapons to the Asian nation. Duterte visited Israel in September 2018, and weapons deals were on the agenda. I attended a protest rally with Israelis in Jerusalem who opposed their government's close ties with Duterte. Britain's international trade secretary, Liam Fox, visited Manila in April 2017 and pledged to build a better relationship between the two countries based on 'a foundation of shared values and shared interests'. Australia's top intelligence chief, Nick Warner, was photographed in 2017 posing alongside Duterte with a clenched fist, the Filipino leader's signature move.

18   Walden Bello, 'Rodrigo Duterte: a fascist original', in Curato (ed.), *A Duterte reader*, p. 78.

19   Megha Rajagopalan, 'How US dollars are helping the Philippines' bloody drug war', *Buzzfeed News*, 28 November 2016. In 2017, the US Senate introduced a bill to restrict military aid to the Philippines and better support the Filipino human-rights community. Washington had planned to send US$5 million to Philippines law enforcement in 2016, and 26,000 assault rifles to the police.

20   Webb, 'Hide the looking glass'.

21   Nicole Curato, 'The Philippines beyond the dark spell', *Asia Global Online*, 8 March 2018.

22   Although many international human-rights group opposed Duterte's drug war,

internet game companies produced countless games that allowed players to kill drug suspects in the Philippines.

23 Alfred McCoy, 'Philippine populism: local violence and global context in the rise of a Filipino strongman, Surveillance in the global turn to authoritarianism', *Surveillance and Society*, vol. 15, no. 3/4, 2017.

24 Police whistle-blowers claimed that officials and police colluded to switch off security cameras and street lights in areas where killings would take place, and planted guns on dead suspects. See Manuel Mogato and Clare Baldwin, 'Special report: Police describe kill rewards, staged crime scenes in Duterte's drug war', Reuters, 18 April 2017. Another Reuters investigation in June 2017 found that police sent dead bodies to hospitals to remove incriminating evidence at crime scenes to obscure the fact that they were killing suspects on the spot. See Clare Baldwin and Andrew R.C. Marshall, 'Philippines police use hospitals to hide drug war killings', Reuters, 29 June 2017.

25 Kate Lamb, 'Philippines secret death squads: officer claims police teams behind wave of killings', *The Guardian*, 4 October 2016.

26 Despite some lawyers' belief that courts in the Philippines were moderately independent, other lawyers pursued different tactics, namely pursuing Duterte in the International Criminal Court (ICC) in The Hague, Netherlands. One lawyer, Jude Josue Sabio, asked the ICC in 2017 to adjudicate on the killing of more than 9,400 people from his time as mayor of Davao City and as president. The ICC announced in February 2018 that it was making preliminary investigations into whether Duterte's drug war fell under its jurisdiction. Duterte said that any ICC investigators who came to the Philippines should be fed to the crocodiles. It didn't take long after this outburst for Duterte to announce that the Philippines was withdrawing from the ICC. The president potentially opened himself up to ICC prosecution by admitting in September 2018 that his government had committed extra-judicial killings. The belief in a strong judiciary, expressed to me by some local lawyers, was shattered when the chief justice of the Supreme Court of the Philippines, Maria Lourdes Sereno, was removed from her position in 2018 after clashing with Duterte.

27 Churches were one of the few spaces that challenged Duterte. A leading archbishop said in 2017 that the Roman Catholic Church would protect police who came forward to give testimony about their involvement in the drug war. The Baclaran redemptorist church, a Catholic institution in metro Manila, openly challenged the violence unleashed during the Marcos era and Duterte period. There were statues and artwork in a garden adjacent to the church that resisted political repression. The 'Desaparacidos', the disappeared, was a mural that featured the Marcos period and beyond. Lady Justice stood next to her child, holding an image of her father, and behind them were panels listing hundreds

of missing and killed citizens from 1971 to 2000. There were no mentions of Duterte's drug war victims, but there was space for more panels. In a different place on the mural were small pointed criticisms of the drug war with painted images of extra-judicial killings and the infamous viral image of Jennelyn Olaires cradling her husband, Michael Siaron, a pedicab driver and alleged drug pusher, who was shot and killed in Pasay City in 2016 during the drug war. The Baclaran church helped many victims of the drug war. I interviewed one of them, 'Cynthia', who used to deal drugs after pressure from gangsters. After her neighbours were killed during the Duterte drug war, she stopped, went into hiding with her children, and was given support and financial aid by the church to rehabilitate her life. She still feared being killed.

28   T.J. Burgonio, 'Offering drug surrenderers a different kind of redemption', *Philippine Daily Inquirer*, 5 March 2017.

29   In April 2018, the Philippine Drug Enforcement Agency (PDEA) released a list of barangay leaders it claimed were involved in illegal drugs. Over 200 people were listed, though the PDEA admitted that the evidence was largely gathered from police and intelligence sources. If innocent people were placed on the list, and their lives threatened or ended by the drug war, the process seemed flawed and open to abuse.

30   Within three months of Duterte taking power in 2016, 700,000 Filipinos had reportedly 'surrendered' to authorities as drug users or pushers. I obtained a copy of the form given by police to people who had surrendered. There was only one option to mark on the page, as a drug 'pusher/user', and the individual pledged to waive all legal liabilities against the state.

31   Jodee A. Agoncillo and Mariejo S. Ramos, 'Rehab or rubout', *Philippines Daily Inquirer*, 9 October 2016.

32   Steve Stecklow, 'Inside Facebook's Myanmar operation', Reuters, 15 August 2018. Facebook commissioned an independent report into its behaviour in Myanmar, and admitted some fault. Released in late 2018, Facebook was 'being used to foment division and incite offline violence,' but the company claimed it was taking action to address the problem. Critics were rightly sceptical.

33   Megha Rajagopolan, 'The country's democracy has fallen apart — and it played out to millions on Facebook', *Buzzfeed News*, 21 January 2018.

34   Lauren Etter, Vernon Silver, and Sarah Frier, 'How Facebook's political unit enables the dark art of political propaganda', Bloomberg, 21 December 2017.

35   The parent company of Cambridge Analytica, exposed as assisting Donald Trump and Brexit in their successful campaigns through data harvesting on Facebook, boasted of helping Duterte win the 2016 election. Strategic Communications Laboratories, or SCL Group, placed on its website, since deleted, that the general public viewed Duterte 'as a strong, no-nonsense man of action, who would appeal

to the true values of the voters'.

36   Etter, Silver, and Frier, 'Facebook's political unit'.

37   Alba, 'Connecting hate'.

38   'Rappler boss condemns "patriotic trolling" on social media', ABS-CBN News, 30 January 2018.

39   I attended an opposition Liberal Party event, where the mood was both defiant and deflated. Duterte had so dominated the political scene since his 2016 election win that political parties struggled to gain support. I was told that the Liberal Party only had around 1,000 signed-up members. A female doctor in her thirties, Yves, spoke to a roaring crowd: 'I shouldn't be here, I'm a doctor. I have to take a stand against he who can't be named [Duterte]. Many people are asleep. He is like Voldemort in Harry Potter. We must make people patriotic and against what's happening.'

40   Duterte acknowledged that his campaign in 2016 paid social-media followers to back him, but claimed that this stopped after he won.

41   Duterte's comments about his foreign policy were contradictory. At times, he said he wanted to 'break up' with the US and become closer to China, including backing its moves in the South China Sea, but Washington still gave huge amounts of aid annually.

42   I interviewed one of the communist rebels opposing the Duterte government by phone on a scratchy line. They were based in the Southern Tagalog region. I spoke briefly to Jaime 'Ka Diego' Padilla, spokesman of the New People's Army's Melito Glor regional command in the Southern Tagalog region of the Philippines and Comrade Kathryn, Office of the Regional Spokesperson. They were at war with the government, had been for decades, and lived in a remote area. I later obtained answers to my questions, via email, on what they saw as the similarities between Duterte's drug war and the violent government-backed vigilante groups that killed alleged communists in the 1970s. Comrade Kathryn told me that, 'Both administrations used paramilitaries and vigilantes against the people. The only difference is that now Duterte uses advanced military weapons and support gained from the imperialist US to attack the revolutionary movement.' In February 2018, Duterte encouraged the army to shoot female rebels in the vagina.

43   Jeremy Scahill, Alex Emmons, and Ryan Grim, 'Trump called Rodrigo Duterte to congratulate him on his murderous drug war: "You are doing an amazing job"', *The Intercept*, 24 May 2017.

44   Aurora Almendral, 'In Duterte's Philippines, having a beer can now land you in jail', *The New York Times*, 21 July 2018.

Chapter Four: The United States

1   Michelle Alexander (author of *The New Jim Crow: mass incarceration in the age of colorblindness*, The New Press, New York, 2012) in a public conversation with

Asha Bandele of the Drug Policy Alliance, 6 March 2014.

2   Thomas Fuller, 'Now for the hard part: getting Californians to buy legal weed', *The New York Times*, 2 January 2019.

3   Julia Barajas, 'A California conundrum: how to crack down on illicit sales without echoing the war on drugs?', *Cannabis Wire*, 4 February 2019.

4   Adam Drury, 'Cannabis activists give joints to Washington lawmakers during rally', *High Times*, 29 March 2018.

5   California is the world's fifth-biggest economy, and its legal marijuana industry was full of potential for businesses and users, as well as risks for smaller players who weren't interested or able to embrace big-scale growing. From 1 January 2018, when cannabis became legal in California, thousands of local growers were no longer legally allowed to run their businesses because they didn't want to get licences. Early reports suggested that the result was mediocre weed products being sold at legitimate shops. There were even marijuana shortages due to the lack of enough licensed businesses. See Chris Roberts, 'California's cannabis industry is facing a crisis of capitalism', *The Observer*, 19 March 2018. Illegal cannabis businesses were still booming, months after the drug became legal in California. The black market remained more profitable.

6   Tim Dickinson, 'The real drug czar', *Rolling Stone*, 20 June 2013.

7   Amanda Chicago Lewis, 'How black people are being shut out of America's weed boom', *Buzzfeed News*, 16 March 2016.

8   Christopher Ingraham, 'Marijuana raids are more deadly than the drug itself', *The Washington Post*, 20 March 2017.

9   DC police announced in September 2018 that they would change how they treated citizens who were caught smoking marijuana in public. It remained illegal, but arrests would be 'non-custodial'. This still meant that an individual would receive a criminal conviction.

10   The legal cannabis industry was predominantly male-dominated, with the major companies having few female managers.

11   Amanda Chicago Lewis, 'The case for drug war "reparations"', *Vice News*, 10 March 2017.

12   Matt Ferner, 'San Francisco to dismiss or reduce thousands of past marijuana convictions', *Huffington Post*, 2 January 2018.

13   The country's most prominent anti-marijuana lobby group, Smart Approaches to Marijuana (SAM), was increasingly successful in raising money in the Trump era to stop or at least slow down the commercialisation of cannabis. See Isaac Fornarola, 'An anti-cannabis crusader ramps up for the mid-terms — and beyond', *Cannabis Wire*, 3 October 2018.

14   Thomas Pellechia, 'Legal cannabis industry poised by big growth in North America and around the world', *Forbes*, 1 March 2018.

15 Max Berlinger, 'High Times has some glossy new competition', The New York Times, 9 January 2019.

16 Jamie Doward, 'Legal marijuana cuts violence says US study, as medical-use laws see crime fall', The Guardian, 14 January 2018.

17 Dickinson, 'The real drug czar'.

18 Benjamin Mueller, 'It wasn't a crime to carry marijuana. Until the police found a loophole', The New York Times, 2 August 2018.

19 Ibid.

20 Baltimore took a different approach to law enforcement after years of arresting huge numbers of people for minor drug offences. Drug arrests dropped by 50 per cent in 2015 after police focused more on large-scale drug-traffickers. See Kevin Rector, 'Battle lines being drawn in Baltimore's war on drugs', The Baltimore Sun, 20 February 2016. After years of struggling with high uses of heroin, Baltimore was now experiencing an influx of deadly fentanyl, causing the deaths of many citizens.

21 Peter Kerr, 'The unspeakable is debated: should drugs be legalised?', The New York Times, 15 May 1988.

22 Jay Gopalan, 'The junkie and the addict: the moral war on drugs', Harvard Political Review, 27 February 2017.

23 Jesse Kornbluth, 'Poisonous fallout from war on marijuana', The New York Times, 19 November 1978.

24 Adam Martin, 'Reagan's war on drugs reduced crime in an unexpected way', The Atlantic, 21 December 2011.

25 Tom Wainwright, Narconomics: how to run a drug cartel, Ebury Press, London, p. 146.

26 Martin, 'Reagan's war on drugs'.

27 Daniel Forbes, 'Prime-time propaganda', Salon, 13 January 2000.

28 Aviva Shen, 'The disastrous legacy of Nancy Reagan's "Just Say No" campaign', Think Progress, 6 March 2016.

29 Mikaela Linder, 'Mass incarceration nation: the truth behind Reagan's war on drugs', Unleashed, Bancroft School, 11 February 2018.

30 Thomas Frank, 'Bill Clinton's crime bill destroyed lives, and there's no point denying it', The Guardian, 15 April 2016.

31 'The Clinton drug war legacy', High Times, 1 February 2001.

32 Bob Dreyfuss, 'Bush's war on pot', Rolling Stone, 11 August 2005.

33 'A brief history of the drug war', Drug Policy Alliance, 2018.

34 Dreyfuss, 'Bush's war on pot'.

35 Mike Rigg, 'Obama's war on pot', The Nation, 30 October 2013.

36 Open and legal research on marijuana for medical and scientific purposes requires cannabis being removed from its status as a schedule-one drug and no

longer prohibited. Research showed that cannabidiol (CBD) helped some people with epilepsy and other diseases. The Food and Drug Administration approved a cannabidiol drug in 2018 for the first time that was designed for sufferers of epilepsy. There were dissenting opinions about marijuana from doctors who argued that the drug contained dangers, especially for the young brain as it developed. Addiction was a problem, as was mental illness, due to excessive cannabis consumption. Driving while stoned was illegal across the country, and in some states that had legalised the drug there were increased rates of cannabis in the blood of people having accidents (although in some studies the connection between driving stoned and increased accidents was inconclusive). See Judith Grisel, 'Pot holes', *The Washington Post*, 25 May 2018.

37   One of the main opponents of the vote to legalise cannabis in California in 2016 were police and prison guard groups, who provided about half of the funds to groups campaigning against it. They feared losing the lucrative government revenue streams that they had been receiving for decades. See Lee Fang, 'Police and prison guard groups fight marijuana legalisation in California', *The Intercept*, 18 May 2016. Alcohol and pharmaceutical companies were also big funders of anti-marijuana ballot initiatives in 2016, fearful they'd lose market share. There was growing evidence in states that legalised marijuana that fewer citizens were buying and drinking alcohol, one of the most dangerous drugs alongside nicotine. See Jon Walker, 'There's real evidence that legalised pot can reduce drinking', *The Intercept*, 20 April 2018.

38   Jessica Glenza, 'Ten million more Americans smoke marijuana now than 12 years ago: study', *The Guardian*, 1 September 2016. US government data released in 2016 found that slightly more middle-aged Americans than their teenage children smoked marijuana.

39   German Lopez, 'Why you shouldn't dismiss the risk of marijuana addiction', *Vox*, 20 August 2018. According to the 2016 national survey on drug use and health, 'the percentage of adolescents with a marijuana use disorder in 2016 was lower than the percentages in 2002 to 2013, but it was similar to the percentages in 2014 and 2015'. In 2016, 2.3 per cent of adolescents aged 12 to 17 had marijuana-use disorder.

40   German Lopez, 'How Obama quietly reshaped America's war on drugs', *Vox*, 19 January 2017. In 2017, Massachusetts threw out 21,587 criminal drug cases after a chemist, Annie Dookhan, pleaded guilty to tampering with or falsifying information over nine years. It was likely the single biggest dismissal of wrongful convictions in the nation's history.

41   Trump released the US government's annual list of nations identified as being 'major drug-transit or major illicit drug producing countries'. Released on 11 September 2018, the countries were Afghanistan, The Bahamas, Belize, Bolivia, Colombia, Costa Rica, Dominican Republic, Ecuador, El Salvador, Guatemala,

Haiti, Honduras, India, Jamaica, Laos, Mexico, Myanmar, Nicaragua, Pakistan, Panama, Peru, and Venezuela.

42 During the Trump era and before, many firefighters, police, and other safety-sensitive employees could be drug tested, and if found to have marijuana in their systems, could be fired. This was even in states where cannabis was legal and even if the drug was the only way to deal with chronic pain.

43 One of the more curious Trump appointments was Taylor Weyeneth, a 24-year-old Trump campaign worker who ended up with a senior role at the government's Office of National Drug Control Policy, despite having no experience for the role. He was fired soon after *The Washington Post* exposed his lack of credentials.

44 California Democrat Barbara Lee introduced a resolution in June 2018, the Respect resolution, that aimed to fight the racial disparity in the marijuana industry. It pushed for expunging the records of people incarcerated for non-violent cannabis offences and for reducing the high fees to enter the legal marijuana industry.

45 Long-time opponents of marijuana increasingly embraced the drug for either medical or capitalist reasons. Former Republican speaker of the House John Boehner announced his support for cannabis, pushed for it be removed from the government's controlled substances list, and became involved in a cannabis business, Acreage Holdings, that aimed to make money from the burgeoning industry. Many in the legalisation movement were sceptical about Boehner's motives after he'd spent his life opposing marijuana.

46 Lara Bazelon, 'Kamala Harris was not a "progressive prosecutor"', *The New York Times*, 17 January 2019.

47 Former vice-president Joe Biden, a former Democratic senator, acknowledged on Martin Luther King Day in 2019 that he had been wrong to back tough-on-crime drug legalisation in the 1980s and 1990s. He helped write and support the 1994 crime bill, under president Bill Clinton, that led to mass incarceration and separate legal standards for powdered cocaine and street crack cocaine. (The latter was more harshly punished, and targeted the black community.) Biden was a Democratic candidate for the 2020 presidential election, and his troubling record on the drug war followed him everywhere.

48 Dominic Holden, 'Inside the Trump administration's secret war on weed', *Buzzfeed News*, 29 August 2018.

49 Asawin Suebsaeng and Lachlan Markay, 'Trump's Disney robot obsession and Anthony Scaramucci's dick joke: scenes from a White House insider', *The Daily Beast*, 24 January 2019.

50 Nicholas Fandos and Maggie Haberman, 'Trump embraces a path to ease US sentencing', *The New York Times*, 14 November 2018.

51 One critic of Trump's criminal-justice reforms, lawyer Keith Wattley, claimed it

discriminated against violent offenders and 'perpetuates the false narrative that people who commit violent crimes are fundamentally different from those who commit nonviolent crimes'. Furthermore, he said that it would only help very few people whose sentences would be reduced, and instead would benefit the private prison industry that aimed to sell electronic monitoring systems when a person was released from jail. See Keith Wattley, 'Trump's criminal justice reform is a step in the wrong direction', *The New York Times*, 4 December 2018.

52 Katharine Q. Seelye, 'In heroin crisis, white families seek gentler war on drugs', *The New York Times*, 30 October 2015.

53 Dan Vergano, 'US overdose deaths will double again in 8 years, scientists predict', *Buzzfeed News*, 20 September 2018.

54 Megan McArdle, 'The incredibly unpopular idea that could stem opioid deaths', *The Washington Post*, 4 December 2018; Zachary Siegel, 'The strongest evidence yet for a highly controversial addiction treatment', *The Atlantic*, 8 December 2018; Dan Vergano, 'The overdose crisis is so bad that some experts want to prescribe heroin to treat addiction', *Buzzfeed News*, 6 December 2018.

55 Felice J. 'Freyer, Emergency rooms once offered little for drug users. That's starting to change', *The Boston Globe*, 10 December 2018.

56 Patrick Radden Keefe, 'Empire of pain', *The New Yorker*, 30 October 2017. Despite Purdue Pharma being a lead cause of the opioid crisis, the company received a patent in 2018 to help treat opioid addiction.

57 David Armstrong, 'OxyContin maker explored expansion into "attractive" anti-addiction market', *ProPublica*, 30 January 2019.

58 German Lopez, 'Drug companies bought doctor's fancy meals — and then those doctors prescribed more opioids', *Vox*, 15 May 2018.

59 Aaron Kessler, Elizabeth Cohen and Katherine Grise, 'The more opioids doctors prescribe, the more money they make', CNN, 12 March 2018.

60 'Why is the opioid epidemic overwhelmingly white?', *All Things Considered*, NPR, 4 November 2017.

61 In 2000, Eric Alvarez had been given a 30-year sentence for distributing crack and cocaine, and for running a smuggling ring between New York and North Carolina. His first clemency application in 2013 was ignored, but he had his sentence commuted by Obama in 2016. When Alverez's son died in 2013, he was unable to attend the funeral. He now lives as a free man in New York City, where I met him at a Starbucks. He had been in and out of correctional facilities for decades, sometimes working legitimate jobs and other times dealing drugs. He worked as a DJ, Chubb Dog (and does so again today). His first clemency application in 2013 was ignored. Today, he installs water heaters across New York. He told me that he would 'give Obama a big kiss' if he met him. 'I would hug the shit out of him. He gave me my life back.' Alvarez was talkative, funny,

and grateful to have been given a second chance in life rather than likely dying in prison.

62   Justin Wm. Moyer, 'A drug dealer got a life sentence and was devastated. So was the judge who sentenced him', *The Washington Post*, 6 May 2017.

63   Michael Collins, deputy director at the Drug Policy Alliance in Washington, DC, told me that it was far easier in the Obama years to convince politicians to push for legislative changes in domestic drug laws, marijuana and sentencing reform but foreign policy and the drug war were too intimately linked to the war on terror. For this reason, Congressmen and women were reluctant to ask too many questions about the role of the DEA internationally as they were afraid that they'd be criticised for being against the war on terror. Collins said that the pro-drug war crowd had cleverly co-opted the 'language and tools' of the war on terror.

64   Keely Herring, 'Was a prison built every 10 days to house a fast-growing population of nonviolent inmates?', *Politifact*, 31 July 2015.

65   Raishad Hardnett, 'The prisoners left behind', *Cannabis Wire*, 7 September 2018.

66   Dinah Ortiz, 'Battle bonded in family defence', Medium, 17 May 2018.

67   Jane Flasch, 'Rochester drug court amid opioid crisis: "It's overwhelming"', 13WHAM News, 22 August 2018.

68   Joseph Goldstein, 'Undercover officers ask addicts to buy drugs, snaring them but not dealers', *The New York Times*, 4 April 2016.

69   Kerr, 'The unspeakable is debated'.

70   Some countries were both hard-line against drugs but also more progressive in treatment. For example, Iran still executed many people for drug crimes, but also provided harm-reduction treatment through its health-care system.

71   Samuel Oakford, 'How Russia became the new global leader in the war on drugs', *Vice News*, 18 April 2016.

72   Ann Fordham and Martin Jelsma, 'Will UNGASS 2016 be the beginning of the end for the "war on drugs"', *Open Democracy*, 16 March 2016. Many US states proposed opening safe injecting centres though the Trump administration opposed them.

73   Samuel Oakford, 'Trump administration plans to UN meeting to ramp up the international drug war', *The Intercept*, 18 September 2018.

74   By 2018, Vincente Fox was director of a Canadian cannabis company in Colombia, and advocated legalisation in Mexico.

75   Tracy Wilkinson, 'Mexico moves quietly to decriminalise minor drug use', the *Los Angeles Times*, 21 June 2009.

76   Doctors from Yale University published a study in *The Lancet Psychiatry* in late 2018 that showed promising results with a new drug that helped cannabis users who had problems with overuse. The drug reduced issues with marijuana withdrawal.

Chapter Five: Britain

1   Comment made to me during interview with Neil Woods on 15 May 2018.

2   David Rhodes, 'Drug and alcohol services cut by 162 million pounds as deaths increase', BBC News, 11 May 2018.

3   Tom De Castella, '100 years of the war on drugs', *BBC News Magazine*, 24 January 2012.

4   Ibid.

5   Damien Gayle, 'Police less likely to find drugs on black people during stop and search', *The Guardian*, 14 December 2017.

6   Simon Jenkins, 'The 1971 Misuse of Drugs act was the stupidest and most ineffective ever passed — but has the PM got the guts to change it?', *Evening Standard*, 15 January 2013.

7   Genevieve Fox, 'From the archive: drugs on the rise in Britain', *The Observer*, 2 December 2018.

8   'Why Britain loves drugs', *Mixmag*, 27 May 2014.

9   Alan Travis, 'Revealed: how drugs war failed', *The Guardian*, 5 July 2005.

10   David Nutt, 'Blair's other war', *Evidence not Exaggeration* [blog], 26 April 2011.

11   Leo Benedictus, 'How the British fell out of love with drugs', *The Guardian*, 24 February 2011.

12   Danny Kushlick, director of Transform Drug Policy Foundation, wrote in *The Times* in 2004 that all drugs should be regulated and legalised, removing the huge amount of money earned by organised crime. See Danny Kushlick, 'Ending the guns-drugs connection', *The Times*, 12 October 2004.

13   '*The Guardian* view on UK drug laws: high time to challenge a failing prohibition', *The Guardian*, 9 March 2016.

14   '*The Guardian* view on drug wars: protect the innocent', *The Guardian*, 14 February 2019. In response to the *Guardian* editorial, some of the country's leading drug reformers, including David Nutt, Niamh Eastwood, Crispin Blunt MP, Neil Woods, and Thangam Debbonaire MP, wrote in a letter to the editor that it was strange that the paper provided no viable alternatives to the drug war. The letter read in part: 'This dismissal of political alternatives sits oddly in a newspaper with a noble tradition of opposing mass violence in pursuit of unwinnable political ends.' 'The "war on drugs" is causing great damage', *The Guardian*, 16 February 2019.

15   Police recorded possession of drugs offences in England and Wales from 2004/05 to 2017/18, Statista, 2018.

16   The Greens pushed for a radical overhaul of Britain's drug laws including non-violent offenders, the majority of people in prison, being allowed to rehabilitate in the community.

17   Ashley Cowburn, 'Government accused of "squandering" 1.6 billion pounds on

anti-drug policy', *The Independent*, 7 August 2017.

18   Franklyn Addo, 'Iain Duncan Smith should stop and search his views on youth violence', *The Guardian*, 30 August 2018. Margaret Thatcher's favourite free market think-tank, The Institute of Economic Affairs, released a report in 2018 that called for the legalisation of cannabis.

19   Damien Gayle, 'Labour peer Charles Falconer apologises over war on drugs', *The Guardian*, 28 September 2018.

20   Michael Allen, 'Inside the secret world of a British undercover drugs cop', *Vice*, 5 September 2014.

21   Decca Aitkenhead, '"I've done really bad things": The undercover cop who abandoned the war on drugs', *The Guardian*, 26 August 2016.

22   'Drugs should be legalised, regulated and taxed', *The British Medical Journal*, 10 May 2018.

23   The Prison Governors Association said in 2013 that keeping Class A drugs illegal guaranteed that criminals controlled the market and pushed people into crime to support their habits.

24   Peter Hitchens, 'There are real laws against smoking — maybe that's why kids switch to drugs', *Daily Mail*, 5 November 2017.

25   Mark Townsend, 'Kings of cocaine: how the Albanian mafia seized control of the UK drugs trade', *The Guardian*, 13 January 2019; and Borzou Daragahi, '"Colombia of Europe": how tiny Albania became the continent's drug-trafficking headquarters', *The Independent*, 27 January 2019.

26   Guy Kelly, 'The real cost of cocaine: Following the drug from Colombian rainforests to British suburbia', *The Telegraph*, 1 September 2018.

27   Jon Stone, 'Former Tory justice minister says he was told to stop asking how much drugs prohibition actually costs', *The Independent*, 3 October 2016.

28   Anushka Asthana, 'Nick Clegg accuses Theresa May of tampering with drug report', *The Guardian*, 18 April 2016.

29   Lester Black, 'Talking weed laws with Crispin Blunt', *The Strangler*, 9 May 2018.

30   James Hanning and David Connett, 'London is now the global money-laundering centre for the drug-trade, says crime expert', *The Independent*, 4 July 2015.

31   Paul Flynn, 'Banning cannabis has failed — now is the time for our MPs to show true courage', *The Mirror*, 11 October 2015.

32   Decca Aitkenhead, 'David Lammy: "Kids are getting killed. Where is the prime minister? Where is Sadiq Khan?"', *The Guardian*, 7 April 2018.

33   Denis Campbell, 'Only one in ten Britons knew that alcohol causes cancer', survey finds, *The Guardian*, 8 January 2018.

34   Denis Campbell, 'Thangam Debbonaire: "I saw the light about alcohol and cancer"', *The Guardian*, 16 January 2018.

35   Thangam Debbonaire and Jeff Smith, 'Labour can afford to be bold on drug policy reform', *Labour List*, 10 July 2018.

36   Tom Newton Dunn, 'Drugs death capital', *The Sun*, 7 August 2018.

37   'Is it high time for a change?', *The Sun*, 30 October 2014.

38   Some of the most powerful advocates for drug reform were parents of children who had lost their lives to overdoses. Anyone's Child is made up of families whose lives have been destroyed by repressive drug laws, and they advocate for drug regulation.

39   Dan Vevers, 'Home Office's injection room refusal "endangering lives"', STV News, 8 October 2018.

40   David Hillier, 'One UK country takes way more drugs than any other country in the world', *Vice*, 9 May 2018.

41   Mike Power, Insta-gram: How British cocaine dealers got faster and better, *Mixmag*, 7 March 2019.

Chapter Six: Australia

1   Comment made to me during interview with Dr David Caldicott on 25 October 2017.

2   The only condition of interviewing users at the safe injecting facility was that I didn't identity their real names and that they had the right to read and amend the transcripts of their interviews if they believed their words could be better expressed. One female drug user, whom I interviewed for the book, backed out months later after she was sent back to prison.

3   European nations such as Germany and Switzerland have drug inhalation rooms where methamphetamine, ice, heroin, or crack can be safely ingested, with medical staff watching on. The aim, as with safe injecting centres, is to support users and offer appropriate treatment and support. In Bern, Switzerland, there's a police-approved 'courtyard system' where registered users can buy and sell drugs among themselves while police observe. See Eamonn Duff, 'The safe room', *The Sydney Morning Herald*, 1 July 2016.

4   'Front Page – The *Tele* Fit Up', ABC TV *Media Watch*, 11 September 2006.

5   Jackson Stiles, 'Australia has "most dangerous" ecstasy drugs', *The New Daily*, 8 June 2015.

6   Jamie Doward, 'Testing drugs at music festivals is a "lifesaver", study finds', *The Guardian*, 9 December 2018.

7   Kevin Franciotti, 'How harm reduction services are keeping festivalgoers safe', *Filter*, 7 December 2018.

8   'History of drug laws in Australia', State Library of New South Wales.

9   Desmond Manderson, *From Mr Sin to Mr Big: a history of Australian drug laws*, Oxford University Press, 1993, p. 12.

10   Desmond Manderson, 'Like men possessed: what are illicit drug laws really for?', *The Conversation*, 3 November 2014.

11   Ibid.

12   Ibid. 'History of drug laws in Australia', State Library of New South Wales.

13   Manderson, 'Like men possessed'.

14   Manderson, *From Mr Sin to Mr Big*.

15   Katie Burgess, '"Drug pushers in suits": why the ACT's bid to "legalise heroin" failed', *The Canberra Times*, 23 July 2017.

16   Steve Evans, 'Drug campaigners gather to remember victims', *The Canberra Times*, 29 October 2018.

17   David Caldicott, 'Pyne's pain', *The Advertiser*, 31 May 2007.

18   Australia is a world leader in regulating tobacco and cutting rates of smoking. The federal Labor government introduced plain packaging for cigarettes from 2012, and despite tobacco companies launching legal action, evidence proves that it is improving public health and reducing consumption. A number of other countries followed Australia's lead.

19   Nicole Lee, 'Three charts on: Australia's changing drug and alcohol habits', *The Conversation*, 1 June 2017.

20   Jonathan Hair, 'Australia has second-highest concentration of dark net drug dealers per capita, new criminology research finds', *ABC News*, 1 June 2018.

21   Michael Heath, 'One part of Australia's economy is booming: illegal drugs', Bloomberg, 11 December 2018.

22   Lucy Cormack, 'Our illicit drug splurge may top our café spend', *The Age*, 20 February 2019.

23   'The drugs debate we have to have', *The Age*, 22 April 2018.

24   ACT Labor politician Michael Pettersson introduced a private member's bill in September 2018 that pushed to legalise cannabis for personal use. He claimed that around 60 per cent of drug arrests in his territory were for marijuana and that these funds could be better spent elsewhere.

25   Justine Landis-Hanley, 'For these Australian prisoners, a 14-month wait without being sentenced', *The New York Times*, 21 August 2018.

26   Angus Thompson, 'Coroner compares drug prohibition laws to racism', *The Sydney Morning Herald*, 5 November 2018.

27   'Weeded warriors: the young veterans breaking the law to treat their PTSD', *Hack*, Triple J, 14 September 2017.

28   Elise Worthington, 'Aura Medical Corporation: Clinics offering ketamine injections to treat depression blame negative publicity for closure', *ABC News*, 15 July 2015.

29   A brave doctor who believes in the benefits of ketamine for depressed patients is Tasmanian-based Dr Stephen Hyde. He told me that he faced constant pressure

from the medical establishment because of his desire to prescribe ketamine. Being in private practice, it was nearly impossible to legally source ketamine, so his patients, many of whom he believed would benefit medically from the drug, could not access it. He thought it was principally 'fear and ignorance' that led the Australian establishment's position. He was cautiously optimistic about the development by pharmaceutical giants such as Johnson & Johnson of a commercially viable ketamine-style nasal spray for depression that could allow large numbers of depressed patients to use it. Hyde told me that ketamine had been 'a life-changing treatment for a number of my patients. It's extremely frustrating that we're not able to prescribe in a way that it should be.'

30   Alex Wodak, 'Australia's drug policy led the world 30 years ago. Now politics holds us back', *The Guardian*, 2 April 2015.

31   Police were obsessed with arresting young people with drugs at music festivals. After the Field Day music event in early 2016 in Sydney, where 184 people were arrested for drug offences, one magistrate took harsh action against 11 of them, imposing fines and finding them guilty, despite some of them having no more than four ecstasy tablets.

32   Miranda Devine, 'A dangerous idea that stubbornly refuses to die', *The Daily Telegraph*, 27 October 2010.

33   Miranda Devine, 'Vale the old Kings Cross, victim of lethal injection', *The Sydney Morning Herald*, 28 September 2003.

34   'Cross Currents: The story behind Australia's first and only medically supervised injecting centre', Uniting Care, 2014.

35   Miranda Devine, 'We are losing the war on drugs', *The Daily Telegraph*, 11 November 2014.

36   Adam Gattrell, 'Alcohol a bigger scourge than meth: doctors criticise "disappointing" drug strategy', *The Age*, 1 August 2017. According to Australian Bureau of Statistics data for 2016, drug deaths reached their highest level in 20 years, mostly from prescription pain and anxiety medication and ice. Heroin was the fourth-biggest killer. The Australian Institute of Health and Welfare found in 2017 that one million Australians had misused pharmaceuticals in the previous 12 months.

37   Miranda Devine, 'This ice age has gone on too long', *The Daily Telegraph*, 24 October 2016.

38   *The Daily Telegraph* never stopped its crusade against drug users and dealers, targeting the weak and powerless in its endless campaign against illicit substances. For example, in May 2018 its target was 'fresh-faced young women' being 'groomed' to smuggle drugs into music festivals. These women were doubtless being pushed into the job, but they were easy targets for the newspaper, instead of it going after the government and police for arresting scores of young people with

small amounts of drugs. In article after article, the violent language of the drug war was used, despite decades of it failing to stop dealing, supplying, or using.

39   Patrick Hatch, 'Marijuana stocks skyrocket, set to "lead world" after export approval', *The Sydney Morning Herald*, 4 January 2018.

40   Tacey Rychter, 'Even Australia's medical marijuana poster boy can't get the drug', *The New York Times*, 11 February 2018.

41   Michael Vincent, 'Medical cannabis "pretty much inaccessible", leaving patients looking to the US', *ABC News*, 24 July 2018.

42   Jill Margo, 'The paradox at the heart of the medical marijuana industry', *The Australian Financial Review*, 10 October 2018.

43   Kathleen Donaghey, 'Australian-made medical cannabis hits pharmacy shelves', *The New Daily*, 11 September 2018.

44   Sean Nicholls, Lisa McGregor, and Stuart Washington, 'Marijuana moguls optimistic about legalisation of recreational cannabis in Australia', *ABC News*, 23 April 2018.

45   Naomi O'Leary, 'Sex, drugs and puke: partygoers turn Amsterdam into an "urban jungle"', *The Guardian*, 5 August 2018.

46   John Silvester, 'How Victoria became Australia's pot capital', *The Age*, 16 June 2017.

Chapter Seven: Solutions

1   Michael Pollan, *How to Change Your Mind: exploring the new science of psychedelics*, Allen Lane, London, 2018, p. 12.

2   The potency of MDMA/ecstasy had rapidly increased over the last years, sold on the street and via the dark net, partly due to drug dealers sourcing different chemicals from China. Deaths due to ecstasy soared. An investigation in *Mixmag* magazine went undercover in China to talk directly with a major chemical supplier, but concluded that the 'problem with MDMA is not purity, price, or availability. It is a lack of understanding — a fundamental, systematic, cultural ignorance of the drug and the way it is used — on the part of the politicians who uphold and extend the illogical laws to ban this, and any drug. *That* is the problem.' Mike Power, 'We went undercover in a Chinese MDMA factory', *Mixmag*, 29 May 2018.

3   James Martin, 'Australia emerges as a leader in the global darknet drugs trade', *The Conversation*, 17 February 2017.

4   James Martin, 'Cryptomarkets, systemic violence and the "gentrification hypothesis"', *Addiction*, 16 October 2017.

5   James Martin, '"Fair trade" cocaine and "conflict-free" opium: the future of online drug marketing', *The Conversation*, 12 August 2014.

6   Kate Wighton, 'The brain on LSD revealed: first scans show how the drug affects

the brain', Imperial College London, 11 April 2016.

7   Ariel Levy, 'The drug of choice for the age of kale', *The New Yorker*, 12 September 2016.

8   Psychedelic drugs could be abused by the wrong people. The Associated Press reported in 2018 about US service members in Wyoming using LSD, cocaine, and other drugs while off-duty in 2015 and 2016; these were individuals who were tasked to guard the country's nuclear missiles. See Robert Burns, 'Security troops on US nuclear missile base took LSD', Associated Press, 24 May 2018.

9   David Nickles, 'It's time to debunk prohibitionist narratives and calls for monopolies within psychedelic science', *Psymposia*, 2018.

10   Oliver Moody, 'Robots may be given anti-depressants to keep their spark', *The Times*, 11 April 2018.

11   Mike Riggs, 'Medical researchers are steps away from legalising ecstasy. Here's how they did it', *Reason*, 18 July 2017.

12   Ibid.

13   Tim Martin, 'The new science of psychedelics', *New Statesman*, 5 September 2018.

14   Ayelett Shani, 'Patients say that ayahuasca is like a reboot for the brain', *Haaretz*, 30 August 2018.

15   Martin, 'The new science of psychedelics'.

16   Jessi Appleton, 'I was in the MAPS MDMA for PTSD study. It freed me from a childhood of abuse', *Psymposia*, 3 October 2017.

17   Stephen Buranyi, 'New trials are using ketamine to treat alcohol addiction', *Vice Motherboard*, 21 July 2016.

18   Eugene Rubin, 'Can craving for cocaine be blocked in addicted individuals?', *Psychology Today*, 2 February 2017.

19   Baum, 'Legalise it all'.

20   Ibid.

21   Steve Rolles, 'Legalising drugs: The key to ending the war', *New Internationalist*, 2017, pp. 50–51.

22   Baum, 'Legalise it all'.

23   Rolles, 'Legalising drugs', p. 66.

Conclusion

1   Max Daly, 'The world's war on drugs has failed yet again', *Vice*, 23 October 2018.

2   Emma Young, 'How Iceland got teens to say no to drugs', *The Atlantic*, 19 January 2017.

3   Robert Muggah and John P. Sullivan, 'The coming crime wars', *Foreign Policy*, 21 September 2018.

4   Alfred McCoy, 'Will China be the next global hegemon?', *TomDispatch*, 21 August 2018.

5   Global Commission on Drugs Policy 2018.

6   When 'migrant caravans' started moving towards the US border from Latin and Central America in 2018, many of the refugees came from Honduras, but most of the mainstream media coverage wilfully ignored the reasons why so many Hondurans had had to flee. I saw barely any discussion of US policy towards Honduras and how it had worsened drug and gang-related violence.

7   Daly, 'World's war on drugs has failed'.

8   German Lopez, 'How one renegade country could unravel America's war on drugs', *Vox*, 20 December 2015.

Select Bibliography

Cockburn, Alexander and St Clair, Jeffrey, *Whiteout: the CIA, drugs and the press*, Verso, London, 1998

Curato, Nicole (editor), *A Duterte Reader: critical essays on Rodrigo Duterte's early presidency*, Bughaw, Manila, 2017

Hari, Johann, *Chasing the Scream: the first and last days of the War on Drugs*, Bloomsbury, Sydney, 2015

McCoy, Alfred, *The Politics of Heroin: CIA complicity in the global drug-trade*, Lawrence Hill Books, New York, 2003

Ohler, Norman, *Blitzed: drugs in Nazi Germany*, Penguin Books, London, 2017

Pollan, Michael, *How to Change Your Mind: exploring the new science of psychedelics*, Allen Lane, London, 2018

Rolles, Steve, 'Legalising Drugs: the key to ending the war', *New Internationalist*, 2017

Scott, Peter Dale, *Drugs, Oil and War: the United States in Afghanistan, Colombia and Indochina*, Rowman and Littlefield Publishers, London, 2003

Wainwright, Tom, *Narconomics: how to run a drug cartel*, Ebury Press, London, 2016

Webb, Gary, *Dark Alliance: the CIA, the Contras, and the crack cocaine explosion*, Seven Stories Press, New York, 2014

Index